A Conflict of Loyalties GCHQ 1984–1991

Hugh Lanning and
Richard Norton-Taylor

Foreword by Mike Grindley

New Clarion Press

© Hugh Lanning and Richard Norton-Taylor 1991

First published 1991

New Clarion Press
8 Evesham Road
Cheltenham
Glos GL52 2AB

New Clarion Press is a workers' co-operative

British Library Cataloguing in Publication Data

Lanning, Hugh
  A Conflict of Loyalties : GCHQ 1984-1991
  I. Title   II. Norton-Taylor, Richard
  327.120941

  ISBN 1-873797-00-1

Typeset in 10/12 Plantin by Orchard & Ind Ltd., Gloucester
Printed in Great Britain by The Bath Press

Contents

This book is dedicated to

Mike Grindley
Graham Hughes   } Dismissed 18 November 1988
Brian Johnson
Alan Rowland

Gerry O'Hagan   Dismissed 5 December 1988

Dee Goddard   Dismissed 12 January 1989

Bill Bickham
Alan Chambers
John Cook   } Dismissed 22 February 1989
Clive Lloyd
Roy Taylor
Harry Underwood

Gareth Morris   Dismissed 2 March 1989

Robin Smith   Dismissed 7 April 1989

With special thanks to their spouses and families, to June
Dimmock and last, but by no means least, to Jack and Iris Hart

**In memory of Chris Dimmock
who died on 26 July 1991**

Abbreviations

AGSRO	Association of Government Supervisors and Radio Officers
CCO	Communications and cypher officer
CCSU	Council of Civil Service Unions
CPSA	Civil and Public Services Association
CSO	Composite Signals Organization
CSOS	Composite Signals Organization Station
CSROA	Civil Service Radio Officers Association
CSU	Civil Service Union
FDA	First Division Association
GC&CS	Government Code and Cypher School
GCHQ	Government Communications Headquarters
GCRO	Government Civilian Radio Organization
GCSF	Government Communications Staff Federation
IPCS	Institution of Professional Civil Servants
IPMS	Institution of Professionals, Managers and Specialists
MPC	Major Policy Committee (of CCSU)
NIPSA	Northern Ireland Public Services Alliance
NSA	National Security Agency
NUCPS	National Union of Civil and Public Servants
OIC	Officer-in-charge
RO	Radio officer or operator
RSRE	Royal Signals and Radar Establishment
SCPS	Society of Civil and Public Servants
SIGINT	Signals intelligence
SRO	Station radio officer
TUC	Trades Union Congress
TUS	Trade union side

Foreword

In 1841 a local Chartist from Cheltenham told the people here: 'Take courage, for there never was a just cause which, begun by perseverance, did not end in triumph.'

It is now the eighth year of the campaign to restore free and independent trade unions at GCHQ. Without the support and solidarity given unstintingly by the trade union movement and by lovers of democracy in this country and abroad, we could never have kept the fight going. To all concerned, our heartfelt thanks. In turn, we hope our stand has been of help in resisting and hampering the relentless tide of anti-trade union actions carried out by the Conservative government and its friends in the private sector. In January 1984 the government not only overturned important and basic freedoms at our workplace; it also began a process of damaging people, families and careers. The choice was stark – your union or your job (or maybe your marriage) – and it was the government that was enforcing it, for motives that have always been suspect and for reasons that bear no credibility.

The unions inside GCHQ before the ban not only provided the traditional benefits as regards pay bargaining, negotiation of terms and conditions of service, insistence on health and safety standards, independent professional advice and legal support; they also provided a window to the outside world, a lifeline to workers whose occupations involved secrecy and reticence, even towards their own families. As one man still working there commented to me bitterly last year: 'Things will never be right there until the unions are back.' Morale in many areas of GCHQ remains low, and macho-management is having a field-day.

Apart from those who never gave up their trade union rights at GCHQ or who rejoined their union later, many of those who did sign the government's document under extreme duress voted with their feet in 1984–5 and left GCHQ in disgust. Highly skilled scientists, linguists, computer experts, mathematicians, telecommunications engineers and administrators were lost to GCHQ as a direct result of the union ban. And all the fault of the Tory government. It is government ministers who should be in the dock for damaging national security. The Thatcher administration carried through the ban and the current Major administration continues it deliberately.

The fourteen of us who were sacked in late 1988 and early 1989 for refusing to yield our membership of a free trade union had individually as much as thirty-two years' service at GCHQ, and half of us had previously done time in the armed forces as well. After a five-year fight from inside our workplace we now carry on the campaign from outside the razor wire.

Apart from the original High Court hearing, the British legal processes have failed us, Lord Chief Justice Lane and the Law Lords having bent over backwards to do the government's bidding. According to these judicial titans, 'national security' is whatever the government of the day says it is and the judiciary abdicates all responsibility in the matter. The European Commission of Human Rights denied our case admissibility and never considered the rights and wrongs of it. The final version of the Social Charter is fatally flawed on basic trade union rights, especially for civil servants. Only the International Labour Organization of the United Nations has consistently found in our favour, and the government arrogantly ignores this UN decision.

We believe that one of the primary importances of the rule of law is to protect workers against the arbitrary power of the state and against the state's removal of basic human rights. Therefore it follows that, if a government attempts to abolish basic rights, even using the forms of law, it cannot claim legitimacy. The Conservative government has been using the rule of law in Britain as a political weapon in the case of workers' fundamental rights at GCHQ and elsewhere.

But they won't succeed. We look forward to a change of government, since all opposition parties are pledged to restore our rights. Free trade unionism, as it existed before the ban, *will* be restored to workers at GCHQ!

> Here's freedom to them that wad read,
> Here's freedom to them that wad write,
> There's nane ever feared that the truth should be heard,
> But them that the truth wad indite.
>
> Robert Burns

Mike Grindley, Chair of GCHQ Trade Unions
Cheltenham, September 1991

Preface

The decision to ban trade union membership at the Government Communications Headquarters in Cheltenham was perhaps the single most authoritarian and unnecessary act of the Thatcher government. It was recognized as such by commentators from both the left and the right. What made it all the more astonishing was the apparent surprise of the government and GCHQ management at the outrage that the unilateral decision provoked. It demonstrated the government's scorn for civil rights, and its extraordinarily arrogant and presumptuous attitude towards a highly skilled, loyal and motivated workforce. Although the government successfully defended the ban both in the English courts and at the European Commission of Human Rights, the removal of trade union rights at GCHQ left a deep wound which will never heal. The government's action, and the way it sought to defend it, was an insult to the entire trade union movement. Any residual belief that the government could treat reasonably with groups representing collective interests in society on the basis of consensus and mutual respect was shattered.

That the issue has not gone away, that GCHQ, an increasingly intrusive part of Britain's security and intelligence network, has become a symbol of both government diktat and individual defiance, is due most of all to the small and courageous group who refused to sign away their union rights. Their fight alone merits a record of the story. But the GCHQ union ban raises a host of other issues: the extent of prerogative power still enjoyed by the executive, the government's abuse of the term 'national security', the lack of accountability of the security and intelligence services, the absence of legal protection for unions and employees, the relationship between the government and trade unions in general, and that between the government and its own employees in particular, which meant that it failed to consult, refused to negotiate and finally took unnecessary and vindictive action against a few brave individuals.

We would like to thank all those, the present and former GCHQ union members especially, who recalled their personal struggles. Some appear in the narrative; many inevitably do not. The latter include Dave McCaffrey, Bill Greenhalgh, Alan Swale, Barry

Sharman, Richard and Anne Gibbens and Glynis Baguley. This book is to a great extent their story. We have of course left many stories untold, and hopefully one day GCHQ trade unionists will have more freedom to recount their own experiences. We also hope that our friends and colleagues will bear with our use of their surnames in this book – a usage with which we have not always felt comfortable.

Union leaders ensured that the issue did not go away. Some – for example, Norman Willis, Rodney Bickerstaffe, Ken Cameron, Campbell Christie, Fred Jarvis, Jimmy Knapp, Roy Grantham and Ron Todd – took an almost personal interest in the dispute. Abroad Hans Engelberts, General Secretary of PSI International, and John Vanderveken of the ICFTU were always supportive. Prominent in the Civil Service union movement were John Ward, former General Secretary of the First Division Association; Alistair Graham and his successor as CPSA General Secretary, John Ellis; Ken Thomas, Alistair Graham's predecessor, who took on the fight at the International Labour Organization; Gerry Gillman, former SCPS General Secretary; Bill McCall, former IPCS General Secretary, and his successor, Bill Brett; Tony Christopher, former General Secretary, and Clive Brooke, the current General Secretary, of the Inland Revenue Staff Federation. Special mention must be made of John Sheldon, the CSU's last General Secretary and now Deputy General Secretary of the NUCPS, and the first NUCPS General Secretary, Leslie Christie, who were present when the dispute started and remain determined to see it through. The amazing support of NIPSA requires thanks to the union as a whole rather than to any one individual. In the CCSU, Peter Jones and Charlie Cochrane have serviced the Major Policy Committee and the GCHQ Working Group for most of the campaign – not forgetting Jean Thomason and everyone else who served on the aptly named GCHQ Working Group. Thanks also to Ben Hooberman and the unions' solicitors, Lawford and Co.

But the campaign could not have got off the ground without the support of the union executives and most importantly the many rank-and-file union members and branch officials throughout the country who gave their support in committee rooms, at their workplaces and at rallies. They are too numerous to mention, but too important to forget. Among local trade unionists from the wider trade union movement – teachers, garment workers, miners, print workers, dockers and many others – one individual stands out, Quentin Tallon of the Cheltenham Trades Council, the inaugurator and organizer of the vigil that takes place on the anniversary of the sackings.

Extra thanks is due to the NUCPS, and its predecessors the CSU and the SCPS, for the commitment they have shown to the campaign, for their co-operation – conscious and unconscious – in the writing of this book, and for the assistance all their staff and officials have given, especially the support staff like Rose Money, formerly Crockwell, Sandra Woolley and Jim Poynter and officials like Mike Barke and Alan Shute.

Cliché though it may be, thanks and love to Fiona and Anna, who have not only put up with us during the campaign, but have also suffered the writing of the book.

We salute the imagination of Chris Bessant and Fiona Sewell, who have chosen this book to be the first published by New Clarion Press. Throughout they showed remarkable patience, encouragement and faith. We – and all those involved in the fight against the union ban and the struggle to restore union rights at GCHQ – owe them a deep debt of gratitude. Inevitably, there will be those who say we have got the balance wrong in our chronicle of the story. We alone take responsibility for this, and for any omissions and errors.

Hugh Lanning and Richard Norton-Taylor
London, September 1991

Introduction

The Rt. Hon. Denis Healey, MP, spoke in the House of Commons shortly after the announcement in 1984 of the decision to ban trade unions at GCHQ.

Let me begin by agreeing on one thing with the Foreign Secretary. No one with any knowledge of the matter can underestimate the importance of this issue. GCHQ has been by far the most valuable source of intelligence for the British government ever since it began operating at Bletchley during the last war. British skills in interception and code-breaking are unique and highly valued by all of our allies. GCHQ has been a key element in our relationship with the United States for more than 40 years.

I am glad that, in his final words, the Foreign Secretary recognized the skill, loyalty and dedication of the men and women who work there...

It is just over four weeks since the Foreign Secretary told the House that he had decided to rob those loyal and dedicated men and women of their right to trade union membership – a right that they have enjoyed throughout their employment there and which has been enjoyed by all employees ever since GCHQ was first set up. It is a right that is enjoyed by tens of thousands of other men and women who do work of equal secrecy and of equal national importance in other government departments and in private industry. It is a right that is enjoyed by more tens of thousands of men and women in the Post Office, the Health Service and in many other parts of the government service on whose continuity of work lives might well depend.

The decision that the Foreign Secretary announced to the House just over one month ago was taken without consulting the representatives of the workers concerned and without consulting even his

1

colleagues in the Cabinet. Since then, I must tell the Foreign Secretary, his daily contradictory statements have made him the laughing stock of the world. When reading through them this weekend I was reminded of nothing so much as the five press conferences given by President Reagan on the Lebanon. The Foreign Secretary has been attacked anonymously by fellow ministers as basing his decision on emotional and not on intellectual judgement. He has been attacked publicly by Conservative back benchers, notably the hon. member for Cheltenham (Mr Irving), in whose constituency most GCHQ workers reside, and by the hon. member for Hendon, North (Mr Gorst) – Gorst of Grunwick as some of us have learnt to call him – who, on radio recently, described the Foreign Secretary's action as 'the nasty thin wedge of Fascism'. The Conservative newspapers have been even more outspoken. The *Daily Telegraph* described the behaviour of the Foreign Secretary and the government as 'little short of shambolic'. The *Daily Express* described their decision as 'highly illiberal and authoritarian'…

The government must recognize that their decision about GCHQ is a kick in the teeth for all those trade union leaders who have been prepared to develop a constructive relationship with the government. Above all, it is a kick in the teeth for Mr Lionel Murrary – *[Interruption]* – Before Conservative members sneer, I hope that they will recognize the significance – I am sure that the Foreign Secretary does and I hope that the Prime Minister does – of the fact that the opposition to the decision is led by Mr Alistair Graham, who compared the Prime Minister to General Jaruzelski, and by Mr Bill McCall. No one who knows them would describe them as mindless militants.

In the past month everyone has been asking why on earth the Foreign Secretary took the decision. It was not because he believed that trade unions were likely to be spies, because he knows, as we do, that most spies since the war have been public schoolboys, masons, scientists or service men. I have no doubt that the government have in hand measures for dealing with that particular threat to our security. The Foreign Secretary told the House this afternoon that he took the decision because the disruption at GCHQ on certain occasions between 1979 and 1981 broke the continuity of work there and might have endangered lives. He concluded – he told us again this afternoon – that membership of the trade union produces an unacceptable conflict of loyalties.

Some hon. members may have been impressed by some of the quotations that the Foreign Secretary read out in his speech from trade union leaders during those periods of industrial action. However, the trade unions have shown that there was no prejudice to the essential operations of GCHQ at the time, and the Foreign Secretary told the Select Committee that there was no evidence that any damage was done.

The most important statement by a minister was made on 14 April 1981, after all those interruptions had taken place. Sir John Nott, the then Secretary of State for Defence, said in the House: 'I do not wish to discuss the difficulties surrounding the dispute, but up to now they have not in any way affected operational capability in any area ... I have the highest praise for the great loyalty shown by the Civil Service to governments of all kinds.' [*Official Report*, 14 April 1981; Vol. 3, c. 136.] ...

Two years after ministers rejected a ban on union membership at GCHQ, the Foreign Secretary and the Prime Minister took a decision to ban the unions right out of the blue. Their only excuse was that the government had not avowed the existence of GCHQ as an intelligence centre until they published the report of the Security Commission on the Prime affair. I have been in the House for more than 30 years and that is the daftest excuse I have ever heard a government give for an act of policy ...

For the Prime Minister and the Foreign Secretary to tell us in 1984 that no one had known – the government had never admitted – until eight months ago that GCHQ was an intelligence headquarters is arrant nonsense, and they know it.

It is difficult to find any convincing reason for this sudden decision by the government – eight months after the publication of the Security Commission report on Prime – except for their fear of staff reaction to the introduction of the polygraph, or lie detector, which is due to begin on an experimental basis in a few weeks' time. The lie detector has been described by a scientist who studied it as wrong on two thirds of the occasions on which it was used, and it was condemned by the Royal Commission on Criminal Procedure as unsuitable for use in court proceedings in Britain for that reason ...

We all agree that there is a powerful case for guaranteeing continuity of operation at GCHQ, but the unions have now offered that in terms of a contract which is legally binding on individual employees. In the evidence quoted at the end of the Select Committee report, Sir Brian Tovey says that had that offer been available when he was director-general, it would have satisfied him. Such an arrangement is far better than a yellow-dog union like a staff association ...

If the government had a spark of common sense, they would have jumped at the offer made by the trade unions, and the next Labour government will do so when the opportunity arrives. But the Prime Minister has behaved in this affair, uncharacteristically, like General Galtieri, who rejected her offer on the Falklands – a very favourable offer – preferred to fight, and lost ...

The Foreign Secretary and the Prime Minister talk of conflicts of loyalty. They have forced on the staff in GCHQ the most damaging conflict of loyalty known to man – loyalty to principle as against loyalty to family. The staff know that in many cases, if they give up work at GCHQ, it will be impossible for them to find work anywhere else without breaking their family life.

One of the results of the government's action has been to give more publicity to GCHQ in the last three weeks than it has had over the past 40 years. The government's action is risking the disruption of the work of GCHQ at one of the most dangerous periods in the post-war world, when the Lebanon is in chaos, when the Gulf war is threatening oil supplies to the Western world, when the United States is warning of military intervention very close to the Soviet frontier, and when there is a new leadership in the Kremlin. What a wonderful moment for the government to choose to put this vital operation in jeopardy ...

It is possible that the government may sack some members of the staff in order to encourage the others, but then they will find that staff pay is made up by the trade union movement, and the government will face legal action. The Civil Service tribunal, as the government know, can award unlimited damages if it finds against the government in favour of an employee who has been unfairly treated.

The unions will also be going to the International Labour Organization because they believe – and I share their belief, although I am not a lawyer – that the government's decision is in flat violation of an ILO convention that the government have signed.

I ask the government to recognize that they have now embarked on a long-drawn-out campaign that they are bound to lose. The campaign will continue until the government change their mind, or until the government are changed by the British people, because there is deep feeling on this matter throughout the trade union movement ...

Every trade unionist in Britain feels threatened by what the government have done. The anger felt by trade unionists was felt deeply by everyone, not least Mr Murray, who attended the meeting with the Prime Minister last week, because she was felt to be accusing the trade unions of lack of patriotism, of being prepared to risk people's lives and to break their promises. The Foreign Secretary made it crystal clear in his speech that that, in his view, is what trade union membership at GCHQ must imply. I ask the government to recognize that they really cannot talk in those terms to people such as Terry Duffy and Kate Losinska, who are now leading the campaign against the government. What a miracle the government have achieved in the trade union movement ...

I have not wasted time on the Foreign Secretary this afternoon, although I am bound to say that I feel that some of his colleagues must be a bit tired by now of his hobbling around from one of the doorsteps to another, with a bleeding hole in his foot and a smoking gun in his hand, telling them that he did not know it was loaded.

The Foreign Secretary, however, is not the real villain in this case; he is the fall guy. Those of us with long memories will feel that he is rather like poor van der Lubbe in the Reichstag fire trial. We are asking ourselves the question that was asked at the trial: who is the Mephistopheles behind this shabby Faust? The answer to that is clear. The handling of this decision by – I quote her own back benchers – the great she-elephant, she who must be obeyed, the Catherine the Great of Finchley, the Prime Minister herself, has drawn sympathetic trade unionists, such as Len Murray, into open revolt. Her pig-headed bigotry has prevented her closest colleagues and Sir Robert Armstrong from offering and accepting a compromise.

The right hon. lady, for whom I have a great personal affection, has formidable qualities, a powerful intelligence and immense courage, but those qualities can turn into horrendous vices, unless they are moderated by colleagues who have more experience, understanding and sensitivity. As she has got rid of all those colleagues, no one is left in the Cabinet with both the courage and the ability to argue with her.

I put it to all Conservative members, but mainly to the government front bench, that to allow the right hon. lady to commit Britain to another four years of capricious autocracy would be to do fearful damage not just to the Conservative party but to the state. She has faced them with the most damaging of all conflicts of loyalty. They must choose between the interests of their country, our nation's security and our cohesion as a people and the obstinacy of an individual. I hope that they resolve this conflict in the interests of the nation. If not, they will carry a heavy responsibility for the tragedies that are bound to follow.

Denis Healey, MP for Leeds East
House of Commons, 27 February 1984

1

The day: 25 January 1984

I have read and understood General Notice 100/84 and wish to continue to be employed at GCHQ. I agree to resign from membership of any trade union to which I belong. I also undertake not to join a trade union or to engage in its affairs or to discuss with its officials my terms of employment or conditions of service or any other matter relating to my employment at GCHQ. I understand, however, that I may join a Departmental Staff Association approved for the time being by Director GCHQ.

Option form attached to General Notice GN 100/84
(see Appendix 1)

On the morning of 25 January 1984 Jack Hart set off for the hundred-mile drive to Cheltenham. In his mind he was calculating whether or not the morning's meetings would finish in time for a few pints before the meeting that afternoon with Anthony Hird, head of E Division. Months and years later small signs, which should have caused unease, were identified; but at the time the pub was the bigger concern as the battered Ford Cortina made its way north.

When the car pulled into Priors Road – on Cheltenham's ring road – lines of cars could be seen as the staff arrived for work. In many ways Government Communications Headquarters (GCHQ) in Cheltenham behaved just like any large government department. Civil servants filed in and out, rushing in before nine in the morning, charging out before five in the evening.

Coming from the Culmhead outstation, near Taunton in Somerset, Jack Hart had to stop and park in the lay-by and go into the security hut to pick up his Cheltenham pass. This would allow him to go about his business on site unescorted. This done, he drove through the gates, turned right and parked the car outside A Block.

Hart now assumed his role as chairman of the trade union side (TUS), the senior lay trade union official inside GCHQ. It was a position he had obtained thanks to the voting power of two unions, the Civil Service Union and the Association of Government Supervisors and Radio Officers.

CSU and AGSRO represented the radio grades, the coal-face workers of GCHQ. The trade union side also included the other non-industrial unions: the Civil and Public Services Association, the Society of Civil and Public Servants, the Institution of Professional Civil Servants and the First Division Association. The CPSA represented clerical staff, the SCPS junior and middle management, IPCS scientific staff and the FDA senior management. The unions representing the much smaller group of industrial staff – mainly the AEU, GMB and TGWU – had their own structure. The division was the traditional split between white-collar and blue-collar workers.

A Block was as far as many visitors got on the Oakley site. It is a shapeless clutch of prefabricated post-war single storey buildings. GCHQ has two sites in Cheltenham, Oakley and Benhall. The Oakley site was built up a hill on the edges of Cheltenham with the more restricted areas placed further away from the road. The most sensitive areas are underground, on floors protected and hidden by an unimpressive superstructure. It was a cramped site for nearly three thousand staff, who complained constantly about the lack of car parking and about the security officers' habit of slapping 'no parking' stickers on their windscreens. Even fewer visitors went to GCHQ's other site in Cheltenham, Benhall, where research and technical work is done.

A Block housed E Division, the Establishments section of GCHQ. As such it was responsible for what passed as personnel management within GCHQ. Its head at the time, Anthony Hird, was called E. His division had five main sections numbered E1–E5. The head of each section used the letter/number code of the section he ran. E3 looked after conditions of service, discipline and negotiations with trade unions.

E3, Don Chidgey, had had a hectic time. The hardest problem, in GCHQ of all places, had been keeping the plans secret. Although the overall level of union membership was only 58 per cent, the unions were well organized in some areas with a good information network.

GCHQ's planning had been long, meticulous and, above all, secret. Political authority had been sought and received from the Prime Minister, Margaret Thatcher. Sir Robert Armstrong, the

Cabinet Secretary and the Head of the Civil Service, had acquiesced. Legal advice had been required from the Treasury Solicitor. The labyrinthine mechanics of the bureaucratic operation had been carefully co-ordinated. Fear of a leak from the CSU members operating the photocopying machines, who were normally used for GCHQ's sensitive printing requirements, led management to arrange for the printing to be done by their cousins across the water, at the US National Security Agency.

With hindsight, they should have used ordinary HMSO envelopes for the letter and General Notice 100/84 that were to be sent to each of GCHQ's seven thousand civilian staff. The different stock was soon spotted. Moreover, senior E Division staff would have preferred not having to unload the van containing the letters themselves. They had been seen, late in the evening, engaged in this unusual activity. It was considered unusual since it was both hard work and outside normal working hours. But its purpose was never guessed.

The most dangerous task, but a necessary one, had been calling home all the overseas officers-in-charge for a briefing. OICs were the senior officials responsible for GCHQ's major overseas stations, notably in Hong Kong and Cyprus. They had to be briefed on management's plans as they were responsible for many key staff. Although these comings and goings had been picked up by the trade union side, once again their purpose had not been guessed.

The cause of all this subterfuge was the four-page General Notice 100/84, which was quickly to become the most notorious circular ever to have been distributed inside GCHQ. It was signed by John Adye, in his role as Principal Establishment Officer, and was accompanied by a covering letter from Peter Marychurch, the recently promoted Director of GCHQ. 'The purpose of this letter', Marychurch wrote, 'is to tell you of an important development which will affect us all in GCHQ. Our future work will depend on its success.' He ended with the hope that all the staff would accept what he euphemistically described as 'the changes' so that they could continue to provide 'the high level of service which is of such vital importance to the country'.

GN 100/84, as it came to be called, stated that the government had decided:

a. that it has become essential to except staff from the provisions of certain employment legislation on the grounds of national security;

b. that recognition of existing trade unions in respect of employment at GCHQ is to be withdrawn;

c. that accordingly GCHQ staff will not be permitted to be members of any existing trade union;

d. that staff who remain at GCHQ will receive a financial payment in recognition of the loss of rights previously enjoyed;

e. and that staff who do not wish to remain at GCHQ are to be given the opportunity to seek to transfer elsewhere in the Civil Service.

GCHQ's work, the circular stated, 'must be conducted secretly and must provide a service on which Her Majesty's Government *and our allies* can rely with confidence at all times' (emphasis added). GN 100/84 went on to inform GCHQ staff that the key provisions of the 1975 and 1978 Employment Protection Acts – namely, their right to take a claim for unfair dismissal to an industrial tribunal and the protection that individuals could not be sacked simply for being members of an independent trade union – would no longer apply. By executive action, Sir Geoffrey Howe, Secretary of State for Foreign Affairs, had signed certificates removing these rights on grounds of 'national security'. Finally, under the archaic absolute power of the royal prerogative, Mrs Thatcher had unilaterally changed their conditions of service, removing their entitlement to belong to and be represented by a trade union.

The circular said that staff could join a staff association, although its constitution would have to be approved by the Director of GCHQ. In return for giving up their statutory rights, staff would get a special payment of £1,000 (subject to tax). Staff had to make up their minds by 1 March 1984. Those who did not accept the union ban would be offered transfers elsewhere in the Civil Service. Those who either refused to sign Option A (accepting the new conditions of service) or refused an alternative posting would have 'their employment terminated from a date to be determined by the Director'.

Unaware of what was going on behind their backs, inside the TUS office Hilda made coffee while the union representatives speculated about the purpose of that afternoon's meeting between Jack Hart and E. The rumours about the OICs being called to Cheltenham made Hart think that the meeting might be to announce further station closures. There were fears among the radio grades that a major British station, such as Culmhead or Cheadle in Staffordshire, might be in danger. When Jack Hart and Pete Bryant, the TUS secretary, had seen the OICs in the canteen the previous Friday their question 'Home for station closures?' had been met with stubborn silence.

Nancy Duffton, treasurer of the TUS and SCPS branch secretary, thought the meeting might be to do with the threatened introduction of the polygraph or 'lie detector'. Ann Downey, from the CPSA, thought it could be about facility time – that is, time off work for union duties – or one of the many arcane disputes going on with the pedantic E Division. No conclusion had been reached by the end of coffee.

On the very morning of the ban, management allowed Nancy Duffton and Jack Hart to give an induction course session on the benefits of trade unionism. The first edition of *Warning Signal* – the campaign magazine started by the unions in early February 1984 – quoted the passage in the GCHQ handbook for new entrants which management so clearly took to heart:

The management has close relationships with the unions and the departmental trade unions and you are encouraged to join the union concerned with your grade. Advice on many aspects of your employment as a civil servant is available to you as a member of your association and, should the need ever arise, representation of your personal problems can be made at the highest level. The names of officers of the various unions and the Departmental Whitley Council are to be found in the pink pages of the GCHQ telephone directory.

The official side secretary Dave Hall normally explained management's formal position about the need for good staff relations and how this was achieved by negotiations with the unions through the Whitley system. The Whitley system was a comprehensive negotiating machinery covering the whole Civil Service, set up in the 1960s to avoid the need or justification for industrial action. In concept the idea was typical of Whitehall: if you talked about any problem for long enough at enough different committees then it would eventually be either resolved or forgotten. In general it worked.

In their talk that day Jack Hart and Nancy Duffton concentrated on the benefits and services provided by unions. In all honesty they recognized that most members joined because they regarded it as an insurance policy, someone to help you out if you got into trouble or had an accident. That morning's meeting was like all the rest.

After the meeting Jack Hart went to one of the highly sensitive areas inside GCHQ to discuss shift problems with the radio officers

(ROs) working there. During the course of this meeting he was telephoned and told that both the venue and the cast for the afternoon meeting had been changed. The meeting was now to be with Adye, not only the Principal Establishment Officer but also titled 'DO', the Director of Operations. He is now the Director of GCHQ, having succeeded Sir Peter Marychurch in 1989. As far as Jack Hart knew, no one else would be present. Nothing had happened to upset his calculations on the drive up. At lunchtime he had his daily fix down the pub.

The meeting took place at 3 p.m. in John Adye's office. Apart from Adye there was the industrial convenor, Ian Hendry, senior shop steward of the industrial unions in GCHQ. The two individuals representing all the unions and all union members at GCHQ were informed of the government's decision to ban independent national trade unions at GCHQ. There was not much argument, just a few questions and a great deal of shock.

The three men then went to a committee room for a second meeting – this time with all the union representatives who could be contacted. While this meeting was going on, elsewhere in GCHQ thousands of envelopes containing GN 100/84 were being distributed to every member of staff on the two Cheltenham sites. By the time the union representatives returned to the TUS office all the letters had reached their destination.

As thousands of GCHQ officials throughout the UK opened the letters the initial reaction was one of puzzlement rather than anger. Robin Smith, an electronics engineer working on communications security, recalls that staff spent the rest of the day discussing with their colleagues what the circular meant and what had sparked it off. Certainly little work was done that day, though few – least of all top management – anticipated the disruption that the government's decision was to provoke in the weeks, months and years ahead. So far everything had gone like clockwork; everywhere – in Cheltenham and at the outstations – the script was identical, the delivery simultaneous. This was true even overseas.

The GCHQ presence had been restored to Ascension Island in July 1978 by the Labour government in order to monitor the growing Argentinian threat to the Falkland Islands. In 1984 John and Vi Cook were halfway through their second tour of duty there. There was so little to do at the GCHQ outstation on Ascension Island – at a place called Two Boats – that staff were 'strongly' encouraged to be accompanied by their spouses. John, secretary of CSU branch 799, was a communications and cypher officer. A CCO's job was to send SIGINT (signals intelligence) material collected by the station back to his or her colleagues manning the Comcen – the communications centre – in W, GCHQ's Communications Division in the depths of the Oakley site in Cheltenham.

At 3 p.m. on Ascension Island staff were given their letters as they sat at work or as they came on shift. The choice they found was either to accept the new conditions of service or to be flown back to the UK, probably to face the sack. No information got through from the unions. Later there were stories of meetings and protests, but it all seemed too distant. At first the only contact was unofficial cryptic messages sent 'down the line' through the communications channels with Cheltenham.

Also at 3 p.m., just as Jack Hart's first meeting with Adye was starting, Sir Robert Armstrong – Cabinet Secretary and head of the Civil Service – began to read a prepared statement to the general secretaries of the Civil Service trade unions, who had been sum-moned at short notice to the Cabinet Office at 70 Whitehall. It was the cue for Sir Geoffrey Howe, the Foreign Secretary, to rise from his place on the government front bench in the Commons. This was the first that the outside world knew of this carefully prepared stratagem. The task of informing Parliament about the union ban fell to Howe since in theory GCHQ was responsible to the Foreign Secretary of the day. In fact, he had never visited the organization.

'Government Communications Headquarters', he told the Com-mons, 'is responsible for intelligence work of crucial importance to our national security. To be effective this work must be conducted secretly. Moreover, GCHQ must provide a service that can be relied on with confidence at all times.' Thus the government immediately set out its markers for the ensuing debate, suggesting that the unions were a potential threat to national security and could not be trusted. In reply to questions, Sir Geoffrey referred to the 'need to avoid a repetition of the industrial action that took place in the three years from 1979 to 1981', which, he claimed, 'faced staff doing this work with a severe conflict of loyalties'. He spoke of the 'need to secure freedom from serious disruption and to remove the risk of strike action' and the need to 'prevent exposure to industrial tribunals' – a reference to the certificates he had signed taking away from all GCHQ staff the statutory rights Parliament had laid down to protect employees from unfair dismissal.

A few days later Alan Watkins wrote in *The Observer*:

Sir Geoffrey made his statement without apparently having the least idea of the enormity of what he was saying. This insensitivity is his great political strength. Those who are acquainted with him know him to be a kindly and decent soul, with no side at all: but, if the government had decided to set up a concentration camp in the Western Highlands for, say, dissident elements who had incurred Mr Bernard Ingham's disapproval [Ingham was Thatcher's influential press secretary], there would be no one more suitable to make the announcement than Sir Geoffrey.

The Foreign Office itself, where the Foreign Secretary is based, is strategically sited in Whitehall, physically separating Downing Street from the Treasury and Parliament. The Foreign Office trade union side traditionally held their meetings at lunchtime. This avoided upsetting management – it meant not taking the time off work even though they were entitled to. The usual business of the TUS was protecting the allowances, perks and way of life of the Diplomatic Service. This was done to the accompaniment of opening sandwich boxes, extracting neat sandwiches and inserting them into well-mannered mouths.

After a typical TUS meeting Hugh Lanning, a trade union officer, was wandering back to CSU headquarters in Praed Street near Paddington Station in West London. On the way he picked up the ingredients for the dinner he was meant to be cooking that night for Fiona, his wife, and her best friend Amanda.

Hugh Lanning was the full-time officer responsible for looking after CSU's communication grades and its members in GCHQ. He had held this position since 1983 when he took over from Fred Phillips, an ex-GCHQ employee who had held the post almost since unions began in GCHQ – some thirty years earlier. Within GCHQ, the CSU had traditionally been the largest and most influential union.

Briefcase and domestic shopping in hand he walked into 5 Praed Street and went up to his office on the first floor. As he entered, Rose Crockwell – Lanning's secretary, and one of the best in the union – announced that he had been summoned by the General Secretary, professional Yorkshireman John Sheldon. He was to go at once to the Council of Civil Service Unions' office near St James' Park tube station.

Lanning, like so many others who had heard the news on the

grapevine, could not believe it when Rose told him. Reluctantly, he took a taxi to the CCSU. He soon realized that it was not simply John Sheldon who was panicking. All the general secretaries of the Civil Service unions were there, along with other officials, asking each other: 'Where is GCHQ? What does it do? How many members have we got there?'

They had just returned from the Cabinet Office where Armstrong had read to them the statement which Howe was at that very moment reading to MPs. CCSU's Major Policy Committee (MPC), the senior committee of Civil Service non-industrial trade unions, was now trying to decide what to do. Not surprisingly this was proving difficult. There was no real precedent for such action by government. They had no idea how their members in GCHQ would react. The broad terms of a statement to the media were agreed and carefully delivered by Bill McCall, MPC chair and the longstanding and cautious General Secretary of IPCS.

John Sheldon and Hugh Lanning were volunteered to travel down to Cheltenham that night, to meet Jack Hart and organize a meeting for union members the next day. A leaflet was already drafted calling on members not to sign away their rights. There was as yet no venue for the meeting, and no time for it had been set. Through the good offices of Endsleigh Insurance Brokers in Cheltenham, a second edition of the leaflet was printed the following morning. It was handed out at lunchtime, informing GCHQ staff that the meeting would be held at 4 p.m. in the historic Pittville Pump Rooms, still alleged to possess the healing spa water for which Cheltenham was famous.

The journey to Cheltenham was uneventful. Sheldon and Lanning went to Reading to pick up Sheldon's car and a change of clothes. Hugh Lanning phoned Fiona to let her know that her and Amanda's dinner was now in Reading and that the chef was travelling on to Cheltenham. Between Oxford and Cheltenham it started to snow very heavily, so much so that they nearly had to stop and turn back.

It was gone midnight when Sheldon and Lanning arrived in Cheltenham. In the bar of the Queen's Hotel they found a forlorn and lonely Jack Hart. The Queen's is Cheltenham's traditional flagship hotel. It has since played host to Mrs Thatcher, but for the next twenty-four hours it acted as the unions' base. They soon went 'downmarket' to the George Hotel after discovering that a bottle of whisky to keep the press quiet at the Queen's had cost over thirty pounds.

Refreshment brought neither inspiration nor hope. The fundamental question remained: how would the members react? Jack Hart
hardly had time to think out his own response while events were
pushing him to the forefront as the 'union leader inside GCHQ'. But
instinctively he was crossing a threshold that was to change the rest
of his life. Many more, over the next few weeks, were to face the same
experience. That night, the only decision they could make was to go
to bed, resolving to fight but not knowing what that meant or how to
do it.

The circular – GN 100/84 – had all the appearance of conclusive
finality; that from the government's point of view, there was no more
to be said. This was far from the case, and in retrospect it is a pity that
MPs, the trade union movement and even senior officials within
Whitehall who were horrified by the decision did not recognize this
earlier. The government was in a muddle. Despite the fact that a
union ban had first been mooted back in 1981 (and had been rejected
by the then Foreign Secretary, Lord Carrington), politically the
decision bore all the hallmarks of being hastily as well as surrepti-
tiously taken, with 10 Downing Street ill-prepared for the legal and
other consequences of its action.

It was not until 2 February that Tom King, then Employment
Secretary, announced that staff who refused to give up their union
rights and move to an alternative Civil Service posting would be
sacked without compensation. This directly contradicted earlier
ministerial statements which suggested that no one would be sacked.

GN 100/84 itself had no legal force whatsoever. The certificates
signed by Sir Geoffrey Howe did not in themselves remove the right
of staff to belong to an independent trade union; they merely
removed their statutory protections as employees. It was as late as 7
February that Armstrong officially informed Marychurch that
Thatcher had given the formal instruction banning unions at GCHQ.
She did so under a 1982 Civil Service Order in Council, which gives
the Prime Minister the power to change civil servants' conditions of
service at will.

Nor did GN 100/84 refer specifically to industrial action in 1979
and 1981, although this was the explanation for the ban given to
Parliament. It was an explanation which, as we shall see, simply does
not stand up to scrutiny. The government argued that it could
impose a union ban only after GCHQ's role as an intelligence-
gathering centre was officially 'avowed' in May 1983 in the wake of

the Geoffrey Prime spy affair (see Chapter 3). As the all-party House of Commons Employment Committee asked: 'Does this mean that but for the exposure of a spy, which led to the avowal, the government would have continued indefinitely to be seriously disturbed about possible threats to national security at GCHQ, and yet be prepared to take no action?' Sir Brian Tovey got round this question by telling the Employment Committee at a private hearing on 8 February 1984 that 'There was no particular reason for choosing January 1984 for making the announcement.' The Employment Committee later called on the government to reconsider the ban in a unanimous report on 14 February.

More astonishingly still, it emerged later that Thatcher had imposed the ban simply by issuing an oral instruction to Armstrong a few days before the previous Christmas, on 22 December 1983. When he ruled in the High Court in July 1984 that the way the ban had been imposed was illegal, Mr Justice Glidewell commented:

Normally when a Minister is empowered to give an instruction or make a direction or decision, he does so in a document. It is highly unusual to have an instruction in so important a matter given orally. I would have expected the Prime Minister's oral direction to be followed by the preparation of a document, which would then receive her signature.

It was a pointed reminder of the cavalier way in which Thatcher and her senior advisers had deprived thousands of civil servants of one of their basic rights. The behaviour of Thatcher's advisers had also been deeply cynical and dishonest. As Glidewell noted, Armstrong was still offering to consult the unions over the proposed introduction of the polygraph to GCHQ in a letter to Peter Jones, CCSU secretary, on 9 January. This was more than two weeks after Armstrong had been told by Thatcher that in future there would be no role whatsoever for unions at GCHQ – in consultations about anything, let alone the benighted polygraph.

The union ban, and the way it was imposed, was to cast a shadow over the remainder of the Thatcher years. It came to be seen as a particularly outrageous example of her attitude towards civil rights and a symbol of her style of government. It was also one issue on which the TUC was united during one of the most turbulent periods in its history.

2

The motives

There is an inherent conflict between the structure of the trade unions and loyalty to the state.

Margaret Thatcher, 23 February 1984

At the Civil Service Appeal Board hearing on 6 July 1989 a number of international events were cited as examples of the potential damage trade unions could cause to GCHQ. Peter Little, who had replaced Anthony Hird as E – head of Establishments – listed the US hostage crisis in Tehran in the late 1970s, the Soviet invasion of Afghanistan in 1979, the Soviet military build-up at the time of political unrest in Poland in December 1980, and a major Soviet military exercise early the following year.

It was a typically robust statement. Yet once the hearing was over, Little quietly asked for it to be excluded from the record. He went out of his way to emphasize that he was not saying how GCHQ had been involved in these events – if it had been involved at all.

Guilt by inference was fundamental to the government's public presentation of its case for banning trade unions at GCHQ. Sir Geoffrey Howe's statement to the House of Commons on 25 January 1984 referred to ten thousand working days lost due to industrial action between 1979 and 1981. These were years in which Civil Service trade unions had taken industrial action over pay and had publicly involved civil servants in GCHQ in the disputes.

The apparent logic of the argument is simple. There were important events – both predicted and unforeseen – happening in the world. GCHQ is a highly sensitive organization involved in intelligence gathering. Trade unions took action in GCHQ during this time. Some harm must have been done.

There is a second thread to the argument: trade unions as national

18

institutions are the problem, not individual trade unionists – and certainly not the staff of GCHQ. The claim is that the industrial action to which the government repeatedly referred involved Civil Service-wide disputes in which the unions had deliberately and unnecessarily involved GCHQ staff. They had done this by bringing pressure to bear on their members in GCHQ. The simple conclusion is that there is a conflict of loyalty in being both a member of a national trade union and an employee of GCHQ. The term 'national trade union', by which was meant a union affiliated to the TUC, had to be introduced to distinguish between the unions that the government was seeking to ban and the staff association that it was hoping to set up.

This neat picture of cause and effect hides more than it reveals about the real reasons behind the government's decision. For the government's theory to hold true, the industrial action in GCHQ had to be national in character; secondly, it had to have the effect described.

'BLACKOUT THREAT TO RADIO VIGIL' screamed the *Daily Sketch* on Tuesday, 16 September 1969. The report under the headline was the result of intelligent guesswork by a journalist based on stories picked out from union journals. It contained a number of inaccuracies, not uncommon in the days before even the existence of GCHQ was acknowledged. But the essence of the story was correct and the guesswork not that wide of the mark.

It described a Whitehall pay battle involving government radio operators which threatened 'to black out Britain's secret world-wide wireless watch'. The 'monitoring of foreign coded broadcasts by the Combined Signals Organisation' was alleged to be 'a vital element of the Foreign Office early warning system'. The reporter, Michael Edwards, the *Sketch*'s industrial correspondent, went on to 'reveal that work-to-rule tactics by these operators recently cut off full early warning information to the Foreign Office'. Finally, he stated that the work-to-rule was in protest against a Civil Service Arbitration Tribunal award rejecting the demand of CSU and AGSRO for a new pay scale ranging up to £1,875 a year.

Certainly the dispute did take place; it did involve Composite Signals Organization (CSO) radio operators; and it did have an effect. One branch, Cyprus, estimated that 'production has been very badly hit, even as much as 75 or 80 per cent in certain sectors'.

At GCHQ's Hong Kong station production of intelligence came to a halt.

To understand the dispute and its effect it is necessary to have a basic idea of the work of the CSO radio operator in the late 1960s and early 1970s. At that time the radio operators regarded themselves as the 'eyes and ears of the world of radio intelligence'. Those present at the closed sessions of the Civil Service Arbitration Tribunal – at which no national union officials were allowed – say that management suggested that the operator was merely the 'fingers' of the organization. The impression was given that the operator did not have to show any initiative or require any brains, and that all the information required to cover the operator's task was available on cards provided by other staff.

It was probably these remarks, rather than the actual award of the tribunal, which sparked off the dispute. Action taken included withdrawing goodwill, banning overtime, withdrawing from asymmetrical watch-keeping systems (shifts which had fewer staff on during the night, the usual pattern for radio officers being full, symmetrical cover twenty-four hours a day), banning unpaid substitution to cover work of a higher grade, and a general work-to-rule. This last included 'working strictly to Headquarters Card instructions; all such working to be strictly confined to Radio grade duties'. The message was: if that is all they think we do, then that is what we will do. We will follow their instructions – no more, no less.

The radio operators (ROs) were civilians employed by GCHQ. But in those days they were described as working for the Composite Signals Organization, the cover-name used to disguise their involvement in signals intelligence. The tasks of GCHQ were stated to be the development and maintenance of an up-to-date knowledge of the radio communications of most countries in the world – their functions, methods of working and equipment. The basic material was provided by the operator, whose function was the interception, identification and recording – if necessary on a continuing basis – of all types of foreign communications and non-communications transmissions. In this task the operator was assisted by a continuing feedback of information from GCHQ in Cheltenham, which would relay information supplied by other communications staff.

The operators normally worked in teams under the overall control of a radio supervisor, who allocated a cover-task to each individual. From that point on the operator was responsible for the radio and associated work involved in the task position. This meant that the operator might be required to undertake any of the following:

- The operation of radio equipment to receive manual morse, radio printer, voice, data and facsimile transmissions and non-communications transmissions, e.g. radar.
- Direction finding, radio fingerprinting and morse operator characteristic analysis.
- Functions in direct support of operators engaged on intercept.
- Outstation intelligence reporting duties.
- The operation of on-line communications equipment.
- Transmission in morse, for which they were trained at twenty-five words per minute.

The very nature of the ROs' work presented exceptional difficulties. They had to receive and copy as accurately as possible transmissions that they were not intended to receive. This has a number of major practical effects.

At the sites used for eavesdropping, conditions of reception were often very unfavourable compared to those enjoyed by the intended recipient. For example, the intercept operator may have had to obtain the wanted signal through heavy interference. The interceptor, unlike the ordinary telecommunications operator, did not work in collaboration with the person transmitting signals, and therefore could not request repeats! If the signal was not intercepted first time, it was probably lost for ever. Clearly this required a wide knowledge of the various codes used by foreign networks.

The interceptor often had to find the 'tasks', searching in frequency and time for the required activity. The RO also needed to be able to recognize transmissions among others that might superficially be very similar. This was especially the case when intercepting targets that had deliberately adopted communications methods and procedures designed to make interception and recognition difficult. Even reports of 'no activity' could be of considerable value, and the chat between foreign operators could often be as significant as the actual messages.

In the interception of manual morse the RO's job was to pick up, follow and copy the transmissions of a group of stations. These might work on one or more frequencies and could change without warning. This called for the simultaneous operation of two radio receivers and the ability to receive morse of differing quality and various speeds.

Many nationalities used additional symbols up to a total of 96. ROs also had to search systematically within a given frequency band to maintain overall knowledge of all morse activity.

By the 1970s, the widespread use of non-morse methods of transmission, both internationally and nationally, required the ability to use a wide range of equipment and techniques. For example, the types of transmission which had to be intercepted ranged from single-channel teleprinters to high-speed data transmissions.

Those employed on 'technical search' had to locate, investigate and report the technical details of all new types of communication and any other types of transmission. Specialized operations meant intercepting, direction finding – that is, finding the direction from which clandestine transmissions came – and searching for very high-speed transmissions, which were often technically compressed as well. Finally, the operators were employed on the preliminary analysis of intercepted material.

In 1969 GCHQ employed 2,200 radio operators alone. GCHQ had moved on dramatically from the now famous image of a few boffin code-breakers unravelling wartime secrets at Bletchley Park (see Chapter 3). During the war the Government Code and Cypher School (GC&CS), the precursor of GCHQ, was a small organization receiving most of its raw material from military signals and intelligence units.

The relationship with the military was described by GCHQ management in 1969 as one of 'full partnership at all levels of planning and implementation'. The armed forces participated in drawing up central equipment plans. More significantly, the way tasks were divided between stations around the world depended on the agreement of the military. In some stations the relationship was even closer – the Cyprus station was, and still is, regarded as a single entity under army operational command, receiving a single task list from (GCHQ) Headquarters.

Despite this tightly knit relationship with the armed forces, GCHQ was by 1970 a major government department – officially under the control of the Foreign Office – but with vast resources of its own, harvesting SIGINT (signals intelligence) from around the world. Whatever their skills, the radio operators were the organization's biggest single grade; they were GCHQ's 'coal-face workers'.

The industrial action in 1969–70 had an immediate effect which demonstrated the impact that the ROs could have as well as their determination to fight for fair treatment on pay. The key to the 1969 dispute had been the 'plus or minus factor', the degree to which the receivers were accurate. The fine tuning by the RO determined whether or not anything was found, and the literal following of instructions could guarantee that nothing was picked up. To assist in finding the target when the industrial action finished the ROs maintained unofficial logs during the dispute. Miraculously the enemy, who during the dispute could not be found, suddenly reappeared!

The ruling of the Civil Service Arbitration Tribunal had become known in early August, and representations were then made to the Director of GCHQ, Sir Leonard Hooper, and to the Treasury. These were to no avail and the action started at 1700 hours on Friday, 29 August 1969. The general secretaries of both the unions involved, CSU and AGSRO, were summoned from the TUC to Cheltenham to discuss the dispute. By 4 September they were able to write to all branches recommending a return to normal working on the basis of a further immediate review of ROs' pay. The action had lasted six days.

Technological change means that radio operators, or officers as they are now known, can no longer have the same effect – indeed, avoiding such dependence on ROs was an added motive behind GCHQ's investment in automatic devices and new technology to replace parts of the RO's job. A union representative in Hong Kong was later informed by a senior management official that the department had 'determined it won't happen again'. So far, however, the devices have had only limited success.

This dispute did not lead to the banning of trade unions. It was not even mentioned in the case put forward for banning unions. Yet its impact was probably greater than any other dispute involving GCHQ. Indeed, during the 1970s – the period immediately following the dispute – unions were consulted perhaps more often and more thoroughly than at any other time.

The government has said that it would have been very difficult to take action against the unions at a time when the role and existence of GCHQ had not been officially acknowledged. This did not happen until the Prime case in 1983. In 1969 there was a Labour government in power. The political climate was very different. This is perhaps reflected in the attitude of GCHQ to the *Daily Sketch* article.

Shortly after the report was printed, the unions wrote to the

Director of GCHQ expressing 'extreme concern and regret' about such an article. It turned out that the journalist concerned had in fact consulted the Secretary of the Defence, Press and Broadcasting Committee, which pointed to a number of passages in the article which infringed D Notices. These were deleted voluntarily by the paper.

The D Notice system, a system of voluntary self-censorship run by Whitehall in co-operation with the media, was set up in 1912. It is administered by the Defence, Press and Broadcasting Committee – the D Notice Committee – consisting of senior Whitehall officials – the permanent secretaries of the Ministry of Defence, the Home Office and the Foreign Office – and a number of senior media executives. Its secretary is a retired senior armed forces officer who has an office in the MoD. He can be contacted by editors and journalists if they want advice about whether information they may want to publish contravenes D Notices. These cover such issues as the movements of submarines carrying nuclear weapons and the activities of the security and intelligence services. The D Notice system has no legal standing and is increasingly ignored as editors prefer to make their own judgements or seek the advice of their own lawyers.

The reply of Sir Leonard Hooper, the Director of GCHQ, to the letter from the unions is interesting:

It is however, rather more difficult to prevent them [i.e. articles of this kind] than may be generally realised. We should be very happy to have a mutual agreement to do nothing to stimulate or inspire press publicity but I do not think it is possible altogether to prevent press publications of this type. The press are at liberty (within the laws) to print what they think is newsworthy, subject only to limitations on any matters which infringe security. Even in this context, adherence to a D Notice is entirely voluntary on the part of the press, and the Government has to rely on the willing co-operation of the press in such matters ...

The Secretary of the D Notice Committee is not entitled to delete or rectify parts of an article which are merely incorrect.

This is a far cry from the later days of the ABC case and Zircon (see Chapter 3).

The radio officers' dispute in 1969 was just one of a limited, though significant, number of departmental disputes which have taken place in GCHQ over the years. Almost as important was the 1979 dispute involving station radio officers – the SROs – whose job it was to supervise the ROs. This dispute was referred to in the House of Commons on 30 July 1984 when, responding to a question from Oonagh McDonald, a Labour front-bench spokeswoman, the Foreign Secretary acknowledged that there had been industrial action by station radio officers between 20 December 1979 and 13 February 1980. The action taken was selective, with small groups of SROs going on strike for limited periods of time.

GCHQ has always been at the forefront of investment and design in new technology to help carry out its tasks. By the late 1970s radio operators were sitting at computer-assisted operating consoles. Obviously pictures of the 'set rooms' in GCHQ are not published. But an impression can be gained from BBC Monitoring (see below), that part of the BBC's World Service – funded by the Foreign Office – responsible for listening to public broadcasts from radio stations throughout the world. In GCHQ each console was equipped with receivers, KEEPNET recorders, a tuning aid (LINELIGHT), a morse recognizer (LIVEBAIT), a keyboard input for copying signals and for access to the computer, and a visual display unit (VDU) both for rapid presentation of data about their tasks and for use as a copying aid.

For morse surveillance and task acquisition, the receivers were accurate to plus or minus 5 kilohertz. Channel watching was assisted by a scanning device such as LIVEBAIT, a morse detector which

This picture of the original BBC listening room at Caversham gives an indication of the set-up at GCHQ.

could monitor up to four receivers at once or configurations of twenty-four receivers. KEEPNET was a new unconventional recorder which, when linked to LIVEBAIT, identified the start of any activity being monitored. Tasks were listed in computer files so that they were instantly available and could be easily updated.

Automatic 'real time' entries could be inserted. Consoles were linked to computers such as the Honeywell 316, which had the now modest-sounding capacity of 32k, or 1 million words. The computer gave warnings at 75, 90 and 95 per cent of saturation. At 100 per cent the system came to a stop.

The SRO was essentially a resources controller, responsible for allocating tasks to the receiving operators, keeping abreast of activity patterns on a minute-by-minute basis, making changes in task-cover according to developing situations in the world and giving guidance – for example, on how to handle new items. If a major targeted event showed signs of developing, the SRO was responsible for recognizing it, reporting it to the analysis section, adjusting tasking accordingly and dropping tasks unconnected with the event. Using judgement and experience, the SRO was responsible for position loading – for transferring tasks between positions to balance the load, taking account of the skill of individual operators.

SROs were all experienced operators themselves. With radio officers refusing to undertake any SRO task, industrial action by the supervisors removed a key component in the chain of command and organization. They were responsible for all liaison from the set room with internal and external operational and cover authorities. Without them there was no way properly to control what was done. The action also restricted feedback on the set tasks. Normally there would have been notes on how long nets had been on cover that day, the extent of recovery of the nets, how many task objectives had been met, what tasks had not yet been observed because of higher-priority activity, and unusual technical developments or any faults occurring in the system.

The very limited action was thinly spread over the period between 20 December 1979 and 13 February 1980. But once again the dispute was resolved quickly and to the satisfaction of the unions. One of the key factors that brought the dispute to a head was the refusal to operate a piece of new equipment. Under normal arrangements new equipment had to undergo thorough operational testing before being introduced. The National Security Agency – GCHQ's

American partner – had applied pressure on GCHQ to speed up the introduction of new equipment to help the NSA monitor the Tehran hostage crisis. Much to GCHQ's embarrassment the equipment under trial was briefly introduced, but was then turned off, although normal facilities continued to be operated. The unions had agreed to the use of the equipment on the understanding that negotiations would continue. However, having summoned union representatives to London ostensibly to settle the dispute, the Treasury and GCHQ management broke off negotiations and refused to make an offer.

The importance of both disputes – the 1969 RO dispute and the 1979 SRO dispute – lies not in their intrinsic impact on GCHQ, which was at least as great as later disputes, but in the reaction to them. Nothing was done; no action was taken. Why? Because they provided no justification for banning national trade unions. Both disputes concerned only GCHQ staff. They were about exclusively GCHQ issues. The pressure for action had come from GCHQ staff. It was GCHQ staff who decided to take action, determined what action to take, controlled the action and decided when to call it off.

The disputes also suggest that the union ban cannot be explained solely by referring to past industrial action. If this had been the case then unions would have been banned much earlier than 1984. Other factors must have contributed to the decision; industrial action could not logically have been the sole or main cause for the ban. Before contemplating what some of the other reasons might be, it is worth considering what impact industrial action in GCHQ might have had on what is now referred to as 'national security'. Ten thousand working days lost as a result of industrial action sounds as if it would have had a substantial effect, but this is a misleading figure if not considered in the context of the workings of GCHQ as a whole.

In November 1988 the new 'E' – Peter Little – heard the internal appeal against the dismissal of one of the fourteen trade union members who were eventually dismissed – John Cook. In trying to justify the fact that the Government Communications Staff Federation – the staff association set up with the connivance of management – was a trade union, but not one that should be banned, he quoted relative membership figures. Little stated that the GCSF had in membership 52 per cent of staff. This compared favourably with the 58 per cent that the unions had at the time of the ban.

Up until this moment, the number of staff whom GCHQ employed was supposed to be an official secret. Indeed, Mike Grindley, the chair of GCHQ Trade Unions – representing staff who refused to accept the union ban – had his positive vetting security clearance removed in November 1987 after being quoted in the press as stating that random searches of staff leaving GCHQ had commenced and for repeating the well-publicized figure of seven thousand employees (see Chapter 6).

The unions know how many members they had in GCHQ. In 1983 the last official figure that management had given the unions for the total number of union members was 4,776. If this was 58 per cent of the total number of staff, it is easy to work out how many staff there were – 8,234. No action was taken against Mr Little for revealing this official secret.

In order to assess the impact of the ten thousand days of industrial action we can use the public figure of seven thousand employees for illustrative purposes. A little more mathematics is then necessary.

Civil servants work 5 days a week.

They have between 4 and 6 weeks' leave a year – let us say on average 5 weeks.

Each member of staff is therefore liable to work 47 x 5 days in the year: that is, 235 days.

Assuming there are seven thousand staff, 7,000 x 235 = 1,645,000 working days a year.

The ten thousand days were lost over three years, 1979–81. During this period there were available to GCHQ 3 x 1,645,000 = 4,935,000 working days.

Therefore ten thousand days represent 0.20 per cent of the total – a fifth of 1 per cent. And this ignores the vast majority of years since the war when there has been no industrial action.

Compare this with the figure for time lost due to weekends over the same three-year period – 2,184,000 working days. Put another way, ten thousand working days represents less than half a day lost each year per employee over the three years in question – far less than would have been lost due to sick leave. However one looks at it, ten thousand days were in absolute terms a drop in the ocean.

This in itself does not answer the charge that national security was threatened by the industrial action. It could quite legitimately be suggested that what is important is not the amount of action, but the sensitivity of the areas where the action took place. These are normally regarded as those areas where there is continuous shift working twenty-four hours a day. At the most only 15 per cent of staff work such shifts.

Throughout the dispute, it was never part of the government's case that individual GCHQ employees were untrustworthy or disloyal. Yet every case of industrial action took place after GCHQ staff had freely voted in favour. Unless it is proposed that the staff deliberately sought to undermine national security, it must be assumed that the staff themselves believed the action to be 'safe'. If it is thought that the staff knowingly connived to undermine national security, then the removal of external trade unions does little to protect it.

The argument was further refined during the appeal hearings. It was not that the staff meant to cause harm; it was that they did not and could not know the damage they were causing. This is a convenient argument backed up by the management's fail-safe clause – 'of course we are not allowed to tell you what damage was done, for reasons of national security'. Equally, no one can tell what damage is the result of mismanagement.

Empirically, the government's claims are hard to prove one way or the other. But they seem unlikely to be true. Even in an organization where everything is done on a 'need to know' basis, it is reasonable to assume that staff in key areas have some idea of the importance of the work they are doing. This is borne out by the fact that certain staff refused to take action. For example, in 1981 the communications and cypher officers in CSU branch 705 unanimously rejected a suggestion that they should take industrial action, although they were asked to do so by their own General Secretary, John Sheldon. There were also areas in which, because of their sensitivity, it was not even suggested that action should take place.

Other precautions were always taken. Before an issue came to the level of an official dispute, the unions always raised the matter with the Director of GCHQ, both to give him a final opportunity to solve the problem and also to allow issues of national security to be raised. Specific notice of particular action was given beforehand to management, allowing them the opportunity to make alternative arrangements. This enabled work to be switched to other stations within GCHQ, or to GCHQ's international partners in the USA, Canada, Australia and New Zealand.

The day on which the greatest number of days were lost as a result of industrial action was 9 March 1981. But this was a 'day of action' throughout the Civil Service, known about weeks in advance. According to the government's own figures 25 per cent, fewer than two thousand staff, would have been on strike that day inside GCHQ. Only gross incompetence by GCHQ management could have allowed the action to have any effect remotely related to national security.

This might sound an exaggerated claim, but there is a simple explanation to justify it: tasking. Tasking determines where the finite resources of GCHQ will be deployed. Since the mid-1960s the department had embarked on a policy that sought to ensure that nothing of consequence went astray. Very largely, a full-take procedure was adopted. This meant that as much information as possible was recorded.

Despite the National Security Agency's desire literally to record everything, selection has to take place. This is done at every level of the intelligence-gathering process. Among the allies – the USA, the UK, Australia, Canada and New Zealand – involved in the international signals intelligence (SIGINT) agreement, different countries are tasked to cover different parts of the world. (See Chapter 3 for a more detailed explanation of the UKUSA Agreement.) The criteria for allocating this division of labour are sometimes technical: for example, based on best reception capabilities (though this is a diminishing problem with the growing use of satellites). Alternatively, the criteria might be political. Britain has had a key role because its colonial past has given it a legacy of secure sites for stations in strategic locations, such as Cyprus and Hong Kong.

With the world thus divided up, each agency then allocates areas to its various stations, and within them specific targets. This process continues until each individual radio officer is given detailed tasks and particular frequencies to monitor.

At each step of the process judgements are made about priorities, about what to cover and what not to cover. These are largely based on military, political and intelligence priorities. Where the crisis is – in Afghanistan, for example, or in the Falklands – will determine the nature of the tasks and how they are allocated. And the importance of the target will vary, according to whether it is the object of routine, commercial, time-critical or highly sensitive monitoring.

The post-war period was one of rapid expansion for GCHQ and signals intelligence. But in 1968 it too was hit by cuts in public expenditure. It was stated that because of general economic pressure, GCHQ, as many other government departments, was being forced to economize in expenditure and therefore also in staff, which was its major item of expense. In June 1968 the head of E Division wrote: 'We therefore cannot afford as much collection effort as in the past.' Clearly selection had to take place.

Resources are always a real constraint on what can be done. One example is the arrangements for Christmas, New Year and Easter bank holidays. Radio grades have traditionally been on symmetrical watch-keeping systems, which ensure that, twenty-four hours a day, there is the same cover of all set positions. This is to try and maintain a capacity to cope with all exigencies. In practice there are quieter times and one of these is Christmas and New Year, not least because the old cold war enemies – the USSR and eastern Europe – also celebrate Christmas, so there is less activity to monitor.

Christmas also happens to be a very expensive period to pay staff to attend. Management therefore forced on the staff and unions a procedure for reduced cover at Christmas, Easter and New Year. In order to save money, normal precautions would be dispensed with. S Division, responsible for radio grades, would determine the extent and period of cover-drops and inform the stations accordingly. Such was the determination of management that they resorted to complaining to the unions about excess attendance – too many staff were turning up!

Furthermore, GCHQ has back-up arrangements. These are designed to cope with breakdowns of technical equipment, adverse weather conditions – for example, typhoons in Hong Kong or snow in the UK – staff shortages due to illness and so on. Essential to this process is the whole question of managing, dropping tasks, changing priorities, and switching them from station to station and from country to country.

In an organization where only 58 per cent of staff were in a union, where the most extensive industrial action apart from 9 March involved 10 per cent of union members at the most, where it was known what action was to be taken and when and where it was to take place, it is simply not plausible to claim that national security was damaged. Sensible reorganization by management, given the advance notice from staff, would have ensured that all key tasks were covered, if any were threatened. All official statements at the time of any action back this analysis up.

This was demonstrated during the 1981 Civil Service strike – provoked, it should be emphasized, by the unilateral tearing up by the government of an established pay agreement. The unions' leadership attempted to apply pressure on a government which, though divided, was led by a Prime Minister who appeared immune to compromise. The cost of the five-month strike cannot be calculated precisely, but it certainly led to a loss of many hundreds of millions of pounds to the Exchequer, mostly as a result of action – in tax-collecting departments – taken after Mrs Thatcher refused to concede the $1/2$ per cent extra pay rise which she was later to accept in the final deal. Lord Soames, the minister for the Civil Service, was a victim of arguments he had with Mrs Thatcher during the dispute and was sacked after the 1983 election.

In April 1981 the Council of Civil Service Unions issued a press release announcing a programme of action in 'the ultra-secret Government communications network'. The action, it said, had caused 'serious embarrassment to the Government by virtue of the extremely sensitive work done within the Composite Signals Organization' – a reference to GCHQ. 'Considerable disruption and inconvenience had been caused', CCSU went on, 'and international relationships between the UK and other governments have been under great strain.' The series of actions – CCSU mentioned GCHQ sites at Bude, Cheadle and Culmhead – illustrated the depth of feeling among civil servants in an area where officials had always been reluctant to engage in industrial action. The monitoring of Soviet satellites and other signals had been disrupted, the unions claimed.

GCHQ management and the government were to make much of this during the controversy over the union ban three years later. Sir Brian Tovey, Director of GCHQ between 1978 and 1983 and architect of the ban, claimed that the effects of the 1981 dispute – and he referred particularly to the day of action, 9 March 1981 – finally convinced him of the need for the ban. What is closer to the truth is that the unions fell victim to the rhetoric of their leaders.

Asked on BBC Radio 4's *World at One* programme on 31 January 1984 how the industrial action had affected national security, Sir Geoffrey Howe responded: 'We cannot prove a single example.' More pertinently, John Nott, Defence Secretary at the time, told the Commons on 14 April 1981, after the action at GCHQ: 'Up to now they have not in any way affected operational capability in any area ... I would not wish it to be felt that I do not have the highest praise for the great loyalty shown by the Civil Service to governments of all kinds.'

In an affidavit to the High Court, the SDP leader, David Owen, stated that industrial action at GCHQ in 1979 – when he was Labour's Foreign Secretary – had had a 'minimal impact' on national security. In his autobiography, *A Balance of Power*, Jim Prior, Mrs Thatcher's former Employment and Northern Ireland Secretary, states that the action had caused dislocation within the security services. But more significantly, he says it had very much upset the Americans.

To conspiratorial minds the Americans have always seemed a likely villain in pressing GCHQ to ban trade unions. The relationship between GCHQ and the USA's National Security Agency is long standing and very close. But it is also one-sided. From a post-Second World War partnership of equals it has evolved into a master–servant arrangement of convenience. It is convenient for the Americans to have another source of ideas and technical expertise. Britain still retains a political edge in some countries which makes it easier for GCHQ to operate. The exchange of information is just as unbalanced, with GCHQ giving the Americans nearly everything of value, while the NSA is highly selective in the intelligence it deigns to give to GCHQ.

It is perhaps fairer to say that the NSA contracts GCHQ to do certain work and in return gives back some information and contributes substantially towards its costs. No figures are available (see Chapter 3) since neither the GCHQ nor the NSA budget is separately identifiable, hidden as they are within those of other departments. But it is clear the British Exchequer does not meet the whole cost of running GCHQ. For example, the deal that was done with the Americans on Bude (officially called CSOS – Composite Signals Organization Station – Morwenstow), the newest GCHQ station, was that the NSA would pay for eleven-twelfths of the construction costs and provide the technical hardware, while GCHQ would provide the staff to run it.

The British government or GCHQ management would probably describe the NSA as a large, valuable and trusted client who merely repaid GCHQ for services rendered. If the NSA is a client, it is only in the same sense that Marks and Spencer is a client of the firms which make its clothes and sandwiches. Marks and Spencer draws up a detailed specification of its requirements, dictates the way the work is to be done, inspects the suppliers' premises and organization, and makes constant quality checks and inspections. If everything is done satisfactorily, then the supplier is paid.

This type of relationship can lead to dependency, since the withdrawal of the contract would mean the collapse of the business. The threat to do so, whether real or perceived, gives enormous power to the dominant partner. It is in this context that we must consider the type of pressure exerted on GCHQ to take action against trade unions, bearing in mind that there have never been trade unions in the NSA, which is essentially run by the US military.

Following the industrial action in the Civil Service in 1981, senior Whitehall officials considered briefly what could be done to remove unions from sensitive areas. Top Whitehall officials, including Sir Frank Cooper, permanent secretary at the Ministry of Defence, discussed the proposal to ban unions in 1981. It had been put to the Joint Intelligence Committee by Sir Brian Tovey, then GCHQ Director. However, it was rejected on the grounds that it was unnecessary and a denial of basic civil rights, and that a ban would be counterproductive. That majority view was accepted by Lord Carrington, who as Foreign Secretary was the cabinet minister responsible for GCHQ. In the end most effort went into contingency plans, diversifying, contracting out work or using military personnel in order to reduce the effect of any industrial action. In GCHQ nothing was said to the unions and no obvious steps were taken to reorganize the work.

However, there was fascinating debate and correspondence within the Civil Service Union's CSO Committee. This was the elected committee representing the CSU's communication grades within GCHQ. For years it was referred to as the CSO Committee in order to maintain the integrity of GCHQ's official cover as the Composite Signals Organization – to do with signals maybe, but nothing to do with SIGINT. One of the members of the committee, Mick Verrion, was also secretary of the trade union side for the whole of GCHQ. In this capacity he worked closely, and on a full-time basis, with GCHQ management in E (Establishment) Division. On 14 April 1982 he circulated a letter to all lay members of the committee. The letter had such a high security classification that its recipients were not able to circulate its contents to other GCHQ staff without breaching security regulations. A sanitized version – that is, one with the sensitive information removed – was made available to the union at the time; the editing makes the grammar a bit strange, but the flavour is clear:

Effects of Industrial Action on the Agreement and Division of Effort

There can be no lay trade union side activist who is unaware of the broad terms of the Agreement and of the consequential Division of Effort [a reference to the UKUSA SIGINT Agreement – see Chapter 3].

In another capacity certain information on the harder line being adopted by Allies came to hand. In the past Allied operational policy was based upon close ties with, and a begrudging reliance on, GCHQ. Time alone has severed many of the close personal ties as hot and cold war colleagues retired, died or otherwise passed on. The need for reliance weakened as the collaborating effort matured in terms of techniques and man-power.

This hard-nosed attitude was becoming apparent during the mid-'70s and onwards as overseas bases became less and less efficient and useful because of technical advances. The loss of bases was not perhaps a significant one in the light of technology. Hong Kong, despite GERANIUM and KITTI-WAKE [code words for two projects at the Hong Kong stations], is today of less importance in the trade-off between allies due, in part, to the cessation of overt military activity in SE Asia and consequential rapprochement between some Eastern and Western countries and in part to BUDE-type installations [that is, satellite-based stations] in the USA.

At one time the UK could offer the allies good, solid real estate. The country was stable and the likelihood of political upheaval resulting in the expulsion of foreign installations considered remote. This is less true today. Accepting this self-evident truth allied governments have been negotiating with the Federal Republic of Germany for base areas and have been offered several reasonably secure sites with adequate protection from the armed forces. These new bases can be readily fitted out with additional operating positions. There is already a major US facility in Germany [presumably a reference to the NSA's facility at Bad Aibling] plus a recently deployed package which has assumed much of Menwith Hill's work [Menwith Hill is an NSA station near Harrogate]. This will undoubtedly have an impact on the agreement which allocates work to Culmhead [the GCHQ outstation near Taunton]. The capacity of the packages exceeds that of a conventional station plus the ability to perform all processing work within the borders of the continental US. [Everything is relayed back via satellite.]

The stress applied to additional positions in the preceding paragraph is there because these extra positions would be tasked ostensibly with low-grade work but will of course provide ready-made operational capacity to absorb UK tasks, allocated under the DOE [division of effort], should the need arise.

Once re-allocated it is unlikely that the tasks would revert to UK resources. At best GCHQ would continue a hopeless parallel action which, without back-up, would not be cost effective. At worst there would be no work to do. This department [GCHQ] is viewed with grave suspicion by the political extremes in this country be they left or right.

The FRG sites then would provide secure bases which would provide sufficient material on which to work. Obviously there can never be enough material and the UK contribution of lively and imaginative human interfacing is highly desirable, always provided that interface is reliable. The US is well aware of the risks it faces in moving into the FRG but are obviously prepared to accept the risk of a leaky BND [Bundesnachrichtendienst – the German Security Service] when compared to the risk – as they see it – of an unreliable GCHQ.

At the moment effort provided by H Division [GCHQ's cryptanalysis division, responsible for breaking complex codes] is the major factor in GCHQ's case. The time difference alone means that material can be on desks first thing in the morning [American time]. A recent management estimate puts the H effort at about 75 per cent of GCHQ's practical worth. Some, but not all, of the material comes from UK sources.

Recently the UK has fitted out surface units of the Royal Navy. These ships will provide a major contribution to NATO's tactical planning and they are, of course, manned entirely by servicemen. TUS [trade union side] training representatives are well aware of the range of training made available to MOD personnel by GCHQ. Much effort is carried out by servicemen and women by land, sea and air. The RAF, in addition to a special surveillance role, which is some 75 per cent of the total effort, provides a limited airborne service which could be expanded.

There is in the process of building a[n] MOD microwave link. GCHQ will have its own trunk into it which implies that sophisticated techniques like AMSS [automatic message-switching systems] and its developments could guarantee the maintenance of vital channels without the involvement of UK civilians, should the need arise.

It is my personal view that trade unions belong on the shop floor be it in a radio station in Hong Kong or a laboratory in Benhall. There must be legitimate concern about the risks to continued employment if, as a result of what could be construed as a politically motivated strike, the supply dries up even for a short time. Steps have been taken by the collaborating agencies to plug the gaps that would appear in the effort if any UK station or link stops work. This plugging act would not be a 'finger in the dike' stop-gap but a permanent repair. Great care should be taken in the application of industrial action. Careful thought should indicate how the best interests of the membership will be served, and that may not be industrial action. Nailing one's colours to the mast or taking part in a kamikaze-like strike is of no use if, after the ship has gone down, there are no life boats around.

Many of the comments at the CSO Committee reflected Mick Verrion's relationship with management, but the most illuminating response came in a letter from Mick Bradshaw, a station radio officer who looked after CSU members at 'closed stations' – stations whose very existence was kept a close secret (see Chapter 3). He said, in a letter dated 19 April 1982:

What is new and quite significant is that the [industrial] action met its aims in that the CCSU won the propaganda war in this area by sending some of our 'friends' up the wall in having them believe that we were taking practical and effective steps. In our department the action was to embarrass rather than harm, and in retrospect this objective we now know was achieved.

Given Mick Verrion's regular contact with the official side, his letter was seen as a clear indication that the relationship with the Americans had been embarrassed, not that any actual harm had been done. The fear in GCHQ, and perhaps in the government as well, was that the NSA would take its ball away and stop GCHQ playing as a major partner in the international game of intelligence. It could be argued that this would have threatened national security, but that is very different from saying that trade unions and industrial action in themselves posed a threat. Many other factors could upset the cosy relationship between GCHQ and NSA. In 1982 something did.

In October 1982 newspapers started reporting stories of a new spying row between Washington and Whitehall. The reports were based on claims made by Alex Lawrie, a former employee of GCHQ, that security at GCHQ was lax. But a statement from President Reagan (*Daily Telegraph*, 26 October 1982), saying that the breach of security involving the British communications headquarters in Cheltenham 'appeared to be serious', was a reference not to these allegations, but to the arrest in July 1982 of another former employee under the Official Secrets Act.

The employee turned out to be Geoffrey Prime (see Chapter 3). Following Prime's conviction Mrs Thatcher referred the case to the Security Commission 'to investigate the circumstances in which breaches of security have or may have occurred arising from the case of Geoffrey Arthur Prime ... and to advise in the light of that investigation whether any change in security arrangements is necessary or desirable'.

The Prime case and the debate which followed it prompted allegations that the banning of trade unions was due, indirectly at least, to American pressure. Sections of the media, including the *Sunday Times* (14 November 1982), quoted NSA officials as stating that Prime would never have penetrated the NSA because he would not have passed the 'battery of psychological examinations' and, crucially, he would have been given a polygraph or lie detector test. Apparently, even before Prime was unmasked NSA officials had been pressing the British to adopt the polygraph (see Chapter 3).

According to James Bamford – author of *The Puzzle Palace*, a seminal work on the NSA and its relationship with GCHQ – one of the goals of the Americans, who sent a special mission to London to make a damage assessment report on the Prime case, was to standardize security regulations and, especially, to convince the British to introduce the polygraph, which had already been used on civilians working in the NSA.

The introduction of the polygraph for a trial period was one of the Security Commission's key recommendations. The proposal produced a hostile response from the unions and civil liberties organizations. The main practical argument against it was its unreliability – the polygraph being as likely not to detect 'liars' as to do so. The government itself admitted that it was intended not to catch existing spies, but to weed out people who could be tempted or forced to become spies through disloyalty or blackmail. The Society of Civil and Public Servants ran a very effective campaign against the polygraph, inviting over an acknowledged American expert, Professor David Lykken, author of *A Tremor in the Blood: Uses and abuses of the lie detector*. Lykken was highly critical of the polygraph as a result of research he had undertaken. The SCPS also produced a well-argued pamphlet, *The Case Against the Polygraph*. The Council of Civil Service Unions urged GCHQ staff not to submit to polygraph tests and promised to support those who refused to do so (although quite how was not clear).

It was widely assumed at the time that it was to overcome this resistance – a resistance which had widespread support throughout GCHQ – that management decided to push for a ban on trade unions. This argument is supported by legal doubts about whether any dismissals based on the polygraph could be sustained at an industrial tribunal. Even if this were possible, the prospect of individual cases being argued publicly was not an attractive one. The certificates signed by Sir Geoffrey Howe, removing the right to go to an industrial tribunal, may have had the polygraph in mind.

It is the view of a significant number of GCHQ staff, including some of those who were subsequently sacked for refusing to give up their union membership, that the polygraph was a key factor behind the ban. Robin Smith, one of the union members who was eventually sacked, looking back to the day when the ban was announced, recalls: 'Someone said polygraph and we all thought about it and it all seemed to fit in.'

One weakness in this argument is that it was well known that senior management in the British Security Service, MI5, had long been sceptical about the value of the polygraph, even though, for form's sake, they agreed to a trial following the Security Commission's report. In the end the polygraph proposal was quietly dropped after a critical report commissioned by the government. It seems unlikely that a mangement doubtful about the polygraph would have taken the far more drastic step of banning unions simply to facilitate a trial of the contested device. Cabinet Office officials responsible for Whitehall security have denied to the authors that opposition to the polygraph was a factor in the ban.

Such a view would be logical, but was GCHQ management logical when it came to trade unions? There is much to suggest that the attitude of the management was closer to pathological, with senior officials desperately waiting for an excuse to get rid of unions. In this context the word 'unions' covered more than just the formal presence of independent national trade unions. Rather it embraced any grouping of staff who resisted what management wanted to do. To understand the outlook of GCHQ management it is necessary to review briefly the history of trade unions in GCHQ.

GCHQ and its predecessors – in particular the wartime Government Code and Cypher School – were always strange creatures in the Whitehall universe. GCHQ worked closely with the military, but as Andrew Hodges notes in *The Enigma of Intelligence*, his biography of Alan Turing, a brilliant mathematician whose work helped pave the way to the construction of the first computers: 'the service chiefs were highly indignant at the condition of creative anarchy ... that distinguished GC&CS's day-to-day work and brought to the front the best among the unorthodox and "undisciplined" war-time staff'.

Civilians brought in from outside worked closely with permanent staff from the intelligence services. They were needed for their particular skills and background. In an article in *Intelligence and National Security* (January 1986) Alastair Denniston, the head of the Navy's code-breaking organization between the wars, describes how senior staff were paid on the basis of the administrative class in the Civil Service and were in due course considered eligible for membership of the Association of First Division Civil Servants, itself the predecessor of today's First Division Association.

Sitting within the secret inner sanctum of the defence and intelligence network was this group of mathematicians, linguists, academics and chess-players. They were important, and to do the job required of them they needed to be the sort of people they were: truculent and independent-minded. They became civil servants in their own right and hence were entitled to become members of trade unions – then referred to as staff associations.

Within GCHQ and its forerunners there was another tension. The administrative civil servants had the job of reconciling the pressures of running the organization as a bureaucracy and dealing with the outside world. Brilliant creative individuals such as Turing could never understand the bureaucratic obstacles placed in their way. This tension remained, but when the modern GCHQ was created another tension was built into the organization. The largest numbers of staff were those directly involved in the collection and communication of signals intelligence. Initially, the number involved in administration and processing was much smaller. Described as 'the Admini' in the union journal of the radio grades, they were resented as a group which did not generate any intelligence yet was always telling the others what to do. With technological developments the number of SIGINT collectors declined, but the processors, analysts and bureaucrats increased. Although there were some attempts to combine the management grades of the specialist, technical and communication grades with the administrative hierarchy, it was nearly always from the latter, from among the generalist, career civil servants, that top management was drawn.

It was this tension, particularly between management and the communication staff, that shaped the industrial relations history of GCHQ.

In 1945 the War Office, the Government Civilian Radio Organization (run by the Post Office and Foreign Office), the Air Ministry and the Admiralty re-recruited the staff – through adverts in newspapers – who had been trained during the war. Communication staff were represented by the Civil Service Radio Officers Association, which was a staff association not affiliated to the TUC and with no full-time officers.

The move to join a trade union came in 1949 following a pay deal by the CSROA which resulted in a substantial number of basic radio grades getting a 10 shillings a week cut in pay, while others, including the negotiators, received an increase. The four main establishments held mass meetings, inviting outside trade unions to address them.

The War Office and GCRO voted to join the Civil Service Union, which was affiliated to the TUC at the time – it was the first Civil Service union to affiliate after the war. Staff in the Air Ministry and the Admiralty remained in the CSROA, which subsequently became the Association of Government Supervisors and Radio Officers.

Management remained silent and did nothing, although they were clearly hostile. Unlike GC&CS and GCRO, which had always employed civilians, the outstations had been run as military organizations during the war. After the war they remained authoritarian – nearly but not quite military. At Scarborough, staff could not leave until the flag was taken down; elsewhere no tea was allowed before 5 p.m. and staff could only go outside for fifteen minutes' lunch-break. At Beaumanor, in Leicestershire, civilian staff had to use the side door, which enabled one former employee to carry on living in the hostel after he had left to work locally, without management realizing.

Then and later – when other staff associations were transformed into trade unions – no action was taken to stop the unions organizing. In the outstations the level of organization was high, with management allowing watch representatives time off to collect the weekly cash subscriptions. The official attitude was set out in the 1956 GCHQ Handbook for the Guidance of All Staff:

A civil servant is free to be a member of any association or trade union which will admit him under its rules of membership. Civil servants are moreover encouraged to belong to associations, for the existence of fully representative associations not only promotes good staff relations but it is essential to effective negotiations on conditions of service.

Despite management observing the niceties of the official Civil Service Whitley system, the 1950s and 1960s saw fights over tea-breaks, status in relation to the army, housing and other day-to-day issues. It was not until 1959 that the radio officers' pay issue – the dispute which had sparked off unionization – was resolved through arbitration. The impact on the local economy was such that a local garage near Beaumanor ran out of cars to sell shortly after the settlement. It also led to the first jointly agreed statement of duties – or job description – for ROs. The 1960s was a period of pressure on pay which resulted in the dispute of 1969–70, but there was also an agreement on New Equipment and Techniques, the forerunner of modern new technology agreements.

According to the Director of GCHQ, Sir Peter Marychurch, trade unions in GCHQ were an enigma, a historical accident that should never have been allowed to happen. This view was expressed at an appeal of one of the sacked union members in 1989. Marychurch thought that GCHQ should always have been regarded as part of the security and intelligence services. More fundamentally, GCHQ management bitterly resented having to discuss what they were doing with staff and their unions. In their minds, and in reality, they did not talk to the outside world; they were answerable to no one. Hardly anyone knew they existed or what they did – yet they had to consult with their staff, get the agreement of trade unions before the introduction of new equipment, answer legal cases for loss of hearing by staff due to inadequate protection from noise, and discuss and negotiate on a wide range of staffing and pay matters. Living in a closed and secret world, unions were barely tolerated. As far as management was concerned, the unions were 'the enemy within'.

Why the government banned trade unions at GCHQ is one of those questions which can be freely speculated about in the secure knowledge that it will be at least thirty years before the official files are opened at the Public Record Office. Indeed, the records may never be released. The key question is whether the official reason given for banning trade unions is true and justifiable. The official reason is that the threat posed to national security by national trade unions required them to be banned. Whitehall never talked about unions being an inconvenience or even a historical accident inside GCHQ. The government alleged that such a fundamental threat existed that it was necessary to remove the freedom of association, the freedom to belong to a trade union, from all staff.

There is little evidence to suggest that what unions had done in the past in GCHQ was a threat. Even Sir Geoffrey Howe claimed that it was the potential threat that was the real danger. But if the official reason is not sufficient by itself then what other explanation is there: the Americans, the polygraph?

It is unlikely that there was one single, simple explanation – more a combination of events and (for the government) favourable circumstances. The starting point for the ban must be GCHQ management. At the appeal against dismissal by union member Clive Lloyd, the ubiquitous Mr Little – head of E Division – stated that a ban was necessary because management was seeking a fundamental change in the staff's conditions of service. It was essential for these to be imposed on staff because voluntary action would not have been successful. He said that the action was initiated by GCHQ management: 'it was a GCHQ proposal'. But he acknowledged that the decision was a political one: 'we couldn't have done it by ourselves from within GCHQ'.

Both sides of his statement ring true. Despite what one of the sacked trade union members, Brian Johnson, describes as Mrs Thatcher's 'pathological hatred of trade unions', it is difficult to imagine her sitting down in isolation and deciding to ban unions in GCHQ. The initiative logically would have come from the department responsible. What made GCHQ management act? The Americans were important players – in terms not of applying direct pressure to ban trade unions, but, in the wake of the Prime affair, of seeking to tighten up security and introduce the polygraph.

More fundamentally, the fears of GCHQ management were crucial. They were concerned that American doubts about GCHQ would undermine its role and importance if the NSA became less co-operative in working together and sharing information. This fear may have been genuine given the British intelligence community's deference to the USA. However, Whitehall has traditionally used the USA as an excuse in the past – for example, over its decision to introduce new vetting procedures in the 1950s. Despite the one-sided nature of the alliance, the USA still needs GCHQ's facilities. But how would they be able to introduce the polygraph without the co-operation of staff? How could they avoid having to deal with trade unions?

In addition the political climate had to be right for the ban to be imposed. GCHQ had floated the proposal before. It was turned down in 1982–3 by Lord Carrington. When Sir Geoffrey Howe replaced him as Foreign Secretary in May 1983, GCHQ management knew that Howe would not stand up to Mrs Thatcher, whatever his personal views. They saw an opportunity to rid themselves of trade unions, and the industrial action of 1981 provided ideal political wrapping paper in which to present the case.

The architect of the ban was Sir Brian Tovey, who was appointed GCHQ Director in 1978 at the age of fifty-two. He had joined GCHQ twenty-eight years earlier. Having first told the media that he would not talk about the ban, he quickly changed his mind. He admitted to the *Sunday Times* on 5 February 1984, a few days after the ban was announced, that the USA had applied 'subtle pressure'. He added:

We do not interfere with each other but, having said that, the Americans could not be unconcerned if a major partner fell down on the job. We noticed a reluctance to enter into work-sharing and we read this as a message. It was the beginning of a reluctant feeling that 'Oh Lord, we don't know whether we can rely on the Brits'.

Tovey went on to say that he had nothing but praise for the 'loyalty and patriotism' of his staff.

Three days later, on 8 February 1984, Tovey gave extraordinary evidence to the House of Commons Select Committee on Employment. Asked whether there would have been no ban on unions without the pretext of the Prime case – and the official 'avowal' of GCHQ's functions in May 1983 – he replied:

I would not use the word 'pretext'. Once again, we are on speculative ground. What is the case is that until Ministers had decided that it was right to avow the intelligence function of GCHQ, *there was no firm and logical ground* for seeking to ban unions [emphasis added].

Tovey, who in common with many other Whitehall mandarins enjoyed a reputation for playing with semantics, denied to the committee that he had used the phrase 'subtle pressure' to describe the attitude of the Americans. He told the MPs:

I am trying to think of the precise words that were used. Words like, 'Well, obviously it is a bit troubling,' or, 'It is a bit troublesome.' Frankly, there was a great delicacy in not trying to push us on this. I would not have entirely blamed the Americans if they had.

It was Tovey who promoted and groomed Marychurch to be his successor. Tovey resigned as Director a few months before his proposal to ban unions was announced and three years before he reached the normal Civil Service retirement age of sixty. He admitted to having fixed up a top job with Plessey, the electronics firm which was one of GCHQ's suppliers. The government claimed that he left early to make way for a younger man. Marychurch was barely a year younger than Tovey.

Marychurch is described by those who have dealt with him as a cold and distant character. 'You've been getting away with it for years, you people,' he told one elected GCHQ union official at their first meeting. One colleague who knew him during GCHQ's early days at Eastcote in West London remembers him as 'fresh-faced, amiable but boring'. He adds: 'Marychurch was hopeless at decoding, but organized a very nifty cricket match. I don't recall that he played exceptional cricket, but he frequently organized a very good game. And it paid off.'

To Mrs Thatcher, in 1983, the proposal to ban unions in GCHQ was a heaven-sent opportunity. Plans were afoot to take on the miners, as the vanguard of the trade union movement. What better than to test the water against the recently defeated Civil Service unions in an area where the national security argument could so easily be deployed? At 58 per cent the level of union organization was relatively low; staff were generally conservative and security-conscious; all had been positively vetted. Surely there would be little or no resistance. Official estimates suggested that only a handful of staff, 'less than twenty', might refuse the new conditions of service and that the whole matter would be settled quickly with little or no fuss. The time was ripe. Thatcher had got rid of her 'wet' opponents in the cabinet. The TUC was on the defensive as she introduced popular reforms in trade union law. And political opposition in Westminster was weak and could not mount an effective campaign – even when many on the Conservative benches, and many in the senior ranks of official advisers in Whitehall, believed that she was going too far.

3

The place

New technology has a great potential for malevolence and for mischief, and ultimately for a kind of electronic big brother.

Prof. John Erickson, World in Action *(Granada TV), 15 July 1991*

The union ban, and the storm which followed, made GCHQ a household name. The people of Cheltenham – where the town maps described the two GCHQ sites at Oakley and Benhall simply as 'government buildings' – had little idea of what the organization was up to. The spouses and families of senior GCHQ officials were told only that it was a secret agency dealing with government communications.

GCHQ's true role was not officially acknowledged – 'avowed' as the government put it – until May 1983 when Mrs Thatcher gave the Commons a sanitized version of the Security Commission's report on the GCHQ spy, Geoffrey Prime. But years earlier, GCHQ had been the half-hidden agency behind two controversial and highly publicized events which demonstrated that Labour was as determined as the Conservatives to prevent any discussion of Britain's intelligence agencies, in particular when co-operation with the United States was involved.

In 1976 Mark Hosenball, an American journalist, wrote an article with the help of a British colleague, Duncan Campbell, in the London weekly magazine *Time Out*. It was a two-page description of how GCHQ intercepted communications, not only those of Soviet embassies and military units, but also those of friendly nations, private companies and individuals. A year later Hosenball was deported, along with Philip Agee, a former CIA agent then living in Britain. In an important test case which has since been cited by the courts whenever asylum-seekers and other non-British citizens have tried to appeal against deportation orders, Hosenball was accused of being a threat to Britain's 'national security', although he was not told how. In a celebrated ruling, Lord Denning, then Master of the Rolls, stated: 'This is no ordinary case. It is a case in which national security is involved, and our history shows that when the state is endangered, our cherished freedoms may have to take second place.'

Earlier in 1977 two journalists, Duncan Campbell and Crispin Aubrey, together with John Berry – a former soldier who had served in the Royal Signals at the GCHQ station in Ayios Nikolaos, Cyprus – were arrested in Berry's flat in Muswell Hill, North London. The meeting had been arranged by telephone, so it was clear that the journalists' phones were being tapped. In what became known as the ABC case, the three men were initially charged under the 'catch-all' section 2 of the 1911 Official Secrets Act. When they were brought to trial at the Old Bailey, they were charged under both section 2 and section 1 – the section which deals with espionage. They were, in effect, accused of being spies.

It became clear as the trial got under way that a great deal of the 'secret' information which Aubrey and Campbell were accused of receiving – the basis of the charges against them – could be obtained from public sources, including specialist magazines. The judge, Mr Justice Mars-Jones, invited the Attorney-General, Sam Silkin, to drop the section 1 charges. This he duly did. But the trial took its course and the jury, which had been vetted, found the three guilty under section 2 of the Official Secrets Act. The two journalists were given a conditional discharge; Berry received a six-month suspended sentence.

The practice of intercepting international communications had long been known. Indeed, Conservative governments and their allies in the security and intelligence services, unable to resist the temptation to use intercepted material to embarrass their political opponents, had readily admitted it. In 1924, for example, a spectacular leak helped to bring down Ramsay MacDonald's Labour administration. On 15 September 1924 a letter purporting to have been sent by Grigori Zinoviev, president of the Comintern, to the Communist Party of Great Britain instructed its sympathizers in the Labour Party to 'strain every nerve' to ensure the ratification of the Anglo-Soviet Treaty (covering mainly commercial issues) and to encourage 'agitation-propaganda' in the armed forces. The letter was leaked to the *Daily Mail* and was published by the newspaper on 29 October, just

four days before the general election. The man who played a key role
in the affair was Admiral Sir Reginald 'Blinker' Hall, former head of
Room 40, the Admiralty's code-breaking unit in the First World War
and the forerunner of GCHQ. At the time of the leak of the alleged
letter from Zinoviev, Hall was the Conservative Party's principal
agent. He had secretly conspired with his former naval colleague,
Admiral Sir Hugh Sinclair, head of the Secret Intelligence Service,
MI6, to leak the document to the *Daily Mail*. Hall was also one of the
founders of the Economic League, the right-wing employment
vetting agency which maintains unofficial links with the security
services.

A few years later the Prime Minister, Stanley Baldwin, could not
resist the temptation to disclose how Whitehall was successfully
intercepting Soviet telegrams. He spilled the beans in 1927 when the
government needed evidence of Soviet espionage and political
interference in Britain to justify breaking off diplomatic relations
with Moscow. By this indiscretion, inspired by domestic politics, the
Soviet Union was thus alerted to the need to protect its secret
communications more carefully in future.

In 1967 the journalist and author Chapman Pincher – often,
though apparently not on this occasion, used by elements in the
security and intelligence services as an unofficial conduit – disclosed
in the *Daily Express* that copies of all private overseas cables handed
in at post offices or cable companies were collected and examined
every day by GCHQ. Pincher was given the story by a former
employee of a cable company who disapproved of the practice. He
consulted Colonel 'Sammy' Lohan, secretary of the D Notice
Committee, which operates a system of voluntary self-censorship in
the media. Lohan failed to persuade Pincher not to reveal this
sensitive information. The government took no action after the story
appeared for fear of exacerbating the controversy stirred up by the
Pincher article. It was particularly concerned because the US National Security Agency – GCHQ's partner in signals intelligence –
was handed the contents of private telegrams which, in GCHQ's
view, might interest Washington. The government did not want this
disclosed.

But still GCHQ remained shrouded in secrecy, enabling the
government to claim that its role as an intelligence-gathering agency
was not officially 'avowed' until 12 May 1983, the day Mrs Thatcher
disclosed to the Commons an expurgated account of the Prime affair.

She told MPs:

Prime was employed in the public service from 1956 to 1977, first in the RAF and subsequently, from 1968 to 1977, in Government Communications Headquarters – GCHQ. The functions of GCHQ, which are carried out under the ministerial responsibility of my Right Honourable Friend, the Foreign and Commonwealth Secretary, are to ensure the security of the United Kingdom's military and official communications, and to provide signals intelligence in accordance with requirements laid upon it by the government in support of the government's defence and foreign policies.

Geoffrey Prime, a Russian linguist at GCHQ with access to its most intimate secrets, was sentenced to thirty-eight years in prison – three for sexually abusing young children, thirty-five for spying for the Russians. He was arrested in 1982, not by GCHQ security officials but by West Mercia police investigating cases of child molesting. It emerged in his largely secret trial that Prime had been a Soviet agent since 1968. Although he had resigned from GCHQ in 1977, there were indications that he had continued to spy for the Soviet Union: when Prime finally confessed to his wife Rhona, she found spying equipment hidden in their bedroom. It also emerged that Prime continued to receive money from the Soviet Union until 1981. After leaving GCHQ, Prime had taken a job in a taxi firm. Known within GCHQ, and still theoretically bound by the Official Secrets Act, he was entrusted with the task of delivering highly classified information from GCHQ to the joint British–American military air base at Brize Norton, Oxfordshire.

It also emerged during the Security Commission's investigation into the case that, despite his paedophiliac tendencies and erratic married life, Prime had passed no fewer than six positive vetting, or PV, security clearance examinations. On one occasion, a woman who had known Prime intimately kept the truth from the PV investigating officer because she was put off by the officer's manner.

The government was most terrified – as it has been with all British spy scandals – about the reaction in the United States, its close intelligence ally on which it relies for both information and cash. 'The alarming thing about the latest scare inside the British security services', claimed the *Daily Mail* in an editorial, 'is the frequency with which the Americans perceive us as the main source of leaks from within the Atlantic Alliance. We have a long way to go before the Americans will really trust us again.' That, as James Bamford points

out in *The Puzzle Palace*, was all nonsense. The USA was simply
better at hiding the extent to which its own intelligence agencies had
been penetrated. While Prime was spying from Cheltenham, two US
defence contractors with top-secret access to NSA material were
arrested for spying. Shortly afterwards, the Walker spy ring was
discovered – the ring had sold the Soviets highly classified naval and
submarine intelligence systems for sixteen years up to 1984.

Since, through Prime, Moscow had known about GCHQ's activities for at least fifteen years – and the government knew this at least
since the time of his arrest and confession in 1982 – the only reason
for hiding GCHQ's role was to keep it secret from British public
opinion. There is a historical self-denying ordinance, sealed by the
Privy Council oath, whereby political leaders of any party do not
discuss the activities of any of the security or intelligence services.
The majority of back-bench MPs either deferentially go along with
it, or resign themselves to the practice of successive governments
refusing to answer parliamentary questions about security or intelligence. In this way agencies which target each other – MI6 and the
KGB, for example – know more about each other than their own
citizens know about them.

We know that the government's claim that it could not ban unions
at GCHQ until 1984 – because the organization's functions had not
been officially acknowledged until the Prime case – is untenable. The
possibility was discussed by ministers and senior civil servants after
the 1981 industrial action and on a number of subsequent occasions.
The delay in imposing the union ban was nothing to do with the
publicity given to GCHQ as a result of the Prime case. As Sir Brian
Tovey, former GCHQ Director, implied in his evidence to the House
of Commons Select Committee on Employment in February 1984,
the ban was dictated by political opportunity. It was only at the end
of 1983 that ministers opposed to the ban had either resigned or been
sacked, and Mrs Thatcher felt sufficiently confident to go ahead.

Secrecy – the ostensible reason for the delay in the ban – was also
abused to hide poor management, inefficiency and corruption. A
former GCHQ radio operator, Jock Kane, campaigned for many
years to expose what he described as 'a disgusting network of
corruption, inefficiency and security betrayal' inside GCHQ and, in
particular, at its base at Little Sai Wan in Hong Kong. His allegations
led to the conviction of a senior Ministry of Defence official in the
colony. But a security investigation conducted by Sir James Waddell,

a former senior Home Office official, was pigeonholed by top GCHQ management. After resigning in 1978, Kane wrote a book, *GCHQ: A negative asset*. In 1984 Special Branch officers seized the manuscript on behalf of government lawyers, who succeeded in obtaining a court order suppressing the book on the grounds that Kane was bound by an absolute, lifelong duty of confidentiality to his former employers.

Kane alleged that widespread negligence and lax security created conditions which enabled Prime to smuggle thousands of pages of secret material out of GCHQ during the 1970s. He said in his manuscript that Prime compromised a sensitive detection operation, codenamed Sambo, used to locate Soviet ballistic missile submarines when they surfaced to communicate with their bases: 'Geoffrey Prime was apprised of GCHQ's successes against this system [i.e. the Soviet submarine manoeuvres] in 1976, and again notified his Kremlin masters, thus jeopardising the entire defence system of Great Britain and the USA.' Prime had also provided the Soviets with details of the US Rhyolite project, a geostationary satellite which could pick up Soviet and Chinese telecommunications continuously. But in the USA, Christopher Boyce and Andrew Lee, two Americans on the NSA staff, were already providing first-hand information about the project to the Soviet Union.

Some former GCHQ officials who left in disgust at the union ban in 1984 and who continue to play an active part in the campaign to restore union membership there dismiss Kane as obsessed and resentful. They are embarrassed by the controversy he provoked, believing it to have diverted attention from their campaign, though they do not deny Kane's allegations. We do not know the full background to his story. But that does not concern us here. His story is another example of the government's hypocrisy. The secrecy surrounding GCHQ is not always related to considerations of national security. Meanwhile, the Prime affair was deliberately used by the government to create a climate in which it could get public and political support for the union ban. It also led to the ill-thought-out proposal to introduce the polygraph or lie detector, an idea that was subsequently abandoned.

The disease of secrecy continued and one episode showed up Sir Peter Marychurch, the Director of GCHQ at the time of the ban, in a particularly unattractive light. Shortly before he died of cancer in 1985, Gordon Welchman, a leading wartime cryptanalyst in charge of the government Code and Cypher School's famous Hut Six at Bletchley, wrote a short essay to put the record straight about the chronology of the School's successes and the role played by the Poles in alerting the British to the German Enigma encoding machine. Welchman, who had published a book on Hut Six three years earlier, was angry about what he considered to be misleading passages in Sir Harry Hinsley's official wartime history of British intelligence. He wrote his essay in 1985 for a specialist journal, *Intelligence and National Security*. It was an article for aficionados, but Marychurch was not amused. The article, he claimed, caused 'direct damage to security'. He went on: 'Each time a person like yourself of obviously deep knowledge and high repute, publishes inside information about the inner secrets of our work, there is more temptation and more excuse for others to follow suit.'

The outburst of Marychurch provoked a curt response from Welchman's successor at Hut Six, Sir Stuart Milner-Barry. Milner-Barry, who made it clear that Marychurch should have shown more respect for such a distinguished man twenty years his senior, described the GCHQ Director's complaint as 'a prime example of the lengths to which GCHQ's paranoias about the preservation of ancient secrets still carry them'. To talk of 'direct damage to security', he commented, was 'surely absurd'. He added: 'To suppose that the battles which we had to wage before the birth of the first electronic computer (which must seem to present-day cryptanalysts rather like fighting with bows and arrows) could be relevant to security now is just not credible.' Official sensitivity may be explained in part by an agreement between the USA and Britain to say nothing about how the German Enigma was broken. After the Second World War, they had sold reconditioned Enigmas to Third World countries assuring them – wrongly – that they would be secure.

The Soviet Union certainly knew all about it: John Cairncross – the 'Fifth Man' of the wartime Cambridge-educated spy ring – passed details of German *Luftwaffe* movements to the Soviets before the battle of Kursk in the summer of 1943. His information, from intercepts collected by Bletchley, helped the Soviet Union to win what was perhaps its most decisive military victory of the Second World War.

The intelligence services, meanwhile, were wondering why Prime's activities had not been picked up by any of their agents. MI6 turned to Oleg Gordievsky, a senior KGB officer who had been an MI6 double agent for a decade before finally defecting in 1985. Anxious to please his new masters, Gordievsky pointed to Cyprus. Early in 1984, military police arrested five young RAF airmen and three soldiers who were working as support staff for the GCHQ station at Ayios Nikolaos. They were accused of handing over to Soviet agents more than two thousand documents and were brought back to Britain. Over a year later they were taken to the Old Bailey for Britain's longest and most expensive spy trial, which cost an estimated £4.5 million.

At the end of the four-month trial, which was held largely in secret, they were all acquitted. So poor was the prosecution case that buildings in which the young men were accused of indulging in unusual sexual practices had not even been constructed at the time that the events were alleged to have taken place. Evidence that their confessions had been forced out of them during their arrest led to an inquiry under Sir David Calcutt, QC, Master of Magdalene College, Cambridge. Calcutt said that while the eight servicemen had been unlawfully detained for a period, and pressure had been imposed on them when they were in custody to force them to make inaccurate statements, none had been subjected to degrading treatment. 'In our society,' Calcutt concluded with a resounding message, 'it is for Parliament and not for investigators, however genuinely and well motivated, to decide if and when, and in what circumstances, the interest of an individual should be subordinated to the interests of society as a whole.' The Ministry of Defence was obliged to pay the young servicemen compensation totalling £19,000, but it had its revenge by withdrawing their security clearance. They left the armed forces.

The government continued to adopt what can only be described as a surrealistic approach towards GCHQ well after the massive publicity provoked by the union ban. Early in 1987 it banned a BBC2 television programme on Britain's first spy satellite – codenamed Zircon – which was scheduled to be part of a series on official secrecy presented by Duncan Campbell. Special Branch officers broke into Campbell's North London home in search of clues which might lead them to his sources. They obtained a warrant from a Scottish judge to make a night raid on the BBC offices in Glasgow where the programme was being edited. The government unsuccessfully tried to obtain a court order to prevent MPs from seeing it.

What was all the fuss about? The Zircon project had already been referred to in a number of specialist journals. It was Britain's first spy satellite and, according to Sir Frank Cooper, a former permanent secretary at the Ministry of Defence who had been interviewed for the programme, it was not before time. Sir Frank adopted a sanguine view: the project might have something to do with macho-politics, giving Britain a new independent intelligence capability, but it was certainly good for British industry which was building it. In the USA, Dr Ray Cline, a former Deputy Director of the CIA, said that the Zircon film was unlikely to harm the national security of either Britain or America.

Zircon was costing £500 million and, under rules agreed between the Ministry of Defence and the Commons Public Accounts Committee, MPs should be told about any new project which costs more than £250 million. There was further embarrassment when it was disclosed that Robert Sheldon, the former Labour Treasury minister and chair of the committee, had been told informally about the project but had not passed on the information to his parliamentary colleagues. The money for Zircon – which is believed to have been put into orbit by the USA early in 1990 – was disguised in the section of the defence budget ostensibly set aside for the Trident missile programme. MPs had been kept in the dark.

The former MI5 officer Peter Wright disclosed in his memoirs, *Spycatcher* – published in Australia and the USA shortly after the Zircon controversy – that the Americans had been pressing GCHQ since the mid-1960s to share the cost of spy satellites. But in 1974 the Cabinet Secretary, Burke Trend, asked Sir Stuart Hampshire, who had been a member of the brilliant wartime code-breaking team, to review GCHQ's future. Wilson's Labour government was concerned about the escalating cost of Britain's share in the SIGINT alliance. A proposal then to build a spy satellite such as Zircon was postponed.

It soon became clear during the row over Campbell's programme in 1987 that the government was also deeply concerned about upsetting the United States, which Britain needed to launch Zircon into space. In an affidavit backing up the government's injunction against Campbell, Sir Peter Marychurch – who revealed that he had been aware of the programme for almost two months – laid particular stress on Britain's close co-operation in intelligence matters with the USA. The revelation of Zircon would be severely damaging, he said, because 'it could cause the US to lose confidence in the United

Kingdom's ability to protect the highly classified information involved and to reduce or withdraw their co-operation (which is
essential to the UK) in this and related fields of great importance to
the country's security'.

In a move which did not augur well for a Labour government's
approach towards the union ban at GCHQ, Neil Kinnock, along
with John Smith, the shadow Chancellor, and Roy Hattersley, the
shadow Home Secretary, were summoned to the Foreign Office and
given a private briefing by the Foreign Secretary, Sir Geoffrey Howe.
They were persuaded that the ban was necessary even though they
had not seen a copy of the programme. At least the Liberal leadership
reserved its judgement until it had a chance to see the evidence.
Eighteen months later, the BBC finally showed the programme in
full – it said it had been advised that the film did not harm national
security after all.

The Zircon episode had another side to it – one which has direct
relevance to the GCHQ union ban. The Ministry of Defence had
agreed to pay for the satellite only after fierce haggling with GCHQ
management and a deal which was struck in 1983. The defence
budget was flush after the Falklands War – a conflict in which Britain
had had to rely on the USA for satellite information. The MoD seized
the opportunity to try and increase its role inside GCHQ, which is
still controlled by civilians and is nominally the responsibility of the
Foreign Office. Since much of the information from Zircon would be
military in nature, the MoD argued that a 'military cell' should be set
up in GCHQ to oversee the operation. It was a tactic designed to
wrench control of GCHQ from the Foreign Office, the intention
being that in order to withstand it, given the government's distrust
of unions, the FO would have to go along with the union ban whether
or not it had misgivings. The MoD knew that if it took control and
if GCHQ was 'militarized' then there would be no place for unions
anyway – there are no unions in the armed forces – giving it greater
appeal to a government looking for help to justify its union ban.
Ironically, elected union officials were among the few who were
trusted enough to have been told about Zircon four years before the
controversy broke over Campbell's film.

The vast apparatus which now constitutes GCHQ grew out of a tiny
First World War code-breaking organization known as Room 40,
which had its office in the Admiralty. One of its greatest triumphs –

as James Bamford describes in *The Puzzle Palace* – took place on the morning of 17 January 1917. Two cryptanalysts handed 'Blinker' Hall, then head of Room 40, what former American code-breaker David Kahn has called 'the single most far-reaching and most important solution in history': the infamous 'Zimmerman telegram'. It was allegedly sent by Arthur Zimmerman, the German foreign minister, via Sweden to the German mission in Mexico. It suggested that if the United States entered the war, Mexico should be offered 'the lost territory in Texas, New Mexico and Arizona' if it took the German side. Whitehall decided to pass the intercepted message to Washington, hoping that it would finally persuade the USA to join the war. It did the trick: President Woodrow Wilson revealed the contents of the telegram to a suitably outraged American public. He referred to it during his address to a special session of Congress called two months later to declare a formal state of war with Germany.

Between the wars, Britain's code-breaking effort, like the other security and intelligence agencies, was run down. It was not a deliberate policy; it was the result of haphazard, and some would say short-sighted, budgetary cuts. Alastair Denniston, head of Room 40's naval section, did, however, have the imagination to set up a peacetime government Code and Cypher School (GC&CS) under the Foreign Office. Just before the outbreak of the Second World War he moved it to Bletchley Park in Buckinghamshire.

One of the first tasks of the GC&CS was to decode the German Enigma encoding system. The initial breakthrough was achieved early in 1939 by a group of Polish code-breakers who shared their secrets, including a high-speed calculating machine called the 'Bombe' which they invented to unravel the Enigma codes. Soon – and mainly due to Churchill's personal conviction about the potential value of code-breaking – Bletchley attracted some of the most original brains in Britain. Among them was Alan Turing, a brilliant mathematician whose work helped to pave the way to the construction of the first modern computers (see Chapter 2). Perhaps more than any other single individual, he enabled Bletchley to continue to break the Enigma cyphers, an achievement which saved many lives during the Second World War. Turing, who was a homosexual, committed suicide in 1954 following pressure from his employers after he resisted a blackmail attempt and reported it to the police. He was a victim of new vetting procedures forced on Attlee's Labour govern- ment by Washington at the height of the McCarthyite period and after the embarrassing flight of the establishment's two Soviet spies – Guy Burgess and Donald Maclean – to Moscow in 1951.

Bletchley's work remained hidden until 1974 when Fred Winterbotham, a wartime signals intelligence officer, published *The Ultra Secret*. The full story has still not been told, but Winterbotham's book showed how the code-breakers provided vital information about German movements, giving the allies a decisive advantage in many key battles of the war, including El Alamein. However, to protect Ultra – the code-name given to intelligence derived from intercepting German Enigma codes – the government would not tell even its own commanders in the field the real source of the intelligence. As a result it was sometimes ignored, as happened when the Germans invaded Crete.

Winterbotham claims that Churchill was forewarned about the devastating blitz on Coventry in November 1940 but was reluctant to take special precautions – for example, by alerting the population – for fear that the Germans would suspect that Britain had indeed broken their codes. This story has been dismissed by other former intelligence officers, including the scientist R.V. Jones. However, Jones notes in his book, *Reflections on Intelligence*, that the claim had a 'widespread appeal because of the ethical problems that it illustrates for an operational commander and his intelligence officer'. The controversy is a reminder of the uniquely privileged, protected – and unaccountable – position enjoyed by members of the security and intelligence services, as well as the enormous responsibility placed on them.

At the end of the war GCHQ – the innocuous-sounding government Communications Headquarters, as the code-breaking organization was now called – moved to Eastcote, on the western outskirts of London. In 1952 it was moved to Cheltenham as part of the government's dispersal policy. The work of GCHQ was considered so important and potentially vulnerable to a nuclear strike that it was decided to spread its stations around the country.

But it was not quite as simple as that. The proposal to move to the home of the National Hunt festival came from Claude Daubeny, the post-war head of signals intelligence and a keen punter. R.V. Jones records that at the end of Daubeny's interview with Whitehall officials for the top job, he was asked whether he had any points to make. 'I told them that I must have plenty of time for meetings. They agreed – but of course I didn't tell them that I meant race meetings.'

By this time, Britain had entered into an agreement with the United States which bound the two countries into a relationship which was to become increasingly significant – and increasingly one-sided – as a pillar of the 'special relationship'. In 1947 Whitehall and Washington signed the UKUSA Agreement, a secret pact whereby the two parties pledged to share the intelligence they gathered from eavesdropping on the communications of foreign countries. The USA was to provide the technology, including spy satellites – money was to become a perpetual source of wrangling – while Britain would contribute the code-breaking expertise which had proved so successful during the war. The intention was to divide up the world between them: the USA would cover the Americas and the Pacific, while Britain would cover the key areas of the north-east Atlantic, the North Sea and Europe – the front lines of Soviet and Warsaw Pact cold war activity. Britain could also offer the United States part of the legacy of its imperial past, giving it indirect access to other useful areas of the world. GCHQ set up listening posts in Hong Kong, Singapore, Bahrain and Oman in the Gulf, Aden, Cyprus, South Africa and the Ascension Islands.

Britain also had its closest allies in the Commonwealth, which had the convenient advantage of being strategically based: shortly after Britain and the United States signed the UKUSA Agreement, Canada, Australia and New Zealand joined the pact as 'secondary partners'. In return for providing facilities for GCHQ and the National Security Agency, these countries received intelligence information from Britain and the United States. Representatives from Canada, Australia and New Zealand (as well as the USA) attended some meetings of the Joint Intelligence Committee (JIC) in the Cabinet Office in Whitehall.

Britain and the United States apply crude pressure on their secondary partners when the governments of these countries adopt policies of which Washington or Whitehall disapproves. It was not entirely coincidental that the Australian Governor-General, Sir John Kerr, intervened to force Gough Whitlam, the Australian Labour Prime Minster, to dissolve Parliament on 11 November 1975. Ostensibly this was because Whitlam could not command the Senate majority needed to approve the country's budget; however, the deadline that Whitlam had imposed for the close-down of America's intelligence-receiving station at Pine Gap was also about to come up. Similarly, when New Zealand's Labour government carried out its election mandate and refused naval warships with nuclear materials entry to New Zealand ports, Whitehall banned Wellington's representatives from the JIC meetings. And the US threat to cut off intelligence information as well as support for sterling was an important factor behind the British government's decision to withdraw troops in the 1956 Suez crisis. This powerful American card is likely to be used against any incoming Labour administration.

GCHQ has a world-wide network of stations: some are controlled directly by GCHQ, some are operated in association with the Ministry of Defence and the Foreign Office, and others are an integral part of the pact with its SIGINT partners – the USA, Canada, Australia and New Zealand. Before GCHQ was officially 'avowed', any connection between the outstations and listening posts and the headquarters in Cheltenham was, if not actually denied, concealed by using the cover that they were part of a separate organization: the Composite Signals Organization (CSO).

Although their precise signals intelligence role was officially denied, the mere size and locations of the stations meant that they at least had to be acknowledged. They were therefore known as 'open stations'. In the mid-1970s, the CSO had nine main CSOSs – Composite Signals Organization Stations – in Britain outside London. They were located at Culmhead, near Taunton in Somerset; Morwenstow, near Bude in North Cornwall; Irton Moor, near Scarborough in North Yorkshire; Cheadle in Staffordshire; Hawklaw in Fife; Brora in Sutherland. Gilnahirk, a GCHQ station in Northern Ireland, was shut down in 1978 and its work transferred to the mainland. The decision was based in part on security considerations, and in part on the fact that Irish traffic could be monitored from mainland Britain. In 1977 Wincombe and Flowerdown were also closed. Later the two Scottish stations were shut – Brora in 1984, Hawklaw in 1988. GCHQ's Central Training School was moved in 1985 from its wartime home in Bletchley to Culmhead. There are two GCHQ stations in London, in Palmer Street close to St James' Park tube station, and in the Empress Building in Earls Court.

GCHQ also has a number of 'lodger' units in establishments run by other organizations, notably the Ministry of Defence – an example is the Royal Signals and Radar Establishment in Malvern – and a presence in the mainly military SIGINT posts in Germany.

The largest lodger unit in Britain is probably at Menwith Hill, near Harrogate in North Yorkshire. Menwith Hill is the US National Security Agency's biggest satellite receiving station in Europe, if not the world. It not only eavesdrops on diplomatic and military traffic in eastern Europe; it also monitors the international communications – telephone conversations and telexes – of companies and private citizens. It is plugged into the international telecommunications network passing through Britain. It is also believed to have the potential to monitor a quarter of a million domestic telephone lines in Britain. GCHQ will, in addition, have a presence at the other main NSA establishments in Britain – Edzell on Tayside, Chicksands in Bedfordshire (both former GCHQ sites) and Brawdy in South Wales. Chicksands concentrates on intercepting Soviet military signals, Edzell on Soviet naval movements in the North Atlantic.

Overseas, GCHQ's acknowledged or 'open' stations were located in Hong Kong, Cyprus, Ascension Island and Mauritius. In 1975 the Mauritius station was closed. Ascension was being run down before concern about Argentinian designs on the Falklands led Callaghan's Labour administration to reactivate it in 1978. After the 1982 Falklands War, a GCHQ listening post was set up on the islands.

Historically, there had been far more small eavesdropping stations overseas, most of them operated by the Admiralty. After the Second World War many were closed down. But the requirements of GCHQ remained and they were covered in a number of different ways. The most common way was to set up small 'closed' – concealed and unacknowledged – stations attached to British embassies, High Commissions and consulates abroad, with the GCHQ staff running them disguised as regular Foreign Office diplomatic staff. 'Closed' GCHQ stations existed – and may still do so – in British embassies in Prague, Budapest, Warsaw, Istanbul and Moscow. They are also present in British missions in Cairo, Accra, Nairobi and Malawi. There are allied SIGINT posts in South Korea, Japan, Denmark and Norway. In southern Africa, GCHQ has stations in British missions in Freetown, Sierra Leone and Lusaka – where it eavesdropped on the African National Congress leaders and passed information on to the South African government. Throughout the period of isolating Pretoria through sanctions, South Africa's SIGINT station at Silvermine, near Capetown, exchanged information with the UKUSA partners.

GCHQ's listening stations in Hong Kong have been valued particu-

Scene of the vigil outside GCHQ's Benhall site in Cheltenham on the anniversary of the first dismissals for belonging to a trade union.

larly highly by the United States – especially during the Vietnam War – and by Australia, which sees itself increasingly as a Pacific rather than a 'western' nation. New satellite relay stations have been built at Chung Hom Kok in South Hong Kong Island and Tai Mo Shan in the New Territories, which are run jointly with Australia's Defence Signals Directorate (DSD) – GCHQ's partner in the SIGINT pact.

GCHQ employs about seven thousand civilian staff, including mathematicians, linguists, computer programmers, engineers, cypher clerks, radio operators and code-breakers. In addition, signals specialists from all three branches of the armed forces work on GCHQ-related tasks. NSA staff are based at Menwith Hill and there are NSA liaison teams in GCHQ.

GCHQ's budget, like those of MI5 and the Secret Intelligence Service, MI6, is not disclosed, but it is well over £1,000 million a year, probably more than half of which is paid for by the United States. The British contribution is hidden in the Foreign Office and (principally) Ministry of Defence budgets. The cost of the Zircon spy satellite came out of the MoD's budget officially allocated to the Trident missile programme.

Under the Director of GCHQ, John Adye, there are seventeen divisions, all of which are denoted by a letter – C, E, F, G, H, J, K, M, Q, R, S, T, U, V, W, X and Z. They are divided into six main groups as follows:

1. The Composite Signals Organization (CSO), GCHQ's intercept arm whose innocuous-sounding title appears on the notices outside GCHQ's outstations.

2. The directorate of Communications Security (COMSEC) – now linked with the Communications-Electronics Security Group (CESG) – which is responsible for safeguarding British communications and is based at GCHQ's Benhall site in Cheltenham. In 1991 GCHQ spent £10 million on a secure, high-speed communications system for exchanging information with America's National Security Agency. The system, codenamed DOJAC, was paid for out of the defence budget and enables GCHQ to send and receive coded information transmitted via satellites in short bursts and on different frequencies. It will also enable GCHQ to apply the same advanced technology to intercept and decode foreign diplomatic, military and economic communications.

3. The directorate of Organizations and Establishment. This has a number of divisions:

   C – Overseas Staff.
   E – Establishment, or personnel matters.
   F – Finance and Supply.
   G – General Management.
   M – Maintenance (Mechanical Engineering).
   Q – Technical.
   R – Security.

4. The directorate of Signals Intelligence (SIGINT) Plans, or P. This is responsible for long-term planning.

5. The directorate of SIGINT Operations and Requirements. This is the largest directorate and includes:

   Z – Requirements, Liaison and Foreign. This is responsible for receiving requests from consumers (the Ministry of Defence, for example), liaison with SIGINT partners, notably the USA, and distributing intercepts to consumers.
   U and V – Search Technology. These are responsible for finding signals on different channels, frequently changed by targets

suspicious of being intercepted. V section, for example, monitored Argentine traffic after the invasion of the Falklands in 1982.

S and T – Statistical Operations. These are responsible for monitoring the change in the volume of targeted traffic.

W – Communications. This is responsible for making sure, from the technical point of view, that consumers get the traffic authorized by Z.

K – General SIGINT. This analyses intercepts from throughout the world (the Middle East, for example, and now including Britain) except the former Communist bloc.

J – Special SIGINT. This is responsible for analysing intercepts from the former Communist bloc (the Warsaw Pact, now effectively defunct, accounted for about 30 per cent of GCHQ's work).

H – Cryptanalysis. This is responsible for breaking complex codes with the help of X.

X – Computer Services. This concentrates on getting computers to break electronic codes.

6. The Joint Technical Language Service (JTLS). This is responsible for research into decoding communications. (The Joint Speech Research Unit, which is developing techniques of automatic speech recognition, was transferred from GCHQ to the Royal Signals and Radar Establishment (RSRE) in Malvern in 1985.)

GCHQ's initial *raison d'être* was to intercept the military and diplomatic communications of hostile and potentially hostile countries (COMINT) and gather intelligence about other countries' countermeasures, including radar (electronic intelligence or ELINT). It intercepted Argentine signals during the Falklands War – through New Zealand's listening posts but also by picking up, through Norway, Soviet messages to Moscow about Argentine movements and intentions. It helped to intercept Iraqi communications during the Gulf War, though most of the intelligence in that conflict was obtained by US eavesdropping and reconnaissance satellites and aircraft. Its outstations were placed to cover particular tasks and particular areas: Ayios Nikolaos in Cyprus, for example, receives intercepted communications from the Middle East and the southern Soviet Union – it forewarned the government about the Soviet invasion of Afghanistan in December 1979.

Developments in satellite technology have brought new possibilities for GCHQ, making it much easier to transmit information from station to station and from partner to partner in the UKUSA pact. Ground stations with no human operators can be controlled by satellite. Equipment for communicating with satellites can now be fitted on the back of a truck. Satellites can handle electronic data, voice transmissions, word-processing data, facsimiles, electronic mail, and audio and video communications. For GCHQ, these developments have opened up a whole new world. Transmissions to satellites are sent through narrow microwave beams. Traffic returned to earth is less directional, more scattered, but still much more difficult to detect than communications sent via traditional radio waves. GCHQ, with the help of universities, is now concentrating research on how to make more effective use of this intrusive new technology through, for example, language recognition software, digital voice coding, direction finding and voice print identification.

Changes in technology have meant that GCHQ has been able to reduce the number of its eavesdropping stations to concentrate on a smaller number of capital-intensive satellite stations. The old labour-intensive stations are disappearing, and there are no longer hundreds of radio officers sitting all day and all night with headsets. But the reduction in the number of stations and radio officers coincided with a growth in traffic. The commercial INTELSAT system had grown from 240 channels in 1964 to 30,000 by 1983. The sheer volume of traffic led GCHQ and the NSA to develop key-word recognition technology, which automatically sifts traffic for words or connections dictated by current security concerns. The idea is to reduce the amount of traffic to be transcribed to more manageable levels, while still harvesting as much as possible. GCHQ has already designed and programmed computers which are capable of scooping up an almost limitless mass of telex traffic in search of specified combinations of key words and names. It now has a network of these computers, collectively known as the Dictionary.

During the cold war, in any conventional view, it was entirely legitimate for the USA and the UK (the European allies, including France and West Germany, literally did not have a look-in) to join forces and listen to as many communications of potentially hostile targets as possible, whether it were top Soviet officials talking in the

Kremlin, Chinese leaders chatting in Peking, Soviet commanders giving instructions to East German leaders or Soviet vessels being tracked from GCHQ's secret station in Silvermine in South Africa. After all, the Soviet Union and its allies were trying to do the same with the West.

It is perhaps understandable, too, that GCHQ uses the technology at its disposal to eavesdrop on communications within Northern Ireland in an attempt to prevent IRA and Loyalist violence. It intercepts Irish communications from disguised premises near Dublin. In the 1980s GCHQ belatedly set up units to concentrate on international terrorism. Through its London stations, it first put MI5 on the trail of Nezar Hindawi, arrested in 1986 for attempting to plant a bomb on an El Al airliner at Heathrow. GCHQ intercepted messages from the Syrian embassy in London to Syrian air force intelligence in Damascus in an operation that enabled Sir Geoffrey Howe, then Foreign Secretary, to speak of 'conclusive evidence' of Syrian involvement with Hindawi.

Satellite reconnaissance has important potential for verifying arms control agreements, as well as providing early warning and accurate information in trouble spots, as happened in the Gulf War. GCHQ also provides security systems, including scrambling mechanisms, to protect British diplomatic and military communications. This work is done by GCHQ's Communications and Electronic Security Group, which moved from London to the Benhall site in Cheltenham in the 1970s. The group advises the whole of Whitehall on computer security through the Central Computer and Telecommunications Agency (CCTA) run by the Treasury.

But GCHQ does much more than this.

Throughout the dispute over the union ban, minister after minister dwelt on the crucial contribution GCHQ made to Britain's national security. They implied that even the slightest disruption, or threat of it, could endanger the nation's security. The fact is, however, that the vast majority of GCHQ staff work a nine-to-five job, analysing, distributing and discarding a mass of information much of which bears no relation to Britain's security. Surprisingly, neither individual union members at GCHQ nor the general Civil Service unions' membership appeared to have much quarrel with GCHQ's activities. Indoctrination and strict 'need to know' rules within GCHQ contribute to an unquestioning attitude, reinforced by the Official Secrets Act. Many of GCHQ's targets have even less to do with national security now that the cold war is over. For years, its technology has been used to monitor three other categories of target: allies or neutral countries; private or state-owned companies; and political groups and individual members of those groups deemed to be 'subversive'. Thus, for example, as *The Guardian* and Granada Television's *World in Action* revealed in July 1991, GCHQ has intercepted the communications of Kathleen Tacchi-Morris, a 93-year-old active peace campaigner honoured for her work by the United Nations; formal exchanges of greetings from East European trade union organizations to Campbell Christie, General Secretary of the Scottish Trade Union Congress; and even the private and diplomatic conversations of the Pope.

In common with intelligence and security agencies throughout the world, GCHQ management – enthusiastically backed by Whitehall – could not resist the temptation to use its resources and technology to expand its empire. GCHQ has advantages over the Security Service, MI5. It has a much larger budget, supplemented by growing contributions from the United States, and it is not bound by any charter. As for GCHQ's other rival – the Secret Intelligence Service, commonly called MI6 – it too has a much smaller budget than GCHQ and officially it does not exist in peacetime.

With the benign, and largely ignorant, acquiescence of ministers, GCHQ has used its lack of accountability to monitor a wide range of targets. In the 1950s, from its station in Aden, GCHQ eavesdropped on Ethiopian traffic for the NSA, which was prevented by domestic political constraints from using its own facilities in Ethiopia, then a non-communist nation. GCHQ gave the Americans information about the Vietnamese stance during the peace negotiations on the Vietnam War and detailed intelligence to guide US bombers on to their targets in North Vietnam. It also supplied the South African government with information about the activities and movements of ANC leaders and guerrillas. In return, Pretoria was asked to continue providing Britain and the United States with information about Soviet and Cuban activities in Angola as well as Soviet shipping round the Cape.

The *New York Times* reported in July 1986 that British and American officials had recently discussed the South African operation at a regular review of intelligence assignments – tasking – at GCHQ in Cheltenham. Seymour Hersh, the respected US journalist, said his source – a former NSA official – described how at one point three South African military intelligence officers were ushered into the room. The participants then exchanged requirements. The former NSA official said that the South African list included the communications of the Angola, Mozambique, Zambia and Botswana governments. The US State Department and the CIA took it upon themselves to deny the story.

GCHQ provided technical help to enable the government to bug Lancaster House, the conference centre near Buckingham Palace, during international negotiations, including the Zimbabwe independence negotiations in 1979. Peter Wright describes in *Spycatcher* how, prompted by the Secret Intelligence Service, MI6, and with the help of the Post Office (which then ran the telephone system) GCHQ bugged the French embassy, enabling the government to monitor every move the French made during the (unsuccessful) attempt by the Macmillan administration to join the European Community between 1960 and 1963. As part of the operation, Britain passed to the United States details of de Gaulle's plans for an independent nuclear *force de frappe*.

GCHQ continues to eavesdrop on the communications of foreign countries and embassies – friendly or otherwise – through its listening stations in the Empress Building in Earls Court, West London – which concentrates on picking up radio signals from foreign embassies – and Palmer Street, central London. 9 Palmer Street intercepts telexes, faxes and international telephone calls made by large companies, especially those dealing with vital commodities such as oil, and banks. Telexes are routed with the help of British Telecom, and computers are programmed to look out for such key words as 'gold'.

On behalf of the Treasury and the Bank of England, GCHQ looks out for decisions which may affect Britain's balance of payments. It will pass on information which may prove useful to British competitors of the bugged companies – BP, for instance, or the chemical giant ICI, or the 'big four' British high street banks. It also intercepts the private communications of British companies, including Rolls-Royce and Marconi – anything seen to be 'an integral part of the British economy'. This is in spite of the wording of the 1985 Interception of Communications Act which, while referring to tapping communications 'to safeguard the economic well-being of the United Kingdom', explicitly restricts this right to 'the acts or intentions of persons outside the British Islands'. The restriction does not suit GCHQ, so it ignores it.

Palmer Street is sometimes referred to as GCHQ's London

station. After the war, staffing problems meant that Palmer Street concentrated on a handful of special targets and the London embassies. Although this was technically a breach of the 1964 Diplomatic Privileges Act and other international agreements on telecommunications, it was trivial when compared to what happened after computers were introduced in the 1970s.

GCHQ's new computerized Dictionary swept aside the cumbersome manual operation. Palmer Street started using an umbilical cable linking it to BT's international telex network to intercept telexes passing into, out of or through London. This covers thousands of supposedly private messages every day: diplomatic cables to and from embassies; a deluge of commercial traffic which is conducted by telex because, unlike fax, it is contractually binding; and a rich harvest of Third World traffic which is simply routed through London on its way to and from different countries. Telex traffic is easily identified by telex call and call-back signs and by numbers.

Yet GCHQ is entitled to intercept a telex only if it has a warrant signed by a Secretary of State on the grounds that it deals with a specified threat to the national interest. GCHQ created a loophole, quite literally constructed one, on the fourth floor of 9 Palmer Street in the 'intercept room'. This room conceals the moment of illegality. It is a GCHQ room. The computer belongs to GCHQ and it runs on GCHQ software according to GCHQ's daily instructions. But after a close study of the law, GCHQ arranged for the room to be staffed by a handful of British Telecom workers. Thus it can pretend that the traffic has never left BT's hands and therefore cannot have been unlawfully intercepted.

The deceit does not stop there. Even though GCHQ has a pact with the United States to share all its intercepts, the truth is that it does not. Some British material is 'for UK eyes only'. But to avoid anyone noticing this and asking any questions, the material is labelled 'special handling' instead. One reason why GCHQ does not want to send all its intercepts to the United States is that some of them contain American communications, breaking another rule – namely, that Britain and the United States should not spy on each other. In the same way, of course, the USA does not share all its intelligence with Britain, and it also spies on its closest ally.

There is one place where Britain and the United States collaborate to bend and evade the law – GCHQ's listening post at Morwenstow, near Bude. The law has been stretched so far that some members of staff started rebelling. Bude's work has been revolutionized by the advent of telecom satellites and has greatly expanded as a result of a reorganization in 1986. The station now spends twenty-four hours a day combing through private, civilian communications on some of the world's busiest satellites – those over the Atlantic and Indian Oceans.

Its routine involves three kinds of work. First, it conducts 'standard baseband surveys', repeatedly trawling through each nation's satellite basebands to discover who is using which channels and what their targets are saying. Secondly, it has developed a 'wildcard' system which enables it to intercept all calls with a particular dialling code so that it can seal off a city or even a switchboard and take every satellite channel that is linked to it. Thirdly, it monitors individual numbers.

Staff were unsure whether any of their baseband surveys were legal. They were particularly worried about the lawfulness of trawling through the United Kingdom channels – so much so that they temporarily backed off them in 1985 until their managers assured them that it was legal. The managers' reasoning is not known. Staff also feared that their wildcard system was not covered by any warrant, and that the only reason for the extraordinary internal secrecy surrounding individually targeted British lines – known as P numbers – was that they were beyond the law.

Through Bude, which was modernized with the help of American money, GCHQ can also pick up communications coming into Britain, while the NSA can pick up communications entering the United States. GCHQ and the NSA can then exchange the information to complete the record of the two-way conversations. This also enables the two agencies to get round the 'one terminal' rule, which dictates that GCHQ should never eavesdrop on a communication which has a British citizen at both ends, and that the NSA should never report a communication with an American citizen at both ends.

There is another way to bend the rule: it applies to GCHQ staff, but not to their equipment. So if an officer from MI5 – installed in GCHQ premises – was to handle Brit-to-Brit intercepts, the rule, strictly speaking, would not be broken. And the rule only forbids 'reporting' the intercept, leaving open the possibility that it could simply be copied and sent on to MI5. Equally, there is no rule preventing GCHQ from lending its technology to other security and intelligence agencies. During the 1984–5 miners' dispute, GCHQ advised the Special Branch about how to intercept the communications of the National Union of Miners and its branches and supporters throughout the country.

The practice is not new. In the late 1960s GCHQ co-operated with the NSA in illegal eavesdropping on the communications of civil rights and anti-Vietnam War campaigners, including the actress Jane Fonda, the singer Joan Baez, and the best-selling baby-book author Benjamin Spock. Under the project, codenamed Minaret, the GCHQ base at Morwenstow – conveniently close to British Telecom's transatlantic ground station at Goonhilly Down – picked up US domestic communications and relayed them to NSA headquarters at Fort Meade, Maryland. The idea was to avoid breaking the US Federal Communications Act by using stations based in Britain to eavesdrop on American domestic traffic. Minaret was discovered by the US Senate's Church Committee on intelligence activities set up in the wake of Watergate. The committee concluded that the NSA's 'potential to violate the privacy of American citizens is unmatched by any other intelligence agency'. By intercepting calls in Britain, the NSA avoided breaking the letter of American legislation. By the same token, the NSA listens to the conversations of British citizens and passes information on to Whitehall.

From time to time, GCHQ is asked by Whitehall to look for particular targets. But so voracious is Whitehall's appetite for information, and so indiscriminate the technology at the disposal of GCHQ, that GCHQ literally harvests communications automatically. Every international telephone call and every domestic call going through the air waves is a potential target for the eavesdroppers.

GCHQ is being used increasingly to intercept the communications of domestic targets – political 'extremists' and pressure groups who were previously left to the Security Service, MI5, and the police Special Branch. Ground lines are tapped: that is, switched to GCHQ with the help of British Telecom. This is technically convenient. It also enables MI5 – its image battered after the revelations of *Spycatcher* and of the former MI5 officer Cathy Massiter – to claim that it is no longer concentrating on domestic 'subversives'. A special unit, K20, has been installed in GCHQ at Cheltenham to monitor the telephone calls of 'internal' targets: British radical groups and British individuals.

GCHQ is free to do this because no outside body monitors its activities. It does not even have the feeble procedure to which MI5 is now subjected – a High Court judge who looks at a random sample of warrants issued by the Home Secretary on behalf of MI5. Internal guidelines say that GCHQ should not intercept communications between one British citizen or group and another. The only safeguard is the entirely voluntary action of the officials responsible for collecting and storing intercepted communications. To take an example: a man with an Irish name, Patrick say, telephones a friend in Chicago who also has an Irish name, Sean. Their conversation is monitored and their names arouse suspicion – it is an entirely private conversation, but GCHQ argues that the two men could be discussing ways of getting money or arms to Northern Ireland. What happens to the recorded tape? A benevolent official may destroy the record, but a malevolent one keeps it and passes it on to officials in the Joint Intelligence Committee at the Cabinet Office in Whitehall. Whatever decision is made about what to do with the tape, the conversation is listened to.

It was against this background that Dennis Mitchell, a GCHQ employee who took early retirement rather than submit to the union ban, wrote to senior MPs and Sir Robert (now Lord) Armstrong, then the Cabinet Secretary and head of the Civil Service, expressing his concern about GCHQ's activities. For thirty-two years he had worked as a cryptanalyst in one of the most sensitive areas of the organization's work. 'I have arrived at the point', he told Armstrong in 1987, 'at which I either make my concerns public, which means breaking the Official Secrets Act, or I fail to discharge my responsibility to account for actions which I believe would be considered unacceptable by the general public were it aware of them.' Armstrong immediately ordered government lawyers to get a High Court injunction preventing Mitchell from disclosing anything about his work at GCHQ. In an article in *The Guardian* in May 1986 Mitchell wrote:

GCHQ is an industrial complex. Its product is intelligence. Intelligence imparts power; power which may be used to withstand a threat – or to apply one; to avert an ill, to bestow a benefit – or to exploit. Intelligence shared is power shared; intelligence withheld confers power over the unaware. GCHQ provides power to the British government; and governments with which it is allied. GCHQ staff have a moral responsibility, both corporate and individual, for the use to which that power is put. The human instruments of the Nazi regime stood condemned at Nuremburg because they shirked their moral responsibility.

Mitchell described GCHQ as a powerful, but unaccountable, arm of government. The only watchdog is the workforce. 'It is they', he said, 'on whom the general public must rely if errors of judgement, excessive zeal or malpractices are to be averted in a department which has considerable discretion and no outside inspection.' The effect of the union ban, Mitchell argued, is that the workforce is now less likely to be representative of the population as a whole. It will be distorted, since people who pay strong regard to civil liberties are less likely to work there, resulting in a GCHQ with more than its share of 'yes-men'.

Trade union representatives at GCHQ had another important role, although perhaps a more humdrum one. Given the secrecy surrounding their work, the 'indoctrination' to which they were subjected – for the most part they did not even talk to their families about it – staff needed an outlet. Union meetings and activities provided such an outlet, while union representatives could also act as welfare officers. The traditional role of fighting for better pay and conditions was only one of their functions.

Union membership, said Mrs Thatcher, was incompatible with 'national security'. It was nonsense, of course. But the phrase is important because it is used as an excuse for government secrecy and is too readily assumed to be self-explanatory. It is also one of the factors allowing GCHQ to do what it does. Ministers have repeatedly defined national security in the following way: 'The term is generally understood to refer to the safeguarding of the state and the community against threats to their survival or well-being.' The Security Service Act which governs MI5 states that its function is 'the protection of national security', adding, 'in particular, protection against threats from espionage, terrorism and sabotage, from the activities of agents of foreign powers' and 'from actions intended to overthrow or *undermine* parliamentary democracy by *political, industrial* or violent means' (emphasis added). This is the official definition of 'subversion' and we may assume that it is used for GCHQ.

'National security' is not defined in the 1984 Data Protection Act, where a 'national security exemption' allows government agencies and the police to refuse to disclose personal information held on computer. Nor, as Lord Justice Lloyd – the High Court judge appointed to monitor official telephone tapping – has noted in his annual reports, is it defined in the 1985 Interception of Communications Act. 'It is narrower', he said, than the term 'public interest', but it is 'obviously wider than the three heads of counter terrorism, counter espionage and counter subversion'. He added: 'Each case must be judged on its merits.' That is what the Home Secretary does as far as MI5 is concerned, and we may assume that the same goes for those who are ultimately responsible for GCHQ. It is entirely a matter for their discretion.

The Interception of Communications Act – the only statute which even remotely applies to GCHQ – allows ministers to issue warrants 'in the interests of national security; for the purpose of preventing or detecting serious crime', defined as an offence which carries a 3-year jail sentence or, more dangerously as far as civil liberties are concerned, potentially criminal 'conduct by a large number of persons in pursuit of a common purpose'; and, 'for the purpose of safeguarding the economic well-being of the United Kingdom', the clause which allows GCHQ to monitor economic and commercial targets.

The term 'national security' was given a potentially extremely broad definition in a White Paper on the interception of communications, issued by the government in February 1985. It said:

The Secretary of State may issue warrants on grounds of national security if he considers that the information to be acquired under the warrant is necessary in the interests of national security either because of terrorism, espionage or major subversive activity, *or in support of the government's defence and foreign policies* [emphasis added].

This suggests that any individual or group opposed to the government's attitude towards nuclear weapons, for example, or towards the European Community, could be regarded as a legitimate target for GCHQ surveillance.

The Interception of Communications Act established a tribunal which theoretically allows individuals to complain if they believe their conversations have been tapped. But the tribunal's terms of reference are cleverly and narrowly defined. It can investigate whether a tap was wrongly authorized – that is to say, whether the criteria for the issue of a warrant were observed. But it cannot take any action in the event of an illegal tap – one that is made without a warrant (when, in any case, the tribunal would itself be kept in the dark). The public cannot know whether their phones are tapped or not, and therefore whether they are the object of illegal interceptions. They are not told the reasons for the tribunal's decisions and have no right of appeal to a civil court. And one warrant can cover an entire organization, pressure group or association.

The Act does not cover modern bugging devices, such as long-distance microphones. And there is some doubt whether it covers the new computer-run telephone exchange system, System X. This system, developed by Plessey – which has close links with GCHQ – uses digital signals. These enable British Telecom and the security and intelligence services to trace and store telephone calls much more easily. The tapper no longer has to tamper physically with individual lines, telephone exchanges or office switchboards. Lines can be tapped by remote interception. Mark Leopold (a former BT employee) and Patrick FitzGerald describe in their book *Stranger on the Line: The secret history of phone tapping* how the system escapes the Act: 'the [digital] tap leaves no physical presence anywhere; it is literally invisible and makes no discernible changes to the telephone circuit being tapped'.

According to GCHQ's unofficial charter, the organization is not supposed to intercept any communication between one British citizen and another. We have seen how this cannot be observed, since GCHQ's technology automatically eavesdrops on communications passing through the air waves. We have seen too how GCHQ can use the American National Security Agency to get round this problem, and how there is nothing to stop officials from the other security and intelligence agencies – MI5, for example – using GCHQ facilities to do their work, including the surveillance of British citizens. GCHQ's unofficial charter covers the staff, not the technology.

Intrusive technology is perhaps at its most dangerous stage. It is at a point where it is powerful enough to enable the security and intelligence agencies to pick up any mechanical communications made by private individuals, private companies or foreign governments. GCHQ and the NSA have more powerful computers than any other organization or corporation – through a 'gentlemen's agreement', the computer manufacturers agree that any encoding systems they provide to GCHQ are more sophisticated than those they sell to anyone else. GCHQ is a uniquely privileged organ of the secret state. Its powerful position, its total lack of accountability, can only cause serious disquiet among those concerned with civil liberties.

4

The battle: 26 January to 1 March 1984

... the nasty thin wedge of Fascism.

John Gorst, Conservative MP for Hendon North

On the morning of 26 January the message to staff at the gates of GCHQ was simple: don't sign. Don't sign the option form attached to the management's letter, GN 100/84. Come to the meeting after work. Several hundred staff stopped to take the leaflet. They were hungry for news and keen to know what the unions would do. The atmosphere was a combination of shock and confusion – GCHQ staff were still not really sure what had happened to them. It was too early for fear or anger.

The pattern for the public campaign was set at that first meeting on the evening of 26 January. Although the meeting was essentially a private one for the members and their unions, it was agreed that the press and television should be allowed in. They saw 1,500 staff from the Oakley and Benhall sites trying to cram into Cheltenham's Pittville Pump Room. The turnout of staff was so high that overflow meetings had to be organized outside. From the 'top table' union officials urged staff not to sign.

More exciting was the response from the floor. The confusion of the morning had turned into indignation. Why had they done this? What have we done wrong? Why is our loyalty being doubted? There were attacks on the government and concern about the erosion of civil liberties. The overall impression was a collective cry of outrage, hurt and puzzlement. It came more powerfully from staff than from the union officials.

Initial press response to the ban was hostile towards the government. And uncharacteristically, it has remained consistently sympathetic to the unions on the issue. This should not be surprising. The government's action was unprecedented – never before had such a step been taken by the government against a trade union in modern times. The ban was imposed without warning – the press had no prior knowledge or briefing. The unions involved – the Civil Service unions – were not a *bête noir* of Fleet Street. Despite the five-month pay dispute in 1981, they were not 'big league' unions like the NUM, which had industrial muscle. In these circumstances journalists and even leader writers acted instinctively; to ban unions, to remove an individual's right to belong to a union seemed wrong. The government's case, vague and muted, was unconvincing even to the impartial outsider.

And the mystery of GCHQ was attractive to the press. What was it? What did it do? These were the standard questions and they were put to GCHQ staff. Staff who had not been allowed to talk even to their own families about what the organization did were now talking to millions of people through the press and television. The picture they gave was important – it was not a concocted image; it was real. They were ordinary people, loyally doing a job which they had been explicitly entrusted to do. Now they had been insulted. This came across in interview after interview. Throughout they responded according to their training – not once did they talk about GCHQ or break the Official Secrets Act. They discussed the ban and how they felt about it, but they did not talk about their jobs despite understandable pressure to do so from the media.

Historically, GCHQ had gone to extraordinary lengths to keep its work secret and out of the public eye. At a stroke the government attracted more publicity and attention to GCHQ than until then could have been imagined. GCHQ had been thrust into the public domain – the government itself had finally shattered GCHQ's shell of secrecy.

The ban immediately provoked hostile criticism from across the political spectrum. James (now Lord) Callaghan, the former Labour Prime Minster, said, 'I was incredulous ... this is an issue of principle which, put in its grandest form, is the right of freedom of association, a right guaranteed under the United Nations Charter and in every other way.' Callaghan maintained his concern. In March 1986, with Sir Geoffrey Howe again havering over whether or not to sack GCHQ staff who had refused to give up their union membership,

Jeremy Windust (SCPS) on the morning after the ban was announced, outside the Oakley site in Cheltenham.

Callaghan told the Commons: 'This disgraceful episode in the government's record will not be wiped out until every member at GCHQ who desires to join a Civil Service trade union shall be free to do so without fear of intimidation, disciplinary action, or dismissal.'

John Gorst, Conservative MP for Hendon North and a member of the House of Commons Select Committee on Employment, made the following comment: 'I have an unqualified acceptance for the right of people to belong to a union. I remain baffled and bemused by what the government has done.' David Owen, leader of the SDP, stated: 'A democracy trusts its government to hold the balance between national security and individual liberty. The Prime Minister and the Foreign Secretary, in depriving civil servants at GCHQ in Cheltenham of the right to remain members of a trade union, have destroyed that trust.' And Hans Engelberts, General Secretary of Public Service International, declared: 'I can find no other example anywhere in a free democratic society where workers have been offered money by the government to leave the ranks of the trade union movement.'

Charles Irving, the Conservative MP for Cheltenham, also opposed the ban: 'The tributes paid to GCHQ between 1981 and the present time, particularly over their efforts during the Falklands War, really do discredit the facts that are being put forward at this very late hour by the Government. If these matters are as true and urgent in the interests of national security as is now being made out, why on earth didn't the Government take action in 1981?' A few days after the ban he said: 'I would not sign my rights away for a mess of pottage.' He won the loudest applause when he addressed CCSU's lobby at the Commons on 23 February. 'Across the party spectrum there is no room for dogma when it loses compassion, justice and fair treatment', he said. He promised his 100 per cent support, but his backing for the GCHQ staff who stood up for their rights gradually melted away.

The initial thought behind the 'don't sign' slogan was to give the unions time – time to think and time somehow to try and reverse the government's decision. But even at the earliest stage it was apparent that if enough members of staff refused to accept the ban then it would be difficult for the government to implement the decision. The best chance was to secure as much support as possible in key operational areas. Not unnaturally, for this is what he was and where he worked, Jack Hart identified the radio grades at the outstations as the most promising target. They were the most organized group of workers in terms of union membership, historically the most powerful, and one of the hardest for management to remove or replace. No one else did the same work. If they could be convinced to stick together, the government's threats would be meaningless.

Significantly, in the light of subsequent debates, the question of GCHQ staff taking industrial action did not really arise. There was an easy consensus that advocating such a course of action would enable the government to claim that the unions could not be trusted. Whatever the moral justification, the overwhelming view was that industrial action was tactical suicide. There was also a more pragmatic judgement – it was acknowledged that there would be no chance of getting a significant number of GCHQ staff to take such action.

By Friday, 27 January, CSU headquarters, just like those of other unions, was a chaotic hive of activity and debate. Circulars had been winging their way to branches. Duties were allocated. Although one of the smaller unions in the Civil Service, the CSU was the 'senior' union in GCHQ. Despite its size, perhaps because of it, the union threw itself into the campaign, probably devoting proportionately more time and resources than any other union, at least until those resources ran out. On the Friday evening – two days after the announcement of the ban – full-time headquarters staff gathered in the office of the CSU General Secretary, John Sheldon.

It was not really a meeting: the drinks cabinet was open and everyone's adrenalin was pumping fast. It was like the night before a big match. It was also a farewell gathering, everyone wishing each other good luck in the tasks they had been allocated. Earlier that day a circular had been sent to all branches telling them that Hugh Lanning had been allocated to the campaign committee the CCSU had established, and that Mike Barke would be assigned to the emergency office to be set up in Cheltenham. Other officers were allocated to take over their work, but in practice the whole union became dominated from top to bottom by the GCHQ issue. It was to be the union's ultimate challenge; one which drained it almost completely.

At the weekend Lanning turned the strategic possibilities over and over in his head. On Friday he had jotted down some ideas, and these were discussed with Sheldon, and with Leslie Christie – SCPS Assistant General Secretary – over the phone at the weekend. The relationship between the CSU and the SCPS was to prove crucial in keeping the unions together through the political disputes that erupted later in the campaign. It may also have contributed to the merger between the two unions in 1988.

The following Monday, at the CCSU Campaign Committee, the

programme of action put forward by the CSU was broadly accepted, with a few elaborations from the SCPS. It argued that the initial strategy should be two-pronged:

Firstly, we must emphasise as much as possible how vital it is for members and other employees of GCHQ not to sign any option form. The objective will be to hold this line until 1st March, with as many as possible not signing. The second and complementary part of the strategy must be to build wider support within the Civil Service and the Trade Union Movement combined with general attempts to build political pressure on the Government.

The Campaign Committee decided to produce a weekly information bulletin for all members, to organize meetings for union members at all GCHQ's UK stations, to set up an office in Cheltenham and to 'establish communication lines which do not rely on official facilities'. The only CSU proposal that was not accepted was a suggestion that the unions should mount a 'counter-options exercise', to encourage staff to fill in forms stating that they would like to retain the right to belong to a trade union.

The priority was the production of a 'statement of case', designed to be a comprehensive union answer to the management claims. The first main focus for action was a lobby of Parliament in mid-February, combined with attempts to have a parliamentary debate and a general 'day of protest'. The CCSU was also to seek support from the TUC and other unions, obtain legal advice and explore international avenues, such as the European Court of Human Rights and the International Labour Organization.

The 'strategy' was really no such thing; it was a reaction to events; a framework perhaps, but not yet a detailed, planned campaign. Crucially, it only considered immediate action in the run-up to the government's 1 March deadline. It did not face up to what the unions should do if, as the deadline approached, there was no change in the government's attitude. The unions were still hoping for a miracle, a U-turn from the woman who was 'not for turning', Mrs Thatcher.

Immediately after the announcement of the ban, on Wednesday, 25 January, the Major Policy Committee of the CCSU sent a letter of protest to the Prime Minister. The letter, signed by Bill McCall, IPCS General Secretary, asked for a meeting at her 'earliest convenience'.

In the Civil Service trade union movement to request a meeting with a prominent figure, either a minister or, in extreme cases, the

Prime Minister, is an almost Pavlovian response. If you do not know what else to do, ask for a meeting. In this case it was crucial.

Mrs Thatcher's earliest convenience turned out to be Wednesday, 1 February – very quick by normal standards and a reflection of the furore the announcement had caused. The basis of the CCSU's argument to be put to Mrs Thatcher was the statement of case, which had been prepared by the Campaign Committee. Most of the drafting was done by Ken Jones, head of the SCPS Research Department. Entitled 'Whose loyalty has been betrayed?', it concentrated on rebutting the government's claim that the unions in GCHQ were a threat to national security.

Press coverage and parliamentary discussion – inspired by Whitehall briefings – now centred on the alleged disruption caused by industrial action within GCHQ. Through the press the government released instances of industrial action between 1979 and 1982. The *Daily Telegraph* printed a 'Catalogue of disruption'. It was a broadly accurate list. The story linked these periods of industrial action with contemporary world events, such as the Soviet invasion of Afghanistan and the Falklands War. Publicly the government did not claim that damage had been done; merely that it could have been. This issue was clearly going to be the battle ground when the meeting took place.

At the 1 February meeting Mrs Thatcher cited four basic factors that underpinned her decision to ban unions:

- GCHQ staff must be denied right of access to industrial tribunals for security reasons.
- There could be no interference with GCHQ operations as a result of industrial action.
- Only GCHQ staff, answerable solely to the staff of GCHQ, should deal with negotiations on departmental issues.
- The maintenance of GCHQ services must not be put at risk by any conflict of loyalties.

In response – and perhaps reacting instinctively rather than in any premeditated way – McCall said that the CCSU was willing to meet the four points raised by the Prime Minister.

The unions pointed out that industrial tribunals can meet in camera and that, if necessary, they would consider the Civil Service Appeal Board as an alternative to industrial tribunals.

The unions offered a 'no-disruption' agreement, while insisting that it was not a no-strike deal. This would be similar to other agreements which, for safety reasons, excluded some areas from industrial action. This time it would be for reasons of national security.

On the third point, the unions reminded the government that full-time union officials did not in any case have access to classified information, and nor were they allowed on GCHQ sites unaccompanied.

Finally, while the unions vigorously denied that any conflict of loyalties had arisen for GCHQ staff, they again indicated that they were prepared 'to discuss sensible arrangements to ensure this did not happen'.

Had it been planned, this response could not have been better designed to wrong-foot the government. The government had not consulted with the unions in advance – the government had not even tried to see if an agreement was possible – and now the unions were saying that they would offer the government an agreement that would overcome all its objections to unions in GCHQ. It was the unions that were, once again, appearing to be reasonable, and the government that was seen as the villain.

Aware, perhaps, of the impact on political and public opinion, Mrs Thatcher proposed another meeting. This was not her original intention – the offer only came after an exchange of notes between Mrs Thatcher and the head of the Civil Service, Sir Robert Armstrong.

At the end of this first meeting, Downing Street issued a terse statement:

In a long discussion each side reaffirmed its position. The Prime Minister made it clear that the government's decision and the offer to GCHQ staff stand. The Prime Minister said that, if the unions wished to meet her again, she would be prepared to do so, and the unions accepted her offer.

The tacit understanding was that, before the next meeting with Mrs Thatcher, secret talks would be held to explore the offer the unions had made to meet her four points.

The impact of the offer was twofold. First, it secured widespread public and political support for the unions, encouraging many doubters, including those within Tory ranks, to urge the government to pick up the offer. After all, had the unions not just offered what the government was really after – a no-strike deal which would set a precedent for the whole of the public services? Secondly, the offer was to strain the unity of the Civil Service unions almost to breaking point.

Ron Leighton, Labour MP for Newham North East, had moved quickly as the chair of the House of Commons Select Committee on Employment. Indeed, the committee decided to consider the question of GCHQ so speedily that it became a player in the process rather than a spectator commentating on events in retrospect, the normal lot for select committees.

The CCSU gave oral evidence to the committee later on the same day of the meeting with Mrs Thatcher. It also gave the committee a note explaining how the unions believed each of her requirements could be met. In essence, the unions were using the select committee as a platform from which to launch negotiations with the government.

In order to understand the negotiation process which subsequently took place, the CCSU's proposals should be set out in some detail.

Part of the government's case rested, as we have seen, on the argument that it could not risk GCHQ operations being exposed by an industrial tribunal. The weakest aspect of this argument was that access to a tribunal had existed for many years and had rarely, if ever, been exercised. The procedure enabled tribunals to hold hearings in camera on grounds of national security. The ban did not and still does not prevent GCHQ from being taken to court through civil proceedings. But hiding behind the question of access to industrial tribunals was the issue of the polygraph. GCHQ management would have had great difficulty in defending the polygraph's credentials as an objective 'lie detector' if they had ever been exposed to public examination and scrutiny.

The unions said that if the provisions for holding the cases in camera were inadequate then they would offer two alternatives. The first was that the powers of the Civil Service Appeal Board should be changed to match those of an industrial tribunal. The CSAB already heard dismissal cases for civil servants, but it could not award compensation or hear cases of sexual or racial discrimination. The second and less attractive option was to use the 'three wise men', the three Security Advisers. This unaccountable body of government appointees had a number of security functions, one of which was to hear the cases of those dismissed or transferred for security reasons.

The unions agreed in principle that the legal right of access to a tribunal could go, provided that it was replaced by an adequate alternative. Their view was that in practice internal Civil Service procedures provided protection as good as, if not better than, the rather limited provisions of the unfair dismissal laws, under which employees lost the overwhelming majority of cases.

The least understood and most controversial of the unions' proposals concerned the maintenance of essential intelligence services. The proposal had three elements, on all of which the unions conceded much. First, they offered to agree 'sensible arrangements to ensure the continuous operation of essential intelligence services in GCHQ, 24 hours a day, 7 days a week'. The 'sensible arrangements' meant machinery to resolve individual and collective grievances – basically some form of guaranteed and binding conciliation and arbitration procedures.

This concession is often portrayed as a 'no-strike' deal, and by its critics within the union movement as a sell-out. Taken at face value, it was not significant. That part of GCHQ requiring continuous operation is a small part of the agency's overall work – about 15 per cent. GCHQ staff knew that essential services had always been maintained and that to guarantee them for the future merely reflected existing practice. Therefore it would have comparatively little impact on the general right of the majority to take action at almost any time. GCHQ union members would anyway not agree to call on essential areas to come out. In practice the unions were conceding little by agreeing to maintain essential services. Indeed, there was some feeling that getting a good disputes procedure would actually strengthen the unions' bargaining position with a management that broke agreements as a matter of routine.

The second and fundamental concession was the CCSU accepting that it was the government's responsibility to determine what were 'essential intelligence services'. Although it was proposed that the government should consult with local representatives in GCHQ before deciding what was and what was not essential, the final decision would be the government's. It was also hoped that a distinction could be drawn between essential *intelligence* services and other work. In logic it could never be maintained that the work of all administrative, clerical, printing and cleaning staff, or even of computer, technical, scientific and communications staff, was essential twenty-four hours a day, seven days a week. If it was, why did management not keep all these services going, all day, every day?

Although logic was ultimately to play little part in the proceedings, the view of the union activists in GCHQ was that industrial action would remain a valuable possibility *in extremis* if they could retain the right to strike in a way that would enable the unions to bring pressure to bear on management. It was not thought necessary to retain the right to undermine essential services or 'national security'. Indeed, it was not something they wanted to do. For GCHQ staff, the right to strike in 'essential areas' was as useful and as meaningful a right as the freedom of eighteenth-century French peasants to eat cake. The *quid pro quo* was that, if the right did not really exist in practice, it was not necessary to take it away.

The final element of the essential intelligence commitment was that the provisions agreed could be included in the conditions of employment of 'those concerned whilst they are employed in providing essential intelligence services'. Given that industrial action is anyway a breach of contract under British law, it must be in doubt whether that was a real concession. There remains no doubt, however, that the unions would have preferred simply to offer a collective agreement rather than one reinforced through individual conditions of employment.

As far as the conditions covering departmental negotiations were concerned, the focus of the discussion centred on the role of the full-time officials of the national unions within GCHQ, and also on who determined union policy on departmental matters – the national union, or staff within the department. The unions' position was straightforward. There were already many curbs on access to GCHQ for any full-time official, and the unions were prepared to enshrine these in a formal agreement. The unions were also prepared to include in an agreement the existing principle that GCHQ staff were sovereign on departmental matters. The only caveat was that GCHQ staff should be able to have a say on national issues: that is, those issues affecting the whole of the Civil Service.

However, once again the stated objectives and concerns of the government disguised their motives. All managements are to some extent hostile to an 'outsider' coming into their organization – all the more so full-time officials who are often seen as, indeed sometimes are, hostile. (Experts hired or brought in by management are rarely seen in the same light.)

But in GCHQ for many years the senior officials had not been proper outsiders. Throughout the 1970s and early 1980s the three officials who had most responsibility for the unions in GCHQ were Fred Phillips of the CSU and Tom Casey and A.L. 'Mac' Macpherson of AGSRO. They were ex-GCHQ employees and had been positively vetted as part of their job. In practice, management did not seek to prevent them seeing anything or having access to information that they would have known about from the time when they worked with GCHQ.

The 1970s and 1980s saw a new generation of officers being employed by the Civil Service trade unions, often with backgrounds that were viewed suspiciously by GCHQ's R (Security) Division. So when Hugh Lanning was due to take over responsibility from Fred Phillips, management wrote to Phillips asking if he 'would kindly weed from [his] files all material concerning this Department which is classified CONFIDENTIAL' and forward it to Cheltenham. It was duly done.

In common with all government departments, GCHQ used the security classification system to control access to information. Not only was this understandable; some union officials regarded it as positively desirable. Their job is hard enough already without having to carry official secrets around as well. For example, in GCHQ they had an early version of a new technology agreement called the New Equipment and Techniques Agreement. Under this agreement all discussions on new equipment were to be undertaken by appropriately cleared lay officials. Only when these discussions could not reach agreement would full-time officials be involved – and then not to be party to any classified information, but solely to try to resolve any matters of 'principle'.

Physical access to GCHQ sites was controlled in the normal way for a highly sensitive government department, and full-time officials were treated no differently from other outsiders. They were not allowed to go into most areas, and were normally restricted to administrative areas, meeting rooms and canteens. They were required to be escorted by a member of staff at all times.

The essence of the CCSU submission was that all of the necessary controls for full-time officials were in place. They could be written up in a formal agreement if that was necessary.

This still did not get to the root of the government's paranoia. Conspiracy theorists who inspire anti-trade union legislation have two conflicting theories. Theory A is that the members are the problem, led on by agitators and activists. Therefore the role of the union and its officials is to control the members, to prevent and denounce any unofficial action and generally not to let things get out of hand. According to the other theory, theory B, full-time officials are the problem. All you have to do is let the members decide through ballots and the normal, conservative instincts of decent folk will prevail.

In one set of circumstances theory A is used, but if the facts do not fit then theory B is brought into play. In the case of GCHQ the government wanted to argue that the reason why staff took action was that the unions – and the full-time officials in particular – forced them to take action against their will. So if you can exclude full-time officials, the problem will go away.

Mrs Thatcher's ultimate stated objective was to remove what she saw as the potential conflict of loyalty facing union members at GCHQ. The CCSU response was that the arrangements they had outlined removed any possible question of a conflict of loyalty: 'The definition of responsibilities and accountability will effectively separate one loyalty from the other, and thus fully meet the Government's requirement in this respect.'

The government, in the form of Sir Geoffrey Howe, also gave evidence to the select committee. His opening statement was a repeat performance of previous official statements, but he concluded with two conciliatory points. First, he indicated that the government remained ready to listen to proposals which the unions might offer. Then he added: 'the Government fully respect the right of civil servants to be members of a trade union ... This is no part of any wider campaign. It is emphatically not the Government's intention to introduce similar measures outside the field of security and intelligence.'

Under questioning from the committee, Sir Geoffrey conceded that if a significant number of staff refused to leave their unions then ministers would have no option but to reconsider their decision. Asked whether the decision was a gamble, he replied that the ban was imposed on the basis of advice from senior management at GCHQ. 'If the advice turns out to be substantially wrong, the matter obviously calls for reconsideration.' While adding that this was not the government's current view, he repeated that the issue remained open for reconsideration at any stage. He also confirmed that Lord

Carrington had considered a ban on unions in 1981 when he was
Foreign Secretary. This left unanswered the obvious question: why
had he rejected it?

Sir Brian Tovey, former Director of GCHQ, was called to give
evidence. The self-proclaimed author of the proposal to ban unions,
Tovey was questioned in secret. He said he could not see how any no-
disruption agreement which lacked the force of law could offer
sufficient guarantees. He claimed that GCHQ had been very seriously disrupted by strike action on one day – 9 March 1981 – while
he was Director, and that this had finally convinced him of the need
to ban unions.

The select committee also sought evidence from Jack Hart,
chairman, and Peter Bryant, secretary, of the trade unions at GCHQ,
and Peter Marychurch, the incumbent Director. On the instructions
of the head of the Civil Service, Sir Robert Armstrong, all were
denied the opportunity to speak to the committee.

While no change had taken place in the government's formal
stance, the tone was more conciliatory and the avenue to talks was
not closed. The government appeared to be shocked by the response
that the ban had provoked. While not reeling, they were taking a
survivalist approach, keeping political doors open, or at least ajar. In
the union camp there was no elation, but some buoyancy. With this
amount of political and public support, if they remained reasonable
and responsible surely a deal was possible – if the unions could only
retain high membership support, if they could get the government
rattled by large numbers of staff still refusing to sign.

While all this activity was happening in London, another battle was
going on inside GCHQ – for the hearts and minds of the staff. In
Cheltenham the office was well established, with Mike Barke and
Jane Hustwitt – the CPSA's 'organizing officer' – fast becoming local
media celebrities, co-ordinating activities from the union office of the
General, Municipal and Boilermakers. They were joined by Chris
Dimmock and his computer. Chris was the editor of *Radio News*, the
CSU communication grades' journal, and – just as usefully – a
former employee of GCHQ. He had responded to a call for help from
union headquarters and had left semi-retirement in Bude for the
front line in Cheltenham.

Contact with overseas stations was still intermittent – information
was being sent out, but it was by no means clear what, if anything, was

getting through. In Cheltenham large meetings, with the media in attendance, were being held regularly. From the outstations in England there had been telephone calls and letters. It was time to meet the troops at the eight GCHQ outstations, which stretched from Bude in Cornwall to Brora, near John O'Groat's, in Scotland.

The tour started on Monday, 6 February 1984 with a meeting in the Four All Hotel in Taunton, where members from CSOS Culmhead were having their second meeting in five days. The main speaker at the meeting was John Ward, General Secretary of the First Division Association. The most welcome contributions from Ward were the examples he gave of support from FDA members in such unlikely places as the Treasury Solicitor's Office and within the Cabinet Office itself. He said that letters of protest that had been sent by his members, often in important policy-making positions, were unsolicited and unprecedented.

After the successful meeting at Culmhead Hart and Lanning travelled up to Cheadle, where they met John Sheldon before the meeting that was to take place in the Royal Oak Hotel on the following night. Although television cameras were not present, there was a healthy cross-section of local and national radio and press, which heard Sheldon explain not only the Downing Street meeting but the importance of members in GCHQ standing firm and continuing not to sign the option forms. Some worries were expressed by members about what action the department might take, but the meeting unanimously passed a resolution supporting the action and campaign being run by the CCSU.

However, the real drama took place at the informal meeting immediately afterwards. While intense discussions were going on concerning whose round it was, a message was received from GCHQ management indicating that a ministerial decision had been made barring Jack Hart and Peter Bryant from appearing at the Select Committee on Employment the following day.

Hart and Sheldon returned to London. Lanning joined Margaret Platt of the IPCS to address the staff from CSOS Irton Moor near Scarborough. The following day – Thursday – Lanning made the journey to Cupar, a station in Fife in Scotland. At Edinburgh Waverley station he was joined by Alistair Graham, General Secretary of the CPSA, who would also be addressing the meeting that night for staff from CSOS Hawklaw, at the Rugby Club in Cupar. The meeting in Cupar was also attended by two busloads of other civil servants, one from Edinburgh and one from the Dundee area, who had come along to show support for GCHQ staff. The meeting was recorded by local radio, and the presence of other civil servants boosted the confidence of the GCHQ employees present. Apart from the usual speeches from the top table, the meeting was spiced with messages of support from local representatives who were present.

In the morning Mark Allan, CSU branch chair at Hawklaw, put Lanning on a train in the middle of nowhere that appeared to be going to the end of nowhere. The train chugged up through the snowbound Cairngorms, revealing sights of abandoned cars on nearby roads. Nowhere turned out to be Inverness, where Lanning was met by Davy Hadden from Brora, chauffeured by the local AGSRO representative. Also in town were Peter Jones, Secretary of the CCSU, and a representative of Radio Moray Firth. After an interview in the hotel lobby and a brief break, they embarked on the final leg of the journey up to Brora for Friday evening's meeting.

The meeting was attended not only by all the available staff, but also by a fair scattering of ex-GCHQ employees who had retired and lived locally. Even in Brora the press and Radio Highland were present for a meeting that showed a traditional determination to stand firm, and a keenness to probe the speakers about the next stages of the campaign. The meeting ended with an affirmation of support for the campaign, a vote of thanks to the speakers and a move to get the guests fed and on the train back to Inverness. After twenty-four hours in London, Lanning took the train west for a meeting at GCHQ's station in Morwenstow, near Bude in Cornwall.

One thing was clear from the trip: although there were worries, there was no sign of the bulk of the unions' membership at the outstations weakening.

The meeting of the Campaign Committee took place on Tuesday, 14 February. The campaign had been going for nearly three weeks and was now entering the crucial phase – the final two weeks before the 1 March deadline for staff to sign their option forms. If the committee had done a balance sheet of the campaign so far, it might have felt quite pleased with itself. The unions had tremendous public, press and political support, often helped by the government's ability to make a blunder every time it acted, generating publicity even when the unions were doing nothing reportable.

As a story GCHQ was big news and it was still running. There were large numbers of staff who were not signing; even some staff rejoining the unions. Those signing were felt mainly to be non-members and management. The core of the membership seemed to be holding up well, in so far as it was possible to tell. Negotiations were taking place, and the Select Committee on Employment was due to report that week. Although Jack Hart and Peter Bryant had been prevented from appearing before the committee, there were still great expectations about what its report would say.

On the negative side, the continuous mudslinging by the government over industrial action and national security was consolidating its position with its natural supporters. Industrial action in GCHQ was also an issue that constantly put the unions on the defensive. More importantly, a growing number of staff – mainly non-union members – were signing and more were considering their position. Some union members were dropping out of contact. Increasingly, there were straws in the wind that things might not be as good as they appeared.

Two other problems exacerbated the difficulties for the unions. The euphoria of the campaign, the regular mass meetings, the ready access to the media, meant there was a danger that the campaign was becoming an end in itself. In addition, there were growing tensions in the unions between the activists and the union leaderships, and among those running the campaign, about what to do next.

But the government had a clear-cut strategy. Its Achilles' heel had been made public by Sir Geoffrey Howe at the Select Committee on Employment: that if 'a significant number of staff refused to leave their unions, ministers would have no option but to reconsider their position'. Therefore, while the government was publicly playing everything with a fairly straight bat, within GCHQ it had to strain every nerve and sinew to get staff to sign. It was also in the interests of GCHQ management to make the plan work. Their advice was that very few would oppose the ban. Ministers would not be pleased if the advice turned out to be substantially wrong.

With little regard to the amount of work being done or lost, every opportunity was used to increase the pressure on staff. The offer of a £1,000 *ex gratia* payment had been enough for some. Technically, the £1,000 had been offered for the loss of statutory employment rights. Perhaps mistakenly, since it diverted attention away from the more significant threat of dismissal, the £1,000 was portrayed by the unions as a bribe – 'our loyalty can't be bought' was a favoured slogan. But for many others it seemed like money for nothing. Why should those who were not members of a union or not particularly bothered give up the chance of a thousand pounds?

The fact that they discussed openly what they were going to do with the money irritated some union members, but it was not critical in deciding what the latter should do. Covert and blatant management pressure was far more significant. Through circulars, meetings of staff, line management, interviews with individuals – in every conceivable way – staff were being cajoled, pushed and shoved towards signing. The message was that refusal to sign would be no good for the individual, his or her career, or GCHQ.

There was no physical coercion. But there was a weapon just as good, if not better. Many years later, at Clive Lloyd's appeal, Peter Little, head of E Division at GCHQ, described the withdrawal of union rights as a fundamental change in conditions of service. It was planned and agreed in advance that – to quote Little – 'there had to be pressure'. Without pressure it was believed that staff would not voluntarily accept the change. The pressure was simple and had been spelt out in GN 100/84. Paragraph 17 is headed 'Staff who refuse to express an option or to accept an alternative posting'. It states: 'Any staff refusing to complete the option form or who, after electing to leave GCHQ, refuse to accept an alternative posting will have their employment terminated from a date to be determined by the Director.'

This blatant threat to sack anyone who did not do as they were told was a crucial part of the government's strategy. In public, it said that anyone who did not want to sign could request a transfer out of GCHQ. Yet this was a meaningless offer for many staff. For example, when the radio grades' pay claim had gone to arbitration in 1969, it had been acknowledged that no one could be found who did comparable work. Establishments Division was telling ROs that they would be transferred as clerical officers. Apart from the fact that they were not doing, and did not want to do, clerical work, there was the small matter that they earned considerably more than a clerical officer, one of the many low-paid grades in the Civil Service. Similar problems affected other specialists. Mike Grindley – who was to become a legend in his own height – was a Chinese linguist. Other government departments came to him when they needed his specialist knowledge of Chinese; they did not employ full-time Chinese linguists of their own. Staff overseas were told that they would be

transferred home immediately. Staff who lived in Cheltenham but
were classed as 'mobile' would be expected to move to anywhere in
the country where there was a suitable job. Locally recruited non-
mobile staff, such as cleaners, security officers and clerical workers,
knew that there was no equivalent size employer in Cheltenham.

In determining the form that the pressure should take management had judged their audience well. Overall, but particularly in
clerical and non-specialist grades, staff in GCHQ were badly organized in union terms – only 58 per cent were union members. Those
grades that were best organized, the departmental, specialist and
technical grades, had nowhere else to go. They were with a unique
employer who monopolized the market. On top of this the staff had
all been positively vetted and had worked all their careers in a closed
security culture. The staff were certainly not renowned for their
revolutionary fervour; indeed, they had a tradition of providing
Conservative members on Cheltenham Borough Council.

However calculated or premeditated the pressure was, it had the
impact that management desired. Among themselves at work, and at
home with their families, all the members of staff who did not want
to sign were weighing up the options. Whichever way they looked at
it, if the unions did not secure a deal before 1 March then they could
either sign or be sacked. More and more were reaching their own
decisions in private. They would give the unions and the campaign
time, but not forever.

Against the background of the battle within GCHQ there was a clear
hole in the union's strategy of 'don't sign'. If no deal was reached, if
the campaign did not put enough pressure on the government, what
was the unions' alternative to the threat of dismissal? In some
industrial climates the history of union solidarity might have been
enough; if we all stick together there's nothing they can do; 'the
workers united will never be defeated'. Although GCHQ staff
understood that by sticking together they could defeat management,
they did not have the confidence in themselves, in each other and in
the unions to believe that the risk to their jobs and families was not
too great.

Although privately they acknowledged and discussed the problem,
the unions' public position was to stand firm and claim that they were
winning. At a meeting of CSU's GCHQ branch secretaries on 3
February, under the heading 'future strategy' it was merely stressed

that at the moment it was important for members not to sign anything. The minutes of the meeting stated: 'At a later stage, future strategy would be considered in more detail.' On 7 February Mike Barke sent a report to Hugh Lanning about a meeting of communication and cypher officers, the staff who ran the nerve centre of GCHQ's communications system. The report stated that members seemed to be standing firm and not signing, but two points were raised for headquarters. 'There is a feeling that the protest day on 28th February is too late. Members *badly* want advice on what to do and what support they will get on 1st March. [They] feel this should not be delayed until the final week.'

Many ideas were being floated. Davey Murdoch wrote down from the wilds of Brora on 9 February: 'Time is now running short but I feel that the unions should strongly advise all members to sign Option B [to transfer out of GCHQ]. The signed forms, and this is the important part, should then all be forwarded to some central union point.' There were also ideas for the unions to collect in all the forms unsigned, or to get a list of all those prepared not to sign. The common theme was that members wanted to see how much support there was, how many people were prepared to stand firm.

On 31 January Lanning had written a confidential memo to the two most senior officials in CSU, John Sheldon and John Randall. Entitled 'Long-term strategy up to and beyond 1st March', it stated:

If the 'Don't sign' campaign is successful and we keep large numbers of staff from signing, the pressure will grow on them the nearer we get to 1st March. I suspect that large numbers are quite prepared to withhold from signing at the moment but want much greater assurance if we are to start urging them not to sign up to and beyond 1st March, as they are then in real danger of facing dismissal.

The first defence is obviously going to be in numbers, and although we should not engage management in a numbers game we will need to have some idea of the numbers who have not signed and also of those who are prepared to carry on not signing. More importantly we will need to have some idea of a base line required to be able to maintain pressure on management.

Secondly, if we do succeed in holding the line beyond 1st March, should it prove necessary, then money is going to become a major problem. It might be that management would not go in for mass dismissal of all those who have not signed but we need to have funds available to pay staff so dismissed.

In essence this part of the strategy is going to be one of nerve/'bottle'. Our only hope is to persuade management that sufficient numbers of people will not exercise one of the options for them to maintain a viable operation, but they will also be waiting to see what happens as we get nearer to 1st March. Over that period our aim must therefore be to provide as much support and reassurance to members in GCHQ [as possible], because if anything goes wrong it will be their jobs that are at risk.

By 12 February the Cheltenham office had written to the CCSU's Major Policy Committee making the same point, and similar discussions took place in the other unions.

Out of these disparate thoughts, ideas and discussions emerged a paper for the Campaign Committee entitled 'Towards 1st March'. The basic assumption was that the talks with Sir Robert Armstrong would break down or fail to produce an acceptable settlement. The paper considered the position inside and outside GCHQ.

To start with the paper examined the major options facing staff and the advice that the unions could give. Staff could be recommended to sign Option B and request a transfer. It was assumed that management would not be able to provide transfers for many staff, so there would be a lot of disruption even though staff had complied with GN 100/84. But this was a dangerous strategy for non-mobile and general staff, who could be forced to move or made redundant. Crucially, management did not have to act, since it was committed only to *seek* transfers. It could therefore play out the process indefinitely.

The defeatist option was to recommend that staff should sign away their rights 'under duress'. This assumed that further action was futile in the short term; the unions would be relying on long-term legal and political remedies.

Neither of these possibilities was taken seriously for long. It was decided to continue the 'don't sign' campaign, but in addition to provide an alternative option, drafted by the CCSU, for staff to send back to management. This would indicate a desire both to continue working for GCHQ *and* to retain trade union membership. It was also suggested that safeguards should be offered by the unions to staff who were dismissed. The safeguards proposed were:

- financial support;
- industrial action, from both the rest of the Civil Service and the wider trade union movement;
- legal action (taking up individual cases);
- political support (seeking formal commitments from opposition parties).

It was argued and accepted that these safeguards would be crucial in convincing members to face potential mass dismissals. If the unions were going to transform a 'don't sign until 1 March' campaign into a 'don't sign ever and face dismissal' campaign then they had to provide an insurance policy for any union member who was sacked. For members the crucial safeguard would be the guarantee of financial support. It was also the crucial one for the unions. If lots of members signed Option C, as it became known (even by management), then the defence would be in numbers. Although the financial liability would be enormous, there was a much smaller risk of sackings. If very few signed, the liability of the unions would be small. In between lay a very large grey area where there might not be enough C signatures to prevent dismissal, yet where there would still be a large financial commitment.

Proposals were put forward for launching the next phase of the campaign on Monday, 20 February, on what was acknowledged to be a very tight timescale. Outside GCHQ the planned parliamentary lobby and day of protest would become the launching pad for the next phase of the campaign. They would demonstrate support and encouragement for those members deciding whether or not to ignore the ban, and a warning to the government not to dismiss anyone refusing to sign. To add strength to this view it was proposed to beef up the day of protest by having the CCSU call for a one-day strike. The Campaign Committee endorsed the strategy, but not everyone's perception of things was quite the same.

In the outside world, trade unionists in the Civil Service and elsewhere were by and large unaware of the debates going on: all they saw was the visible product of the campaign. The ban was greeted by protests and walk-outs by civil servants in nearly all Civil Service departments – except, of course, in GCHQ where no action was called. There had been protest meetings, publicity and, in London, a large lunch-time rally at Central Hall. So far the only further action involving union members that had been announced was a lobby of Parliament on 23 February and a day of protest, with lunch-time meetings and rallies, on 28 February. Among tens of thousands of civil servants there was a genuine feeling of outrage and frustration. They were eager to take action, but only supportive protest action was being requested. The view of the CSU's communication and cypher officer branch meeting as reported by Mike Barke was widely held – the day of protest was too little, too late.

In the world of the phased, gradual build-up of pressure and activity, there was a showpiece rally of union leaders at the TUC on 16 February, designed as a significant media and political event. The TUC had got involved in the campaign almost as soon as the ban was announced. The TUC Finance and General Purposes Committee had formally supported the CCSU campaign at its meeting on 30 January. It had also agreed a levy of all TUC constituents to support anyone dismissed from GCHQ. Len Murray, TUC General Secretary, had attended the meeting with the Prime Minister on 1 February. From very early on, TUC representatives sat on the CCSU Campaign Committee.

The TUC rally was attended by the executives of affiliated unions and the media. Perhaps the most significant speech of the evening came from the former Prime Minister James Callaghan, for the first time announcing his wholehearted support for the campaign. There were also speeches from Len Murray, Neil Kinnock, David Penhaligon, Bill McCall, Lord Wedderburn and Lord McCarthy. The best received contribution of the night was made by Jack Hart speaking on behalf of GCHQ staff, for whom standing ovations were to become a way of life.

All fine stuff – but it did not meet the demands for a 'general strike now' chanted outside. A newly re-elected Tory government was rampant, spoiling for a fight with the miners and any other union prepared to offer it one. In fact Hugh Lanning had been dragooned into an NUM meeting in Dover Town Hall the weekend after the ban was announced and had the unenviable task of following Arthur Scargill in addressing the meeting. At the time the NUM President was doing the rounds preparing the miners for a head-on clash which he was sure was imminent.

For many in the wider Labour and trade union movement GCHQ provided an ideal vehicle to take on the government. It was an unlikely scenario given GCHQ's role and the lack of 'militant' trade unionism in GCHQ. But with such widespread support for the unions on the issue of the freedom to belong to a union, surely there was scope for more action than the TUC and the CCSU had proposed?

The initial dilemma centred on the role of GCHQ staff. If it was thought wrong tactically and politically to call out GCHQ staff, if GCHQ members said it was undesirable and impossible to get GCHQ staff out on strike, then what could you call on others to do? The received wisdom was that you could not get other trade unionists to take solidarity action – still legal at the time – unless those on whose behalf they were taking action were on strike themselves or had been treated exceptionally badly. At that moment, neither was the case in GCHQ. Until 1 March GCHQ staff could still be union members, they were still at work, and no one had been dismissed. For many trade unionists outside GCHQ all the staff had to do was stick together and they could defeat the government.

On the other side of 1 March, if there were enough members left in the unions, then a whole new range of possibilities would arise. What GCHQ members did or did not do would not be a problem – the government would have failed to listen and would have to decide whether or not to sack the union members. In these circumstances, who knew what would happen? All the unions could do was speculate.

In the real world the London Co-ordinating Committee of the CCSU, the local committee organizing the protest activities in London on 28 February, had called for a one-day strike for that day. Scotland, Manchester, South Wales, South Yorkshire and Humberside local CCSU committees had already made similar calls. Speaking on behalf of the CCSU's Major Policy Committee, Bill McCall said:

The local committees of the Council have no authority to call for industrial action. It is not the policy of the Council of Civil Service Unions to call for any industrial action whilst negotiations with the government are continuing. The CCSU has called only for lunch-time rallies and demonstrations on 28 February. Further advice if necessary will be given to members after the discussions with the government have been completed. We understand the anger and indignation of members, but, in the meantime, all members should follow the advice of the Council.

The *Shorter Oxford English Dictionary* defines 'to negotiate' as 'to confer (with another) for the purpose of arranging some matter by mutual agreement; to discuss a matter with a view to a settlement or compromise'. There was certainly much conferring going on between Sir Robert Armstrong and Bill McCall, but to this day it remains a moot point whether or not this amounted to real negotiations. The government did not formally acknowledge that talks were taking place. Armstrong made it clear that he was only exploring the possibilities and did not have the authority to negotiate. Despite this, clear signals were being received that a deal might just be possible if terms acceptable to the government could be found – at least that was the clear impression within the upper echelons of the CCSU. Drafts of possible agreements between the CCSU and the government were circulated among the members of the CCSU's Major Policy Committee. More concessions were made after further contacts with the Cabinet Office.

The backdrop for the discussions had been set by the report of the House of Commons Select Committee on Employment, which was published in the week ending 17 February. The report was prepared in record time and was a damaging reverse for the government, particularly as the select committee contained a majority of Conservative MPs. John Gorst was one of the committee's members who turned out to be a particularly eloquent opponent of the union ban. Tory MP for Hendon North and a supporter of the right-wing Freedom Association, he had a reputation for being 'anti-union'. But people had as much right to be members of a union as they had not to be members, he argued.

Gorst resigned as leader of the Tory group on the committee in protest against the government's attempt to persuade MPs on the committee to tone down their criticism of the GCHQ ban. He also sharply criticized the government's decision to prevent three GCHQ employees – Jack Hart, Peter Bryant and the Director of GCHQ, Peter Marychurch – from giving evidence to the committee, either in public *or* in private.

Gorst drew attention to the average £4,529 compensation given to people who refused to belong to a closed shop under the 1982 Employment Act. Comparing this with the £1,000 offer to GCHQ staff for giving up their statutory rights, he said that the government appeared to value differently the freedom to associate and the freedom not to associate. He also criticized the Employment Committee for not calling for an outright and immediate 'ban on the use of the polygraph' in its report published on 20 February 1984. The issue, he said, related to 'protecting the rights of the individual'.

There had in fact been a split in the committee, with some Tory members claiming that the government had acted correctly in preventing the three witnesses, Jack Hart, Peter Bryant and Peter Marychurch, from appearing before it. Despite this, however, the committee had recommended unanimously:

(1) that the concessions offered by the unions as set out in their note to the Committee submitted after the meeting of 1st February be thoroughly

examined by the Government to satisfy themselves that they meet every requirement of national security;

(2) that the unions offer whatever legally binding assurances the Government require in order to make these arrangements totally effective;

(3) that if arrangements which involve setting precedents that would in other circumstances be unacceptable to trade unions have to be demanded, these arrangements will be applied solely in matters relating to national security at GCHQ;

(4) that representatives of the TUC and the CCSU should immediately accept the Prime Minister's open invitation for talks in order to reach agreements along the lines recommended above.

The report briefly raised hopes that a deal was on. But in the discussions that were taking place the going was getting tough. It remained unclear whether the CCSU was talking to the government or not. Did Armstrong really have no brief from Thatcher? Had no words passed between them, or was Armstrong just being 'economical with the truth'? Whatever the basis of the talks, they were not going well. The CCSU, having set out such a reasonable initial negotiating position, was finding it hard to prevent or argue against further concessions.

In the final draft of a possible agreement, which the CCSU subsequently published (see Appendix 2), the CCSU was the Emperor with no clothes. The draft agreement had been broadened to include the maintenance of essential intelligence *and security* services, a concession that would be hard to limit. In the discussions which followed it was Armstrong's view, and presumably would be the government's, that the whole of GCHQ would be covered, not just parts of it. As the agreement conceded the right of the government to determine what were essential intelligence and security areas, the unions would in practical terms be left with little or no room for manoeuvre.

Staff's conditions of service would be phrased to prevent them taking any action which would or *might* interfere with the uninterrupted operation of essential intelligence services. The unions would not instruct or ask members employed in or *under* GCHQ to take any action which would or *might* put at risk the continuous maintenance, twenty-four hours a day, seven days a week, of essential security and intelligence services. There would be no disputes procedure as such, but a clause providing for GCHQ management and the GCHQ trade union side to consult together to provide agreed machinery. Full-time officials would 'take no part' in departmental negotiations, merely provide information on national agreements which might be relevant.

However you looked at the final published proposals, management had been tough in these 'non-negotiations', these 'clarificatory' talks. Every 'i' had been dotted, every 't' crossed, all to the government's advantage.

During the negotiations some of the unions were getting increasingly apprehensive about the slippery slope down which the talks were going. The SCPS were controlled at the time by the 'left'. Instinctively, they did not want to be associated with anything that smacked of a no-strike deal. They and many others had real and genuine fears that a precedent would be set for other parts of the public services. They were worried that restrictions would be put on the right to strike in other essential services. There was a view, particularly among those unions with only a small percentage of their members in GCHQ, that it would be better to suffer a glorious defeat over the right to union membership at GCHQ than to retain that right through shoddy compromise.

The IPCS was solidly behind the deal – after all, it was their General Secretary who was conducting the discussions. Bill McCall had run and controlled the IPCS for twenty years and was not going to lose control during his finest hour. AGSRO was almost bankrupt and just about to merge with the IPCS. They had little choice but to follow their new paymasters. The FDA supported the discussions and the agreement. The unions with no members in GCHQ (NIPSA, POA, IRSF) would follow the majority of those unions with members inside GCHQ. This left the CPSA and the CSU.

The CPSA was split. Alistair Graham, the 'new realist' General Secretary, supported the concessions to get an agreement. His membership and National Executive Committee were another matter. Whatever Graham was saying at the CCSU Major Policy Committee, there were severe doubts whether he would in due course be able to carry his executive and conference with him. In fact both the CPSA and the SCPS rejected the draft agreement at their conferences. But at the time there was no opportunity for democratic consultation with union members. Unlike the later miners' strike, there were no media calls for a ballot of members on the issue. The process was being settled in rooms – less smoke filled these days – by telephone calls and at the various union headquarters. Soundings were being taken with executive committees or whoever was available.

The piggy in the middle of this process was the CSU. Often described as an 'officer-led' union, it was crucial to any agreement. Given the number of members the union had in GCHQ and the grades they represented – operational and communication grades – no agreement would have any credibility if the CSU were not a party to it. John Sheldon, the CSU's General Secretary, was part of the left-wing club of general secretaries in the TUC. A former Post Office engineer, he became a full-time official at the IPCS after a period at Ruskin, the trade union college at Oxford. His brief spell at the IPCS had created a mutual dislike between him and Bill McCall. Sheldon, a pragmatic member of the Labour Party, was also a close friend of Campbell Christie, Deputy General Secretary and heir apparent of the SCPS. Politically, therefore, there were pressures on the CSU to maintain the 'pure' line. And there were also other pressures on the CSU.

From a peak of forty-eight thousand, the CSU's membership was declining rapidly under the impact of the Conservative government's cuts in the Civil Service. The instant loss of 1,500 members would be a major blow. The communication grades were an important and powerful part of the union. Organizationally and emotionally the CSU had probably committed itself more completely to the campaign than any other union. It was too far down the road to turn back. Perhaps most crucially, the message that the CSU was getting from its members in GCHQ, despite misgivings about recent concessions, was that the draft agreement was broadly acceptable if it was the price to be paid for continued union membership.

With the CSU supporting an agreement, there was a clear majority among the unions with most members in GCHQ; although large in the Civil Service as a whole, both the CPSA and the SCPS had relatively small memberships in GCHQ. The CCSU formally endorsed the deal, a decision that has never been revoked despite the subsequent votes of the CPSA and SCPS conferences. However, although one side of the deal had been struck, there were quite a few on the union side hoping that the agreement would not be picked up. Whether it would be or not was very unclear.

The Establishment itself was divided. In a letter to *The Times* on 4 February, a few days after the ban, Lord Bancroft, Armstrong's predecessor as head of the Civil Service, described the government's handling of the issue as 'breathtakingly inept: a further exploration of the bloody fool branch of management science'. He added: 'Altogether it is a sad and serious turn of events for Crown Service.' Bancroft's letter provoked a stinging response from Tovey. 'As former Director of

GCHQ', he told readers of *The Times* two days later, 'and hence as the individual largely responsible for drawing up the original proposals, I do not consider that any other means of presentation and implementation could sensibly have been put forward.'

John Somerville, a former Director of Organization (DO) at GCHQ, effectively the GCHQ Deputy Director, also went on the record: 'When the unions put their teeth on the table in February 1984, I cannot understand why the Prime Minister didn't pick them up', he said.

The First Division Association, which represents about seven thousand Whitehall officials, including ministerial advisers, gave its support to the CCSU campaign, taking initiatives which would have been unthinkable a few years earlier. In the week following the announcement of the ban it had recruited eight new members in GCHQ – a figure which might be considered modest except that it had recruited less than that number in the whole of the previous year. The executive committee unanimously passed a resolution at its February meeting condemning 'in the strongest terms the Government's arbitrary and brutal withdrawal from staff at GCHQ of rights of access to industrial tribunals and the right to belong to an independent trade union'. The official report of its annual delegate conference in May of that year recorded: 'The debate on GCHQ was the most emotional one of the day and the delegates demonstrated their feelings by giving a standing ovation to Mike King', FDA branch secretary at GCHQ until the ban was imposed. While a standing ovation may not be unusual at other union conferences, it is uncharacteristic of FDA annual delegate conferences. In his speech King said:

What has happened has been a tragedy. Not only for GCHQ, which has been dragged unnecessarily into the world's spotlights when it works best in quiet obscurity, and where morale has suffered badly, but mainly for the whole nature of the relationship between the government and the governed and in particular [its relationship] with its own employees ... We have been shabbily treated and the full financial and other implications of the refusal to sign are now becoming clear ... Whatever noises the government makes about the way the Civil Service trade unions have behaved, it pales to nothing compared with the government's behaviour to their staff.

At a well-attended meeting shortly after the ban was announced, the FDA GCHQ branch, which included many senior staff and line

managers, sent a unanimous motion to Sir Geoffrey Howe. It said
that, while accepting the government's declared objective to achieve
arrangements to guarantee the undisrupted functioning of GCHQ,
it expressed 'its extreme dismay that the measures which were chosen
to achieve this objective, and the method of their implementation,
have been such as to provoke at all levels a profound loss of
confidence in senior management, and a crisis in staff morale'.

In an unprecedented initiative, the FDA branch in the Cabinet
Office wrote to the Earl of Gowrie, the minister for the Civil Service
who adopted a hard line during the period of negotiations. 'As senior
managers whose responsibilities include policies to improve standards of management of civil servants, our members expressed
astonishment at both the action taken by the Government and the
precipitate way in which it was taken', the branch said, adding: 'It has
been entirely counterproductive and an extraordinarily inept piece of
management of loyal and patriotic civil servants which is bound to
have far reaching consequences for the management and commitment of the service as a whole.'

Trade union members at GCHQ were also supported by the
Bishop of Gloucester, John Yates. In a letter to *The Times* he asked:

Is it too late to hope that the Government will be strong and wise enough to
alter the terms of this crude and inhuman ultimatum before it expires at the
end of the month? Those who framed it would seem to have assumed that
principles can be abandoned for cash and that family life can be cursorily
disrupted in the interests of state policy. I would want to argue that cynical
assumptions of that kind about the value and dignity of human beings,
coupled with power, are more of a threat to our way of life than current
anxieties about the security of GCHQ.

A second meeting with the Prime Minister had been scheduled for
Thursday, 23 February, the day of the planned parliamentary lobby.
Although the CCSU's Major Policy Committee had seen and
broadly endorsed the Campaign Committee's proposals for launching 'Option C' and calling for industrial action on 28 February, no
formal decisions had been taken. Authority was given to make
preparatory arrangements. For example, dates and venues for meetings with GCHQ members were finalized. Option C forms were
printed with carbon paper, one copy for management, one for the
union and one for the member. A letter outlining the safeguards to
members was drafted. But nothing further was done.

The reason for this was spelt out in the CCSU press release concerning calls for industrial action on 28 February. Despite the fact that the CCSU was itself formally considering industrial action, it was not thought appropriate to make it public while negotiations with the government were taking place. Whether they were called 'negotiations' was not the point – the judgement was that nothing should be done to rock the boat. This meant not calling for industrial action and not launching Option C.

Perhaps inevitably, those involved in the negotiations and those involved in organizing the campaign placed most emphasis on that part of the process they were most involved in. There were perhaps two schools of thought. First there were those who believed that a negotiated settlement was the unions' only chance; that if they could not get a deal before 1 March then they were lost anyway. The alternative view was that the only chance of securing a deal was to retain enough members to force the government to talk. The key players, though, were on the government side.

Over the weekend of 18–19 February, government announcements became more hawkish. It appeared to many that the hope of a deal was diminishing rapidly. In the battle of numbers into which the unions had unfortunately been dragged, it was clear that more and more GCHQ staff were signing Option A or B.

This was the key period. For one observer, the delay between the two February meetings was fatal. Referring later to the unions' 'no-disruption' offer, Hugo Young, the *Guardian* columnist, wrote:

The unions thought that by paying this high price, they could carry on at GCHQ. So did Sir Robert Armstrong, with whom they first negotiated. So, at one time, did Mrs Thatcher herself. For a fleeting moment, and after much resistance at the crucial negotiating session which she personally conducted in early 1984 [the 1 February meeting], she was evidently impressed by the unions' offer. Had the session carried on to a conclusion, it is possible that, with Armstrong standing behind her, she would have accepted the arrangement.

By the end of February, others in her Downing Street court had got to work – she had been persuaded to tough it out. Bernard Ingham, her powerful Press Secretary whose influence as a political adviser belied his status as a civil servant, describes his role in his autobiography, *Kill the Messenger*. Explaining how he played a game of 'spot the U-turn' with political journalists, he says:

If I felt the Government's credibility was in danger of being undermined, it was my duty to say so. I did my duty, for example, when a compromise was proposed over trade union membership in the Government Communications Headquarters (GCHQ) at Cheltenham where it had been banned after industrial action. Union membership remains unacceptable.

In a later interview Ingham – who was knighted by Thatcher in her resignation honours list – told Richard Norton-Taylor that he would not have been doing his job had he not warned Thatcher that the media was 'looking for weakening'.

The Earl of Gowrie, who combined his job of minister with day-to-day responsibility for the Civil Service with that of minister for the arts, also advised Thatcher to reject the unions' offer on the grounds that she had to maintain her credibility. Sir Robin Butler, her principal private secretary (now Cabinet Secretary and head of the Home Civil Service), also advised her to turn down the draft agreement which had been accepted by Armstrong, his predecessor. Thus, on the basis of the most superficial of considerations – mere political presentation – was decided, behind the closed doors of 10 Downing Street, a fundamental issue involving civil rights.

Meanwhile, without solid inside information, the unions clung to the hope that a deal was possible. Holding back, they created a lull in the campaign and failed to give clear-cut and unequivocal advice to their members.

On Thursday, 23 February the parliamentary lobby took place, involving two thousand civil servants from virtually every government department. It was an organized rather than a mass lobby, and observers at the time regarded it as one of the most successful of the period – success being judged by the number of MPs, Conservatives included, who made themselves available and appeared to listen. The Labour Party had by now agreed to use some of its parliamentary time to debate the issue. The debate was scheduled to take place the following Monday afternoon.

While the lobby was going on the general secretaries of the Civil Service unions, joined by the TUC General Secretary, Len Murray, slipped quietly away for their fateful meeting with Mrs Thatcher. The troops waited anxiously in the Commons and the nearby pubs. As soon as they returned it was clear that the unions' worst fears had been realized: the meeting had been a disaster, there was no deal, the unions had delayed in vain.

The benefit of the CCSU's proposed draft agreement was that it left the government no easy way out. All of the points Mrs Thatcher made at the first meeting had been met. Although it was suggested that the unions were still arguing over what was and was not essential, since the agreement gave the final decision to the government this was not a valid basis for rejecting it. Indeed, given previous government statements there was no logical or consistent reasoning behind the rejection. Perhaps in these circumstances the government, or at least Mrs Thatcher, had no option but to reveal the truth.

'There is an inherent conflict', she said, 'between the structure of the trade unions and loyalty to the state.' She was not only saying that officials of independent and free trade unions could not be trusted, that everything about them smacked of potential treachery; she was also saying that GCHQ staff – vetted, indoctrinated, enthusiastic – were in danger of becoming disloyal by simple virtue of the fact that they were members of a trade union.

Thatcher went further. The gap between the government and the unions, she said, was 'a gap which cannot be bridged by words'. It was an astonishing statement. There was no scope for a compromise because, no matter what the unions offered or did, they could not meet her objections – or at least they could do so only by ceasing to be trade unions, by ceasing to be themselves. As John Ward, FDA General Secretary, told his annual delegate conference three months later, Thatcher's language had 'serious implications for the Civil Service, for trade unions and for the country'. And not one of her civil servant advisers, not one of her ministers (including some still in power), batted an eyelid.

Immediately after the one-hour meeting, Bernard Ingham gave an off-the-record briefing to political journalists. Union membership at GCHQ, he insinuated, involved 'the risk of even putting people's lives in danger' – an apparent reference to the death of GCHQ officials who had been killed by bandits in Turkey, an incident far removed from anything over which the unions had influence.

The meeting was also a turning point in the government's relationship with the TUC, wrecking the prospect of improved industrial relations. At just that time, Len Murray – in the face of opposition within the trade union movement – was offering an olive branch to the government. This 'new realism' now became impossible, and a deeply saddened Murray took early retirement later in the year.

Jim Prior, in his memoirs *A Balance of Power*, links the GCHQ union ban to the efforts of Len Murray to come to terms with the government policies of the time. He comments:

The Government's decision caused uproar throughout the union movement. It struck at their very heart; the right of people to join a trade union. Even the most rabid right-wingers in the union movement were appalled.

Only a few days before, Len Murray had been telling trade union members to respect the laws passed by a Tory Government and now that same Government had done this. Len tried desperately to reach some compromise, even going as far as to offer a non-strike agreement at GCHQ – precisely the type of agreement which we had been saying for years we wanted to see in the public sector. Yet this, in an act of further stupidity, was turned down. Len Murray was lost. In the short term this may not have hurt the Government, but in the longer run a strong and wise leader like Len Murray is invaluable to any government or society which is seriously concerned to promote better industrial relations.

Coming out of Downing Street, Len Murray took the unprecedented and courageous step of placing his own personal authority and prestige behind a TUC day of action the following Tuesday – to coincide with the CCSU day of protest. He asked all trade unionists to do 'anything they can', and said that it was up to the courts to decide whether supportive action was unlawful. What he was doing, he said, was calling for 'just and proper action in defence of a freedom intrinsic to democracy that is and must be our paramount concern'.

After consulting members of the TUC's Finance and General Purposes Committee – the 'inner cabinet' – Murray said that it was not for him to call a strike. That was a matter for individual unions. The TUC was simply urging trade unionists to get together in what he described as a 'common cause' with their Civil Service colleagues, since the government had tarred them all with the same brush.

Option C was also finally launched, along with the all-important guarantee of financial support to anyone dismissed for being a union member. The guarantee, a brave one in the circumstances, was indefinitely to make up the take-home pay of anyone who was sacked. The option form itself read:

I have read and understood General Notice GN 100/84. I wish to continue to be employed at GCHQ and to retain the right to be a member of a civil service trade union with recognition rights established as at 24th January 1984.

Another tour of GCHQ's outstations had become necessary. But the circumstances were now vastly different from the first round of membership meetings. They were due to take place on 24 and 27–9 February, the last four normal working days before the 1 March deadline. In this last desperate round of meetings the unions were implementing the new strategy of trying to persuade members to sign Option C and ignore the government's deadline. The view at this stage was that if five hundred or a thousand members stayed firm then it would be very difficult for GCHQ to implement the threat of dismissal.

The unions had two other big problems. For the past month they had been engaged in a battle over the numbers signing Option A. They had maintained that a majority had followed the union call 'don't sign'. Psychologically, sights were not set so much on the numbers required to frustrate the ban. They were not even concentrated on the number of union members who had signed, which was probably still a minority. Sights were on the total number signing Option A, which by now was over half of all GCHQ staff.

The second problem was that the unions had essentially three days to tackle for the first time the task of persuading members to face up to the possibility of being sacked. Management had spent five weeks capitalizing on the fears and conservatism of staff, pulling every emotional string. Their argument was that it was safer to remain within the club, that management would look after them, that the unions could not be relied upon to support them.

The first meetings were scheduled to take place on the Friday evening, starting with Cheltenham and Culmhead, which were felt to be most promising. John Sheldon took the Cheltenham meeting and appeared to get a good response. The meeting at Culmhead was taken by Jack Hart and Hugh Lanning. Hart, who chaired the meeting, made the contribution the members were waiting for. For many years, Culmhead had been his domain. On returning as a youngish rebel from Cyprus, he had risen up the union ranks to the position of senior statesman. Now, after a characteristically short speech, he took an Option C form and signed it. Lanning and Hart had never discussed whether or not the latter would sign Option C when the time came. Quietly, with the support of his wife Iris, he made his decision. Where Hart went thirty or forty others followed, either signing forms there and then or taking them away to sign them later. Others who were working or on night shifts were to be contacted over the weekend. When Sheldon was phoned from the pub, it was thought that overall there might be two hundred or more members prepared to sign Option C.

As Hart and Lanning sat in the pub, they thought that, if only the unions could keep the ball rolling, get everyone who had taken a form or signed one to stick with it, reach the people not at the meetings, then maybe, just maybe, the impossible could be on.

But over the weekend things did not go well. People who had made a commitment at the meeting went home, thought about it and discussed it further with their families. Union representatives could not be sure if everyone signing an Option C form would in fact hand it in to management. By Monday morning their hopes were fading fast; a more realistic assessment put the figure between fifty and a hundred, depending on whether or not you included those who had signed Option B requesting a transfer. Option B signers would be allowed to continue being union members until they were found a job in another government department or were offered premature retirement, the Civil Service euphemism for redundancy.

On Monday afternoon there was the first set-piece parliamentary debate on GCHQ, although there had been many questions in the House. The debate was on an adjournment motion tabled by the Labour Party. Of the twenty-three speakers only eight supported the ban. MPs from all parties spoke against the government, including a number of Conservative MPs. At the end of the debate the Labour Party deliberately abstained from voting. The purpose of this was to allow the government only a hollow victory, since the Tory majority in the Commons would anyway ensure that Labour lost the vote. The government duly won by 201 votes to 25, the 25 being mainly Alliance MPs. The Alliance – the electoral pact uniting the Liberals and the SDP – had not agreed with the Labour tactics and had voted against the government. Many of the Conservative MPs who had actually listened to the debate conspicuously failed to vote.

Meanwhile, at Cheadle station in Staffordshire, Lanning was once again met by Mick Bradshaw. The latter was secretary of both the Cheadle branch and the CSU branch representing the 'closed' stations. These were the clandestine stations that were not even acknowledged to be part of the Composite Signals Organization. Bradshaw had had a few brushes with R Division because they felt he might have inadvertently given away the location of one or two closed stations in Turkey and Africa as a result of the way he took up their problems. In fact union headquarters could only guess their whereabouts: any information for the union was sent to them via Bradshaw through GCHQ's internal mail system. Unknown to management,

Bradshaw was also one of those who had used the *nom de plume* 'Scribe Laziro' (Lazy RO, lazy radio officer) in the ubiquitous *Radio News*. The column regularly irritated management and had provoked it into threatening legal action on more than one occasion. But management was never sure who wrote the column.

Over dinner the conversation settled only once on that evening's meeting, merely covering when and where it was to take place. The venue was the same as last time, the Royal Oak pub. Ever since the radio grades had first become organized, they had always held their meetings away from official premises. It was a sensible precaution against management's ability to misuse the technology at its disposal. But evening pub meetings were also more accessible to those off duty. Depending on the pressure of work, some of the staff on shift duty could get away for the meetings as long as they left behind enough people to cope with the shift's tasks.

On the way to the meeting Mick Bradshaw told Hugh Lanning that he felt he had to sign Option A. Lanning was not surprised, Bradshaw had been intimating as much for a while, but he still had hopes that some others would come forward to sign Option C. But although Cheadle was a well-organized and active branch, as soon as he walked into the pub Lanning knew this was not to be. In the bar the atmosphere was cordial and polite, but no one was looking Lanning in the eyes. The reason for this later became clear. During the previous week the local committees of both AGSRO and the CSU had got together and come jointly to the decision that they were all going to sign Option A. They had then notified this decision to all their members. In the absence of any guidance from the union, Cheadle had come to its own decision.

Apart from Bradshaw, who opened the meeting, no member of the committee sat on the top table. Lanning made his prepared speech, a now forlorn appeal to the members to trust the unions and to stick out for their right to remain members. It was clear, however, even to Lanning, that his message was falling on deaf ears. The radio grades were professionals at pretending to listen to things – the members had come out of politeness to the union, in recognition of what it had done in the past. They had also come in sorrow to say their farewells. At the end of the speech, in contrast to Culmhead, none of the known union activists came forward to sign Option C. Then a bespectacled, weathered person stood up, muttering phrases like 'I don't know what's the matter with you all', moved to the table, took a form and signed. It turned out to be Stan Wright, a quirky vegetarian with a complicated private life, who could not stomach being told he could not belong to a union. In fact a lapsed AGSRO member at the time of the ban, he had rejoined to make his point.

After the meeting there was some brief discussion in the bar, some not unjustified criticism of the unions for leaving them unguided until so late, some self-justification, some 'if onlys', but no bitterness or rancour, just sadness. Early the next morning Lanning was taken to the station to catch a train to London to speak at a rally. This was Tuesday, two days before the deadline. It was the TUC's day of action.

The first sign of the day of action – 28 February – was the lack of trains. In a masterstroke of planning, Lanning had not thought how he would get from Cheadle to London if the NUR organized strike action. Would going by train be strike breaking? Cutting through this philosophical knot, he asked the time of the next train. One was expected sometime and was due to get to London later that day. Relying on this accurate information, he took a gamble and waited for the train.

Throughout the country support for the day of action from civil servants and other trade unionists was excellent, particularly given the short notice. The CCSU had organized over fifty marches and rallies. The Treasury was afterwards forced to admit that at least a quarter of all non-industrial civil servants – about 150,000 – had taken action. It was unprecedented, perhaps with the exception of the 1981 pay dispute. These figures did not include those who just attended the lunch-time marches and rallies. Thousands turned up to the London march, making it the most successful protest the Civil Service trade unions had ever organized in the capital.

On the train from Cheadle to London Lanning had to write a speech for the rally. All the pent-up anger and frustration poured out. The anger was at the government for what it had put everyone in GCHQ through. Loyal members of staff, ordinary trade union members who had done nothing wrong, were being forced to make impossible, unnecessary and heart-breaking decisions. It was not so much that they had to choose between their unions and their jobs, families and careers; rather they were being forced ignominiously to do something they did not want to do, something in which they did not believe. They knew they were having a freedom taken away and felt less of themselves that they had to sign. It was a resentment that those who signed unwillingly or reluctantly were never to lose.

The frustration Lanning felt was knowing that the battle for the hearts and minds of GCHQ staff had been lost. At that very moment tens of thousands were taking action not knowing that it was futile, at least in the short term. Those whom they were trying to defend had disappeared, had been whisked out of the public limelight and back into the closed world of GCHQ.

The rally was taking place in Jubilee Gardens, on the South Bank facing the Houses of Parliament. It was a cold, damp and windy day. By the time Lanning got to speak, the crowd had dwindled, not least because they could not hear anything. He was reduced to shouting through a megaphone, so they only got an edited version of the speech. But *Radio News*, ever quick to spot a scoop, printed the full unabridged version, under the headline 'Close to tears – the speech I would have made, by Hugh Lanning'.

I'm naturally quite placid, but today I'm angry. Last night I had the worst meeting of my life. Trade union members of 20–30 years standing were close to tears trying to decide between the threat of dismissal and loyalty to their families and their belief in and loyalty to their trade union. Then this morning coming down to London, I read the report of the parliamentary debate in which Sir Geoffrey Howe stated that: 'The Government's overall objective was to ensure that staff at GCHQ were not in future subject to the kind of pressure that had been deliberately put on them in the past.'

On that count he is a *hypocrite*.

Then he says: 'There is not one word of truth in the wild and extravagant claims that have been made. The decision is not part and should not be seen as part of any wider campaign.'

On that count Sir Geoffrey Howe is a *liar*.

The ban on trade unions in GCHQ is part of at least two campaigns. The first is the general campaign against the civil service. Since this Government came to power in 1979 it has mounted attack after attack on its employees.

It scrapped the pay agreement.

It drastically cut, with no regard as to the effect, the size of the civil service.

It is continuing that process by its plans for privatisation which are directly aimed at the pay and conditions of the employees. They also see privatisation as a means of undermining union organisation.

Through their rewriting of the Facilities agreement, the limitations they are imposing on the private political activities of civil servants, their abuse of annual leave agreements, they are seeking bit by bit to undermine the right of trade unions in the civil service to organise effectively.

When Sir Geoffrey Howe made his allegations about the effect of industrial action in GCHQ from 1979–1981, he did so in the safety of the knowledge that his arguments could not be refuted unless staff in GCHQ revealed information they were not allowed to publicly.

When they realised that the Trade Union Side representatives, Jack Hart and Pete Bryant, might actually tell the Select Committee the truth they banned them from giving evidence, ensuring that the full trade union case was never heard.

The OTHER campaign the decision is a part of is the general attack on trade unions. The Government doesn't merely want to curb trade unions, it wants to destroy trade unions as we know them. Utopia for the Government is one where there are no trade unions, merely state approved staff associations.

Employment legislation is trying to do this in two ways, firstly by reducing legal protections for employees and meddling with the rule books of trade unions. Secondly by legally limiting our rights to take collective action.

The press are now trying to describe today's action by the TUC as political action. The Government is trying to prevent one trade unionist from helping another. If the law says that it is illegal for trade unionists collectively to defend the right of others to belong to a trade union, then the law is wrong.

At GCHQ the Government is setting up its model, its ideal for others to follow.

FIRST you take away their legal rights.

SECOND you use union busting techniques to bribe and bully staff to leave their union.

THIRD you set up a tame, state approved staff association.

Other employers in this country, management in other parts of the public sector and other parts of the civil service are going to look at the example the Government has set and say 'what's good enough for the Government is good enough for us' – and the Government will encourage them.

The Government is trying to pretend that because of the numbers signing the option forms in GCHQ, the staff are choosing to give up their trade union rights.

Over the last month I have visited Cheltenham and every other UK outstation at least once and many of them more.

The truth is that trade union members and non-members are being forced, bullied and intimidated into signing the option forms. It is not the £1,000, it is the threat of dismissal.

The Government cannot and must not win on this issue.

It is time that we woke up and took our heads out of the sand. This Government is not going to go away, it is not going to change its spots, Mrs Thatcher will not wake up one morning and say 'Enough is enough, I think I've kicked the unions and the civil service enough.'

She will carry on as far as we let her.

Trade unionists in GCHQ aren't militants or revolutionaries. Far from it – many voted Conservative.

At this moment they need to know your support is there.

BUT just as importantly we need to decide ENOUGH IS ENOUGH, the time has come to start fighting back.

I hope this campaign is the start of the restoration of our pride. When we say we're proud to be civil servants, when we say public services are a good thing, when we start saying I'M PROUD TO BE A TRADE UNIONIST and when we say to Mrs Thatcher 'We're not going to let you take away that right NOT NOW, NOT EVER!'

After printing the speech, *Radio News* quipped: 'Perhaps it's just as well it was never made, it's much too long!'

5

The war: 1984 to 1986

As a result of coercion by my employer, GCHQ, I regret that I have to inform you of my resignation from the Civil Service Union. Although I would prefer to remain a Union member, as you know, this would result in my dismissal. I simply cannot afford to be unemployed and unemployable.

It is with considerable regret that I now have to terminate my 30 years association with the Civil Service Union.

At 4 p.m. yesterday, with the most extreme reluctance, I signed option A.

I wish to record my profound thanks for all the CSU has done for me in the past, and in spite of the wording of Option A I intend to continue supporting CSU by paying my monthly subscriptions as normal.

I most sincerely hope and pray that the appalling action taken by this Government will be recalled and widely publicised at the next general election. To date, I have been an unshakeable supporter of the Conservative Party, but not any longer. Mag the Hag is a blot on society and a disgrace to the Conservatives. I believe she has probably won this battle, but has definitely lost the war.

Firstly the bad news, I have today signed Option A. I write to you not to make any excuses for doing so, as I know you will understand the agonising choice I had to make, a choice that many of us have had to make after thinking about little else since 25 January.

The reason for my writing is to thank you for the magnificent effort you and others have made on my behalf to try and protect my civil rights.

During the last few days I have heard the government claims of increasing numbers of people signing Option A. I think that they must now realise that they can take little comfort in the fact that they have removed a basic civil right from many thousands of loyal people by threats and coercion and playing on the genuine concern of people for their families – a tactic I know most thinking people regard as despicable. This at best is a very hollow and doubtful 'victory'.

Over the next few months, or even years, I know you will be challenging the government action in both the courts in this country and abroad, and I would like you to know that I, and many others, will be monitoring developments with great interest. Even if we are prevented from taking an active role our thoughts will be very much with you – perhaps over the coming months when things start getting tough and looking hopeless you may be able to take some comfort in this and draw strength from it.

I am sure, at worst, that this is only a temporary loss and in the long term a change of government or legal decision will enable me to rejoin my union.

They may be able to force me to give up my trade union rights in name, but they seem to forget that I am a trade unionist in my heart and they CANNOT take that away from me.

Fight on brother. WE WILL WIN.

Extracts from letters received at CSU Headquarters,
early March 1984

Interviewed in 1986, Mike Grindley – a GCHQ union member who did not sign Option A – talked about his personal feelings:

Much of those five weeks is a bit of a blur, to be honest. When the fateful envelope arrived on my desk on 25 January 1984, I was racked with an alternating mixture of incredulity, anger and anxiety. I remember thinking that no way would I take any of their filthy money, and that the word must be spread on what had happened. So I left work early, leapt on my bike and pedalled round to Alex Lawrie's house in Hayes Road.

Lawrie had been pushed out of GCHQ in 1982 for indicating publicly that the organization had an intelligence role – this was five years after the ABC trial – and for refusing to accept line management's security role: secretly reporting 'untoward' habits of his subordinates. GCHQ management also told him that he could only continue his county councillor work if he avoided anything to do with 'national political controversy'. Grindley continues:

Having helped get Alex elected as the Labour councillor for Pittville ward in 1981, he was the first person I thought of to contact. I remember the look of amazement on his face as he scanned through Marychurch's letter, the 'option' form, and GN 100/84. He asked to borrow the documents and rang the *Gloucestershire Echo*, Cheltenham's evening paper, which sent a taxi to collect them.

The full enormity of what the government had done took a little while to sink in properly. This wasn't really happening! Then when it *did* fully sink in, the pressure started. The only time it lifted was when you were asleep. I remember waking up each morning and there followed a few seconds of normal tranquillity. Then *wallop*! An acquaintance of mine described it as like being bereaved.

After a time, I got to think: 'I'll have to transfer elsewhere.' But all the time underneath I was regrouping. I have never been an establishment man, and stubbornness is to me as beer is to a glass. What finally persuaded me to stand firm here, rather than to shift hearth, home and family, was the trip to Tolpuddle on 22 February 1984. This must sound very corny, but it's nevertheless true. Six of us went down in a full-sized coach and were met by two members of the Agricultural Workers' section of the T&G. We laid a wreath on the grave of James Hammett, the only Tolpuddle man who didn't end up in Canada. I thought to myself afterwards that what that poor devil went through makes our situation seem like a bloody cakewalk on a spring morning.

Once my mind is made up, that's it. Probably comes from being part Yorkshire, but more so from being half-Irish. My family on my mother's side are from the kingdom of Kerry. They say of the Kerry people that 'they are the last into a fight, but, by God, they're also the last out'. To understand a man you must know his memories.

Brian Johnson, then a member of AGSRO, echoed a view expressed by other union members. He said they had refused to sign away their union rights because they felt they would be letting down those who had died in two world wars fighting for the freedom which the government was now denying GCHQ staff. Others felt they would be letting down the whole trade union movement which had rallied to their support.

Graham Winton, a member of the SCPS who applied for a transfer, told *Warning Signal*, the GCHQ members' journal, in March 1985:

I did not relish moving from a part of the country where I would have been happy to spend the rest of my life, and most importantly, I would be leaving all the friends I had made in and out of work. I had to accept that, in material terms, almost a quarter of my life so far had been wasted ... those employees who lived through early 1984 will not forgive and forget so easily. However, over the years the department will change and this is what worries me most. Many younger people to whom the new conditions of service are unacceptable are leaving already; older staff who can't find alternative work so easily will eventually retire. And who will be left? Either those who actively support the kind of illiberal attitudes and actions we've seen over the last year, or those (just as bad) who simply don't care ... But it has been inspiring to see how adversity can bring out the best in people.

Claire Hengeveld, an SCPS member who also signed Option B, wrote in the same issue of *Warning Signal*:

GCHQ is no longer an establishment in which I could contemplate a career ... I have come to realise that if I had not stuck my neck out and said 'I will remain a member of my union', then nobody would be there to represent me and protect my basic rights.

Terry Benstead, a CSU stalwart from GCHQ's station at Irton Moor, near Scarborough, who opted for special early redundancy terms, wrote:

May I say that it has been a privilege to be associated with those who, despite all the threats and many pressures, remained true to their high principles not to relinquish their rights as free men and women. They have stood up to the wickedness of politicians who have sought by stealth and deception, and the use of taxpayers' money in issuing huge bribes, to deprive those employed at GCHQ of basic rights of association. Their attempt to enslave hearts and minds will not succeed whilst there are those who are willing to fight for freedom.

In the first days of March – when the dust had settled – the CCSU Major Policy Committee had to admit that there were not enough union members left to prevent the ban being implemented. The unions claimed to have a hundred and fifty members: just over one hundred had signed the unions' option, Option C, with a further forty or fifty signing Option B. Although it was a request for a transfer out of GCHQ, those signing Option B could remain members until such time as they were transferred – in some cases this turned out to be over a year. Subsequently, in March 1989, GCHQ management said during an appeal at the Civil Service Appeal Board that 'originally 130 did not sign or later did not accept conditions'.

At the time neither side could be sure of the precise figures. There were those who delayed, deferred and prevaricated over returning their forms. Some staff may have acted as 'double agents', telling management one thing and the unions another. Some suggested that there might be a few management 'plants' among the members. And the unions could not be sure that all those who had remained in a union had got in touch and made themselves known.

Prior to 1 March the unions had given some thought to how to organize if the ban was confirmed, but most effort had been concentrated on how to react if management decided to remove all union members from GCHQ the quickest way – by sacking them. The CCSU drew up detailed plans for industrial action. Questions were asked by the members about how much financial support anyone sacked would get, how it would be calculated and whether the unions would really guarantee to make up their take-home pay for ever.

There was some hope that the government might be silly enough to sack everyone – it would be the surest way to stimulate the campaign, providing the unions with a clearer rationale for strike action. But if calmer counsels prevailed and management bided its time, what were the unions to do? They were committed to legal action, and lawyers were preparing a case for the High Court. But what about the campaign itself? The prospects looked rather forlorn. Massive support had not shaken the government and the unions had lost the overwhelming majority of their members in GCHQ. Surely it was pointless to carry on?

If this was the way some union leaders were thinking then they were wasting their time. There were nearly a hundred and fifty union members in GCHQ who had no intention of giving up or going away. Maybe because they had made their decision – from which there was no easy way back – they were less despondent than those involved in running the campaign, whose heads were definitely down. This was to become a recurring feature. When union morale was at its lowest ebb in years to come, it was always the members who recovered most quickly from the latest setback. Now they wanted to know what the unions were going to do with them.

On 27 February the CSU had written to the CCSU Major Policy Committee proposing that as soon as possible after 1 March, trade union membership and organization within GCHQ should be formally declared. The proposition was that the unions should jointly and openly establish a GCHQ Free Trade Union. Bill McCall and Peter Jones floated the idea of a GCHQ Supporters Club. The two ideas were not necessarily mutually exclusive, but there was real trepidation about the idea of an open trade union organization within GCHQ, not least because of the pressure it would put on the members.

At about this time the TUC made one of its most positive and constructive contributions to the campaign. In informal discussions Brendan Barber in the TUC Organization Department made it clear that, in the opinion of the TUC, if the campaign was to have a future then the members would have to become the focus of the campaign. It was vital to prevent them from being sacked and to take action in their defence if they were. But the TUC also counselled that if this was to be done then a clear agreement should be obtained first from the remaining union members. This would ensure that there was a solid core of members prepared to adopt a high public profile. They would have to be warned of the pressures such a role would place on them.

Not for the last time, the TUC provided some backbone to the

CCSU's deliberations. In future years proposals were sometimes floated through the TUC to give them added weight and status when they came back to the CCSU. In much the same way, unpopular or silly suggestions were leaked to the GCHQ members so that they could be killed off by the emotional blackmail that members were unconsciously – at least to begin with – able to exercise. The members' first positive use of their power was to kill off the idea of a supporters' club, which they described as a diversion.

Meanwhile, the CCSU organized a private meeting on Saturday, 10 March. It was held at the Great Western Royal Hotel at Paddington. On that day GCHQ Trade Unions was born. As with all good unions it had a committee, made up of a Cheltenham Committee and outstation representatives. Its membership was as follows:

Cheltenham Committee
    Brian Johnson   AGSRO
    David McMillan   CSU
    Ann Downey   CPSA
    Mike King   FDA
    Richard Alexander   IPCS
    Jeremy Windust   SCPS
Outstation representatives (all CSU except Stan Wright)
    Alan Rowland   Bude
    Stan Wright   Cheadle (AGSRO)
    Jack Hart   Culmhead
    Mike McClinton   Earls Court
    Mark Allan   Hawklaw
    Terry Benstead   Scarborough

The name GCHQ Trade Unions had in fact been selected from among several suggestions at the first 'Monday meeting' for Cheltenham members on 5 March at the Park Place Hotel.

With the establishment of GCHQ Trade Unions, the members and the unions had a purpose and specific tasks with which they could proceed. Infrastructure to support the idea was quickly put in place. Nancy Duffton, treasurer of the SCPS branch, had decided to leave GCHQ and agreed to work as full-time organizer for the unions in Cheltenham. She also became secretary of GCHQ Trade Unions. An office was rented by the CCSU, and Janet McCaffrey, the wife of a member, was employed as a part-time secretary. Mike Barke and

Jane Hustwitt were relieved of Cheltenham duties, to be replaced by a rota of full-time officers from union headquarters on two-week stints.

The members themselves did not sit idly by. In Cheltenham regular Monday night meetings were organized. Tables were established in the GCHQ canteens in Oakley and Benhall to give out union information, and they were staffed by a rota of union members. The canteen was neutral territory, under the control of the Civil Service Catering Organization (CISCO). *Warning Signal*, the union publication brought out during the first weeks of the campaign, was transferred from London to Cheltenham. Its title was the brainwave of the IPCS Press Officer, Charlie Harvey, who also contributed the campaign slogan 'No, Prime Minister'. Jeremy Windust became its first editor. So far it has only had two, Jeremy Windust and Robin Smith – a better record than most national newspapers over a similar period.

Within two to three weeks the unions had bounced back from rock bottom. A new organization and structure had been set up, and the members were busy in their new roles. The difference was that it was now the members' campaign. The unions could plan and plot, give standing ovations and pay for everything, but at the end of the day the members were the campaign.

On the other side of the fence, life had not been so easy for the staff association that management was trying to create.

On 26 January Anthony Hird, GCHQ's Establishment Officer, had written to trade union representatives within GCHQ. The letters related to paragraph 5 of GN 100/84, which described how staff might wish to put forward proposals to form a departmental staff association. The staff association would be consulted and negotiated 'within a system modelled on the present Departmental Whitley pattern, covering the same range of subjects as under existing arrangements'. There was to be one key difference: 'the precise form of the association would be for staff to consider and make proposals for approval by the Director'.

The letters were all similar; Jack Hart's contained the following invitation:

You have in the past been elected by your colleagues to represent them and are experienced in discussions and negotiations with management. Such experience might be of particular value during the initial period when a Staff

Association, or similar organisation, was being established. Assuming that you will elect to remain with the Department, you may wish to consider continuing as a staff representative and to play your part in drawing up proposals for submission to the Director, at least until such time as any Association is agreed and functioning. During that time you would of course be eligible for facility time etc. [facility time is time off from work normally to undertake trade union duties].

The attempted subtlety failed to persuade anyone to come forward, and by the beginning of March no progress had been made in establishing a staff association. Management could force staff to leave a union, but how could they make them set up a staff association? Even GCHQ management must have appreciated the irony when they decided, having just banned trade unions and subjected their staff to a tremendous ordeal, to call in an industrial relations expert.

The unfortunate individual who received this poisoned chalice was John Lambert, a senior official with the Advisory, Conciliation and Arbitration Service, which had been established to help settle industrial relations problems. The move caused a furore among staff working for ACAS and drew official complaints from both the TUC and the CCSU, who felt it undermined ACAS's independent role. In an unprecedented initiative, ACAS released a press notice stating that it attached great importance to its reputation for integrity and even-handedness in disputes, and to the impartiality of its staff. It said that the government's decision to instruct Lambert to advise GCHQ management on how to try and undo the damage created by the ban placed ACAS 'in an invidious position'. Lambert never did return to ACAS.

Inside GCHQ the first visible product of this activity was an Information Notice (No. 4/84) to all staff, dated 3 April 1984. The notice recognized that there were arguments in favour of management not taking any initiative, leaving it entirely to the staff to take the first steps. This would remove the danger 'of it being perceived as a creature of management'. But there were a number of issues on which decisions were needed, so management went on to outline how the staff association could be run. The first step was for line management to make time and accommodation available for meetings to elect representatives.

The unions responded by issuing a leaflet entitled 'Staff association – no thanks'. It urged staff not to 'collaborate' with the setting up of a staff association, arguing that it added credibility to the ban and that the staff association would not be able to improve or defend staff interests. It was not and could not become truly independent, since its very existence relied on the approval of the Director. Having banned unions, management needed another body to legitimize its actions and decisions. It also needed input and feedback from staff, a resource that was to decline dramatically, along with morale.

By May people's thoughts and hopes were moving away from events inside GCHQ to the courts. The unions had succeeded in obtaining a judicial review of the government's actions. This was to be held in the High Court beginning on 21 June. The judge was Mr Justice Glidewell, who was rumoured to be relatively liberal. He described his recreations in *Who's Who* as 'beagling, walking, spasmodic interests in the Arts'.

The journey through the courts was dominated by arguments about whether the Prime Minister had the right and the authority to ban unions unilaterally, without any consultation. When to its surprise and embarrassment the government did not get its way on this, it fell back on its last resort – raising the flag of national security.

The legal challenge began in June 1984 in the High Court, where the argument centred on whether the government had a duty to consult GCHQ staff, and on the way the decision to ban unions was taken. The cavalier attitude Mrs Thatcher adopted to fundamental rights – and the way her ministers succumbed – was illustrated by the way in which she imposed the union ban. She used what were, in effect, ancient royal powers in the way a medieval monarch might have done. Like a latter-day Henry VIII, she simply told Sir Robert Armstrong – a latter-day Cardinal Wolsey – to ban unions at a meeting a few days before the previous Christmas, on 22 December 1983. As we have noted already, Mr Justice Glidewell pointedly remarked in his High Court judgment:

Normally when a Minister is empowered to give an instruction or make a direction or decision, he does so in a document. It is highly unusual to have an instruction in so important a matter given orally. I would have expected the Prime Minister's oral direction to be followed by the preparation of a document, which would then receive her signature.

Even by 16 July 1984, the day Glidewell delivered his judgment, the document had not appeared. In his ruling he said:

It is in my view clear that General Notice 100 [GN 100/84] was, as its title says, a notice giving information, not a set of regulations or instructions. There is no other document containing any regulation or direction amending the terms and conditions of service of GCHQ staff. Thus no such regulations have yet been made.

The regulations were not formally issued until 1985. Glidewell added in a telling passage:

The 'direction' with which I am concerned is the oral direction – the precise terms of which I have not been told – given by the Prime Minister on 22 December 1983. For some reason which escapes me, it was thought desirable for Sir Robert [Armstrong] to confirm the making of the direction in a letter dated 7 February 1984 to the Director of GCHQ.

Marychurch's GN 100/84, signed by John Adye, was firmly put in its place – it was perhaps a pity that GCHQ staff and the unions had not grasped that before the 1 March deadline.

The key argument at this stage centred on the 1982 Civil Service Order in Council, a remnant of the royal prerogative which gives the government of the day executive, discretionary power to act without legislation and even without consulting Parliament. This reads: 'the Minister for the Civil Service may from time to time ... give instructions ... for controlling the conduct of the Service and providing for ... the conditions of service' of all persons employed therein. Simon Brown, counsel for the government, called it the 'residue of arbitrary power'. The issue here was whether, in 1984, ministers could act in an arbitrary manner; in particular, whether the government should have consulted GCHQ staff, its own employees.

Brown argued that the Crown – i.e. the government – had 'untrammelled' power to determine what should be done to protect the public safety of the realm; that the prerogative gave the Crown the power of 'uncontrolled discretion' and the right, therefore, not only to change civil servants' conditions of service, but to dismiss them at any time without notice and without giving a reason. A civil servant remained in his or her job merely 'at the Crown's pleasure'. (This point was challenged by the CCSU not least on the grounds that civil servants were employed by individual departments, not by the government as a whole.)

The Order in Council, Brown said, gave the Prime Minister complete discretion as to the form and content of any instructions to be given to civil servants. This power could not be reviewed – indeed should not be questioned – by the courts. 'The principles of natural justice do not apply in the exercise of prerogative power,' he said. The view of Lord Denning – the former law lord – that common law included the right of freedom of association was dismissed by Brown as 'radical and contentious'.

Questioned at one point by Mr Justice Glidewell, Brown argued that the government even had the *power* to insist that only those with red hair could be employed at GCHQ – for that was the logic of the government's case. Commenting on Brown's thesis that the prerogative effectively gave the government absolute power, Glidewell remarked: 'It is an unusual way to legislate these days. No doubt it happened quite frequently 500 or more years ago.'

The government relied heavily on the affidavit of Sir Robert Armstrong, the Cabinet Secretary and head of the Civil Service. It would have been both ' inappropriate and unproductive' to have consulted GCHQ staff beforehand, he argued. Prior consultation would have exposed the intelligence-gathering centre to potential disruption. Armstrong added in a key passage: 'To have entered such consultations would have served to bring out the vulnerability of areas of operations to those who had shown themselves ready to organise disruption and consultation with individual members of staff at GCHQ would have been impossible without involving the national unions.' Predictably, he referred in a hurriedly drawn-up second affidavit to motions passed by the CPSA and the SCPS annual conference in May – after the ban – criticizing the unions' leadership for offering a 'no-disruption' agreement.

Although at this stage the government was concentrating on its right to do whatever it wanted under the Civil Service Order in Council, it tried to bolster this case by referring to the needs of 'national security'. In his first affidavit, Armstrong claimed that 'the events of 1979–81 showed that the existing trade union position at GCHQ posed very real and exceptional dangers to national security'. Brown echoed this claim: 'There is no higher constitutional responsibility of the Crown than to secure the interests of national security,' he said. If the government lost its case 'then the Crown would be powerless irrespective of the impact on the safety of our shores'.

For the unions, Louis Blom-Cooper, QC, argued that the now famous GN 100/84 had no legal standing. It was not signed by any minister. The Order in Council did not refer anywhere to national security. And while, in his certificates taking away the statutory right of

GCHQ staff to appeal to an industrial tribunal, Sir Geoffrey Howe had referred to national security, the certificates themselves did not stop GCHQ staff from continuing to belong to independent trade unions. He referred to the affidavit by Jeremy Windust, committee member of the SCPS at GCHQ, that only 10 per cent of staff took action in 1981; to the affidavit of Ann Downey, one of the few remaining CPSA members, that industrial action had not caused any disruption to operations and that adequate notice had been given to management, who had prepared contingency plans; and to the affidavit of John Sheldon, General Secretary of the CSU, who said that the purpose of the 1981 campaign was to gain maximum publicity to strengthen the unions' negotiating position. At no stage, Sheldon said, did the unions threaten GCHQ's operational capability; nor did they put any pressure on their GCHQ members to do so. 'Simply to put up the flag of national security and shut out any consideration of the matter is much too facile,' Blom-Cooper told the High Court. There was a difference between the real security of the country and the political security of the government of the day. Though he described the industrial action as 'irresponsible', David Owen, the former Labour Foreign Secretary, said in an affidavit that he would have engaged the unions in 'proper consultation'.

It had been established in common law, and through what amounted to contractual rights, that staff in the position of the civil servants at GCHQ had 'a reasonable expectation' to be consulted. The government had a duty to consult GCHQ staff fairly, said Blom-Cooper, especially since both their statutory and their fundamental rights had been taken away. The government had no power to terminate these rights 'at will'. The government could have consulted with the unions in 1981 about new working conditions, as it had done before the ban about proposals for psychological tests in vetting procedures, random searches and the polygraph. Quoting a comment by a judge in an earlier case, Blom-Cooper said: 'Convenience and justice are often not on speaking terms.'

On 16 July 1984 the courtroom was packed as Glidewell slowly read out his 64-page judgment. He referred to an affidavit by Peter Jones, Secretary of the CCSU, who said that Armstrong had discussed with national Civil Service trade union leaders aspects of the 1983 Security Commission's report on security procedures, including the polygraph. This, according to Armstrong's own affidavit, was after the government had decided to ban unions at GCHQ. 'In the discussions on security matters prior to 25 January 1984, there was no indication either formal or informal of any proposal to ban unions at GCHQ or to remove employment legislation rights from the staff at GCHQ,' Glidewell noted.

The judge made a point of dwelling on the way the decision to ban unions was taken. The issue, he said, raised matters 'of considerable constitutional importance'. In a seminal ruling with widespread implications for government claims in the future about its powers under the royal prerogative, Glidewell said:

I see no reason in logic or principle why the exercise by a minister of a power conferred by an Order in Council should not be subject to the same scrutiny and control by the courts as would be appropriate to the exercise of the same power if it had been granted by statute [in other words, by Parliament].

As he went through the judgment, it remained unclear which way Glidewell was going to jump. He agreed with the government that civil servants could be dismissed 'at will', and he agreed that ministers were not bound by contract to consult staff. Ominously, he said that any decision about what activities constituted a potential threat to national security were 'solely for HM Government'. He avoided the issue of whether the union ban was in breach of the conventions of the International Labour Organization, the United Nations body responsible for employment standards.

The key point for Glidewell was that GCHQ staff had a 'legitimate expectation' to be consulted before their union rights were withdrawn. He pointedly referred to Armstrong's letter to the CCSU confirming his intention to consult the unions about the possible introduction of the polygraph. Armstrong's letter, he noted, was sent on 9 January 1984 – more than two weeks after Thatcher's oral instruction to him to ban unions from GCHQ. 'If consultation was promised about changes in conditions of service of this kind,' Glidewell said, 'it would certainly in my view be a "legitimate expectation" that the right to be a member of a trade union would not be removed without prior consultation.' He concluded by declaring that the instruction 'purportedly' issued by Thatcher on 22 December 1983 was 'invalid and of no effect'.

His ruling was greeted with shrieks of delight from the back of the court – most audibly from Nancy Duffton. But the euphoria was short-lived. The government immediately asked for an early hearing at the Court of Appeal. And this time, it would concentrate on 'national security'.

The CCSU and its lawyers rehearsed what had now become familiar arguments. Any residual prerogative power the government might have had in this area was superseded by the 1927 Trade Disputes and Trade Unions Act, and had not been revived by the 1946 Trade Disputes and Trade Unions Act. No reasonable minister could have concluded that it was necessary to ban unions since past industrial action at GCHQ was insufficiently disruptive to prompt fears that national security would in future be jeopardized. There was a delay of three years before the government took any action, and the official 'avowal' of GCHQ in 1983 was not an adequate reason for the delay since the intelligence-gathering functions of GCHQ had been given wide publicity at least by 1978.

In the Court of Appeal a few weeks later Lord Lane, the Lord Chief Justice, sitting with Lord Justice Watkins and Lord Justice May, overturned Glidewell's High Court judgment. 'Ministers are the sole judges of what the national security required,' they said, 'and consequently the instruction and certificate were not susceptible to judicial review.' Prior consultation, they added, might have provoked the 'very trouble which by their decision [the government] was seeking to avoid'.

During the case the unions argued that this point had never been raised by Brown during the High Court hearing. Indeed, they added, the government must have known that the way it took the decision was just as likely to cause disruption – which, of course, it did. And it was clear that the government's motivation was to prevent a hostile reaction in Parliament as well as among GCHQ staff. Moreover, the unions pointed out that Howe himself had described as 'serious and meaningful' the talks in February 1984 to seek a compromise, thus giving the lie to the argument that consultation would have been a sham.

Simon Brown, for the government, claimed that 'The interests of the state require that staff employed at GCHQ should not be members of national trade unions.' He spoke of 'this indiscreet age' and claimed that operational efficiency of intelligence operations had in the past been affected. There was no consultation because the government did not want to 'disturb GCHQ's high vulnerability to industrial action'. GCHQ operated 'in an area where only the minister can judge the national needs. That is a fundamental duty from which the government must not shirk and for which it alone must ultimately bear the responsibility.'

Ultimately the arguments of Brown held sway. Though the government took on Robert Alexander, one of the most abrasive, successful and expensive barristers in the country, when the case went to the House of Lords, Brown was soon rewarded for his role. He became a High Court judge and in 1990 was appointed president of the Security Service Tribunal, a timid body with limited powers to consider complaints against MI5.

The case in the House of Lords was heard by five law lords: Lord Fraser; Lord Scarman, who had a reputation as a liberal; Lord Diplock, a former chairman of the Security Commission and the author of the no-jury trial system in Northern Ireland; Lord Brightman; and Lord Roskill. Robert Alexander (who also acted for the government in the ill-fated *Spycatcher* saga and is now Lord Alexander, a Conservative peer) argued that Whitehall had no legal duty to consult GCHQ staff before it imposed the ban, and that the tradition of consulting staff about pay and conditions simply reflected good, but entirely voluntary, management practice.

For the unions, Blom-Cooper insisted that the government had provided no evidence to back up its claim that the ban was motivated by the need to protect national security. It was not enough for the Prime Minister simply to utter the words 'national security'; the government had to come up with some evidence to support its case. He cited section 10 of the 1981 Contempt of Court Act, which states journalists should not disclose their sources 'unless it be established to the satisfaction of the courts that disclosure is necessary in the interests of national security'. Blom-Cooper optimistically interpreted this as a reflection of the 'growing willingness of the courts to look into an issue relating to the public interest, including national security'.

The unions lost 5–0. 'National security', that much-abused concept and the greatest of all excuses available to organs of the state, had triumphed. 'The decision on whether the requirements of national security outweigh the duty of fairness in any particular case', Lord Fraser pronounced, 'is for the government and not for the courts. The government alone has access to the necessary information, and in any event the judicial process is unsuitable for reaching decisions on national security.' The sentiment was echoed by his peers. 'National security' was too much of a hurdle even for Lord Scarman. Even in cases involving national security, he conceded, the courts had to act on evidence. In this case, he said, accepting the government's claims about the potential effect of future action if GCHQ staff had been consulted about the ban, the evidence had been established.

The law lords' judgment was nonetheless significant in a way that might benefit other public servants – and even members of the public. It established that, in general, decisions taken by the executive under prerogative powers without consultation can be challenged in the courts through judicial review. Lord Roskill, quoting the words of Lord Atkin, an earlier law lord, warned governments not to resort to 'the clanking of mediaeval chains of the ghosts of the past'. Blom-Cooper, writing pseudonymously as Justinian in the *Financial Times*, took some comfort from what he regarded as a step forward in administrative law. He quoted Lord Roskill, who said:

I have little doubt that were management to seek to alter without prior consultation the terms and conditions of civil servants in a field which had no connection whatever with national security or perhaps, though the matter does not arise in this appeal, with urgent fiscal emergency, such action would in principle be amenable to judicial review.

Blom-Cooper added:

This may prove to be a legal obstacle to attempts by Mrs Thatcher, or any future minister for the civil service, to force through the slimming down and reorganisation of the civil service. It puts a large question mark over the government's conduct of the 1981 pay dispute, when it disregarded procedures which it had agreed with the civil service unions.

But that was cold comfort then.

1984, George Orwell's year, was a long one. Its high point was the victory in the High Court. The celebrations outside were followed by an attempt by the unions to recruit back more members, as Glidewell had ruled the ban illegal and invalid. Unwisely, perhaps, the unions chose to do this through public recruitment meetings – a more subdued approach might have been more encouraging for potential members who still felt exposed to the keen eye of management. About a hundred members nevertheless sneaked back through the window of opportunity created by the High Court – until it was slammed shut by the Court of Appeal.

1985 began with a march and rally in Cheltenham to mark the first anniversary of the ban. Between five and six thousand civil servants and trade unionists came from all over the country. The main speaker was Neil Kinnock, who made a slightly equivocal promise to restore trade unions. The Liberal MP David Penhaligon made a typically rousing speech on civil liberties. The annual January rallies were to become a regular, albeit incongruous, feature of the Cheltenham scene. Unpopular among some sections of the resident population, they were certainly embarrassing for GCHQ management. The *Gloucestershire Echo* of the day took to publishing a special supplement to mark the occasion. The *Echo* for Saturday, 23 January 1988, for example, had messages of support from individuals and groups including the Northern Ireland Public Services Alliance, the Lincolnshire Federation of the NAS/UWT, ACTT, NALGO, the Fire Brigades Union, the NUM Northumberland area, CCSU Highlands and Islands Local Co-ordinating Committee, USDAW, the IPCS Ordnance Survey Branch and Eric Hammond of the EETPU. Frickley Colliery Band and the Musicians' Union provided entertainment most years, although one year George Melly lent the proceedings a slightly different style.

The union ban was the one issue which united the TUC. The rallies were an occasion for union leaders to highlight the government's attacks on civil liberties in general and on unions in particular, whether it was pay for nurses or ambulance workers, negotiating rights for teachers, or employment legislation.

The ban was also an issue which united the opposition parties: Labour, Liberal Democrat and (before the break-up of the SDP) Alliance speakers promised, with varying degrees of certainty, to restore union rights at GCHQ. At the CSU's annual conference at Blackpool in May 1985, Roy Hattersley promised that 'on the election of a Labour government the rights [of the Cheltenham workers to join the union of their choice] will be restored'. Hattersley later cited what was to be the swift dismissal of the unions' case by the European Commission of Human Rights as an example of the dangers of basing a British bill of rights on the European human rights convention.

At the January rally in 1987, a general election year, Paddy Ashdown, the Liberal Democrat leader, promised that when Richard (now Lord) Holme was elected Liberal MP for Cheltenham – he did not make it – he would fight for the immediate restoration of trade union rights at GCHQ. He added that the Alliance would propose 'negotiations with the unions for an agreement to minimize disruption and disturbance to vital security operations'. Liberal Democrats spoke of a 'no-disruption' agreement at GCHQ combined with what they called a 'matching responsibility allowance'.

During the same period Neil Kinnock's pledges were also slightly circumspect – measured, no doubt, by the possibility of being seen as 'soft' on a national security issue. He set out his considered view to *Warning Signal* in March 1985, adopting a form of words which he was to repeat. He said:

Our attitude is greatly influenced by the proven record of GCHQ trade unionists, who have always accepted the need for continuity of security cover and who in the past made considerable efforts (including during the period 1979–1981) to avoid any disruption of security cover whilst at the same time preserving their fundamental rights as trade unionists. It is that record which is at the heart of our pledge to restore trade union rights at GCHQ.

The Labour Government will naturally ensure continuity of security cover and I am perfectly certain that we could reach an agreement with the trade unions involved which would safeguard the rights of their members as well as the needs of national security.

Following the House of Lords decision, the government had a problem. In theory the ban had been imposed and the government could claim to have been legally exonerated; the CCSU's commitment to take the case to Europe was a distant prospect. The real question was what to do with those trade unionists who remained in GCHQ. The government's answer was simple, if hypocritical. It sought to divide and rule, first by taking action against those union members who had rejoined following Glidewell's ruling. They were identified as a soft target not only because they had originally signed the new conditions of service, but also because they had received the £1,000 payment.

On 1 April 1985 the uneasy silence broke when nine members of GCHQ Trade Unions were sent letters requiring them to give an undertaking, within ten days, that they were no longer union members. The deadline expired; none of them complied. A further letter arrived threatening 'to institute disciplinary proceedings' if an assurance was not received – this time within five days.

The media descended on the members, and the unions threatened to take industrial action if any of them were dismissed. The general secretaries trooped off once again to see Sir Robert Armstrong, on 9 May. The purpose of the meeting was to discuss what the government actually meant by disciplinary proceedings. The meeting broke up with no agreement and – more significantly – without dismissal being ruled out. The two sides agreed to further talks, but apart from informal to-ings and fro-ings nothing materialized.

In August, Armstrong wrote to the CCSU saying that union members who had signed GN 100/84 must resign from the union or face disciplinary action for breaching their conditions of service. The letter was taken by the unions as a clear statement of intent by the government to proceed, probably with dismissals. A meeting with Tim Renton – a junior Foreign Office minister – clarified nothing, although afterwards an official press release suggested that Armstrong's letter only meant that they *could* be fired, not that they would be.

The first week of September, as usual, was time for the TUC conference in Blackpool. Congress overwhelmingly passed a motion calling on the TUC to organize a campaign of support and a day of action if anyone was dismissed for being a trade union member. It recognized that further action, including strikes, might be necessary to restore trade union rights to GCHQ.

Perhaps the most significant speech was made by Eric Hammond of the Electrical, Electronic, Telecommunications and Plumbing Union (EETPU). Two weeks earlier Hammond had grabbed the headlines by saying that he would ballot, along with the GMBATU, for industrial action in the electricity supply industry if anyone was dismissed. At the TUC conference he restated his position:

Our union fully supports the motion but it understands that if its objectives are to be achieved then more is needed from all of us than the mere raising of hands at the end of the debate. It is no good calling from on high for days of action, wringing your hands at the miserable response but experiencing a self-satisfied glow because you personally have had a day off. That reinforces government and diminishes our force. GCHQ must and will be different, and the way to do that is to base action firmly on the decision and understanding of our members, not of the General Council, not of the executives, no not even of Congress, but of our members.

We in our union resolved yesterday to ask our power workers for a decision to stop work if those that stood firm and remain loyal to their union are sacked at GCHQ. The ballot to secure that decision will be a campaigning one. The campaign to win a 'yes' vote begins now. All of our officials concerned have been summoned to Blackpool tomorrow for a briefing meeting. They will immediately arrange a programme of campaigning visits to branches, depots and power stations. I am more than confident that our members, if required, will return a massive vote to support the civil service unions' own action.

The motives of the EETPU were much impugned – the union was unpopular with some in the TUC because of its right-wing image and aggressive recruitment tactics – but the threat of industrial action by power workers certainly added much-needed impact to the day of action the TUC were committed to calling in the event of any dismissals of GCHQ union members.

One of the most interesting developments during this period of cat and mouse between the unions and the government was the TUC decision to fund an advertising campaign. In the run-up to a TUC day of action adverts on GCHQ would be placed in the national press showing why the government was wrong. Advertising agencies were invited to bid for the contract, which was won by Delaney, Fletcher and Delaney. The agency would swing into action as soon as it was clear the government was going to proceed with dismissals. In the event it remained on standby for three years.

By October 1985 the feeling of crisis was beginning to recede. GCHQ management had now threatened dismissal or disciplinary action six times since 25 January. A favourite occupation at the time was speculating on the government's motives. Was it trying to frighten off more staff from rejoining a union, or just testing the reaction of the unions? Perhaps it would just keep on threatening but never reach a decision before the next general election. Finally, it was possible that the government had been intent on dismissals but had been surprised by the response, in particular by the statements of intent from the power workers.

Whether the unions would have delivered the threatened action is debatable. But GCHQ was by no means the main industrial news. The years 1984 and 1985 were dominated by the miners' strike, and as GCHQ Trade Unions' second anniversary approached, another dispute grabbed the headlines – the battle of the print unions with News International at Wapping.

The official count of the second anniversary march and rally on 25 January 1986, held once again in Cheltenham, was over eight thousand – 50 per cent larger than the previous year. In many ways the TUC and CCSU were better organized, but as far as union activists were concerned they blundered by inviting Eric Hammond to speak. In the weeks preceding the rally he had gone from the potential saviour of GCHQ to the villain of Wapping. His prize was to be heckled, as was David Steel, who pledged the high-flying Alliance to restore trade unions, but with a no-strike agreement.

It was an occasion deep in irony. Hammond's EETPU, already bitterly attacked by other union leaders for backing the Thatcher government's employment legislation, was facing the prospect of suspension from the TUC because of its role in undermining the print unions by recruiting members employed by News International newspapers during the Wapping dispute. Yet Hammond's decision to campaign for a power black-out in the event of dismissals at GCHQ was one reason why the government backed away from sackings in 1986. In his speech, which was almost entirely drowned by hecklers, Hammond said that his union had firmly resisted the use of its industrial power for political purposes. He added:

But our pledge to defend fundamental human rights is as strong as our commitment to parliamentary democracy ... If the government presses ahead and punishes GCHQ workers for their traditional unionism, then I can tell them that our members will vote to strike – we have debated, argued, persuaded, and we know that the majority of our members are at one with us.

Though he was scarcely heard, Hammond was loudly applauded by some GCHQ union members – not a little upset at their rally being disrupted by events outside their control.

For the Labour Party, it was the turn of Roy Hattersley to give a commitment to restore trade union rights when it was elected the next government. He also said a Labour government would, if necessary, 'underwrite the indemnity' suffered by staff who had refused to give up their union membership. The rest of his speech concentrated on trying to bring down the government over the Westland affair.

The march and rally were the high point of GCHQ Trade Unions' calendar. Supporters, members, their families, full-time officers, politicians and journalists all mingled in the social afterwards. It was an opportunity for members to relive the previous year and to relieve the pressures of working in GCHQ, threatened with dismissal, one of the small active band of trade unionists still having to work normally and co-exist with their non-union colleagues. But GCHQ Trade Unions spent the whole year round trying to boost morale among the union members, creating new bonds at the weekly Monday evening meetings in Cheltenham and also in social events. A GCHQ Trade Unions skittle team was set up, and its successes (and occasional defeats) were being regularly reported in *Warning Signal*.

Meanwhile, among GCHQ staff as a whole morale was plummeting. Almost as soon as the ban was announced, a number of the country's biggest electronics companies – including GEC-Marconi, Racal (with a factory nearby) and Plessey (Tovey's new firm) – placed advertisements in the *Gloucestershire Echo* to attract disaffected skilled GCHQ staff with lucrative offers. Marconi hired rooms at the Golden Valley Hotel on the edge of Cheltenham – the setting for the *Crossroads* television soap.

So great was the turmoil that Marychurch felt obliged to issue another circular to all GCHQ staff. Officials found the memo on their desks on 19 March 1984:

I should first like to make it clear that I and my Directorate colleagues fully appreciate that some of you have been deeply disturbed by being faced with what is recognised as a genuine question of principle. This I readily acknowledge and I sympathise with staff finding themselves in this position. The intense public debate which has taken place as a result of the 25 January announcement has I know exacerbated the difficulties and I wish this had not been so. Let me say here that I have been deeply impressed by the way you have avoided being drawn into this public debate and by the way in which throughout you have all continued to carry out your normal work.

The fact remains that the important and unique character of our work are such that GCHQ needs to be insulated from external pressures ... My hope now is that we can all get on with the job we are here to do without the glare of publicity we have been subjected to. And, even more importantly, that we can together soon re-establish the friendly and cooperative atmosphere which has so characterised GCHQ in the past. This will be among the highest priorities of my colleagues in the Directorate and myself.

The circular was a clear acknowledgement from the top that all was far from well.

More than a year later, in April 1985, Robin Smith, an IPCS computer scientist at GCHQ (now an energetic IPMS recruiting official), reported that a flood of talent – mainly scientists and engineers – was leaving GCHQ, with departures as high as 50 per cent in some areas of GCHQ. He described the recruitment rate in specialist grades as 'practically zero'. In 1984 GCHQ had lost half of its higher executive officer (HEO) computer experts, a figure which compared with a loss rate of just 7.5 per cent for the Civil Service as a whole. In 1983 the Civil Service had lost 2.7 per cent, GCHQ none. 'The fact is that certain of GCHQ's operations, and by implication the national security that the Government claims to hold so dear, are suffering great damage,' Smith told *Warning Signal*. Two years later, he told the IPCS annual conference that, in view of these arguments about national security, it had seemed unlikely that services would be contracted out at GCHQ. But that had happened: one GCHQ trade union member who left to earn a great deal more in the private sector had ended up in a company doing work for GCHQ.

Early in 1987, *Aerial Views*, GCHQ management's in-house journal, admitted for the first time that the ban had damaged the organization's operational capability. It acknowledged that 'certain highly skilled personnel in GCHQ were being lured away by the prospect of better pay in outside industry. This problem was not helped by the de-unionisation and its attendant media coverage.'

In the summer of 1989, Mike Grindley reported some of the unsolicited comments he heard from staff in the course of his bicycle rides through Cheltenham:

It's all so tortuous up there nowadays – nobody tells the truth. I've decided I'll probably leave [executive officer].

It's not the same as it used to be – I've decided to leave [executive officer].

Anybody with a conscience shouldn't be there [linguist].

The place is going to the dogs rapidly. It's a f...... nightmare for me. We have a new system now – they tell us what to do and we do it [outstation radio grade].

We have been told that if we are seen reading *Warning Signal* it will be a black mark on our report [J Division worker].

This last observation was reflected in management's moves to ban union journals inside GCHQ. Senior staff took a particularly dim view of the presence of the NUM's journal during the 1984–5 miners' strike. In July 1984 Gerry O'Hagan showed a copy of *The Miner* to a GCHQ colleague. The colleague made a verbal complaint to the management. 'I am now banned from bringing onto the station [Hawklaw] any paper printed by any trade union and especially prevented from showing these papers to the staff', O'Hagan told *Warning Signal*.

In autumn 1987 John Cook enquired at GCHQ's library whether *The Whip*, the CSU's journal, was available. He was told it was withdrawn following the union ban, although GCHQ management was still reading it. 'What really intrigues me', Cook wrote to *Warning*

Signal in November 1987, 'is why management should have regular access to trade union literature, yet members of staff are denied the same opportunity. We are now being subjected to stop and search procedures. What will happen to members of staff who are caught with a copy of *The Whip* in their possession?'

Random searches were part of the package the government introduced in the light of the Security Commission's report on the Geoffrey Prime affair. A pilot polygraph – or lie detector – scheme was another. Whitehall made much of the argument that Prime, under interrogation, had said that he probably would have been found out had he undergone a polygraph test. Curiously, it seemed to give credence to the views of a spy. One category the polygraph was certain not to discover was the trained spy. The proposal was, of course, the result of pressure from the USA, where President Reagan was setting great store by the polygraph even though its reliability and ethics were already being questioned by independent experts. This did not stop Whitehall and GCHQ management from bowing, like latter-day Don Quixotes, to the strange instrument. A special building was constructed in GCHQ's Oakley site to house it. The Cabinet Office announced in a letter on 29 November 1983 that it hoped the scheme would start 'early in the new year'.

The House of Commons Select Committee on Employment and the British Psychological Society savaged the polygraph as unreliable, especially for security screening. The latter concluded that 'so far as security vetting is concerned, the polygraph test seems to us to be an irrelevance'. Charles Irving, Cheltenham's Tory MP, presented a Commons early day motion saying that 'the willingness to ignore the damning evidence against the polygraph represents a cynical disregard for the interests of those civil servants ... covered by the positive vetting procedures'. One person who refused to co-operate with the Employment Committee's inquiry was Sir George Terry, former chief constable of Sussex and then chairman of Britain's only commercial 'lie-detecting' company, Polygraph Security Services. Soon afterwards, Terry announced that he had resigned from the company.

The Employment Committee said it could not comment on the Security Commission's judgement in recommending a pilot scheme since the commission refused to disclose the results of its contacts with US authorities. Marychurch also refused to give evidence to the committee during its 1985 inquiry. Whitehall had the bright idea of testing the polygraph on senior members of the Security Service, MI5. It proved to be an embarrassing initiative. The *Sunday Telegraph* reported on 2 June 1985:

Whitehall security chiefs have been shaken by results of secret tests using polygraph lie detectors on about 200 members of the MI5 counter-intelligence service which show a 37 per cent failure rate. Leaks of the preliminary findings before the polygraphs are introduced in a pilot experimental scheme at the Cheltenham intelligence communications centre are a setback for experts who want them to be introduced in other Government departments.

The polygraph increasingly became the focus of comment. In 1985 a senior KGB officer, Vitali Yurchenko, defected to the USA, where a polygraph test suggested that his intentions were genuine. Shortly afterwards, to the great embarrassment of the Reagan administration, he returned to Moscow. 'It sure as heck didn't do much in the Yurchenko case. I personally like thumbscrews,' commented Patrick Leahy, vice-chairman of the Senate Intelligence Committee. Leading British psychologists warned that the careers of innocent people could be ruined by misleading polygraph readings. Later that year, the Secretary of State, George Shultz, threatened to resign after being asked if he would willingly submit to a lie-detector test. 'The minute in government that I'm told that I'm not trusted is the day that I leave,' he said. Polygraph tests, he said, were not reliable and could implicate innocent people. Spies and other professional leakers of sensitive information could train themselves to avoid being exposed by such tests. Participants at the polygraph conference organized by the SCPS in 1983 had described how placing drawing pins, or even a slice of cold ham, in your shoes could confuse the machine.

George Toulmin, a widely respected statistician, contributed devastating criticism of the polygraph in *Warning Signal*. The government finally disclosed at the end of 1988 that it had decided to abandon the polygraph pilot scheme – conveniently after the sackings. It announced its climbdown – and vindicated the five-year campaign by the CCSU – in a written parliamentary answer released late in the evening of 8 December. Mrs Thatcher said that as a result of a report commissioned by the Cabinet Office from the Medical Research Council, the scheme would not go ahead. Toulmin told *Warning Signal* readers that the author of the report, A.B. Levey, could not be blamed for the fact that it tells most of us little more than we knew already. The polygraph, he added, was essentially an

American phenomenon, 'though many intelligent Americans must bitterly regret the fact'. The long report, Toulmin suggested, could be summarized as follows: 'the polygraph as a lie-detector is indeed scientific nonsense; the more we learn about it the more useless it looks; the idea of a "pilot test" was rubbish all along'.

Despite the union ban, the CCSU was able to continue defending the civil liberties of GCHQ staff on another contentious issue. In 1985 the government picked up another of the Security Commission's proposals – namely, that civil servants undergoing positive vetting tests should be required to allow access to all their medical files. The CCSU approached the Central Ethical Committee of the British Medical Association, which immediately opposed the move. They suggested as an alternative an arrangement whereby an individual's doctor – acting as an impartial expert – could write a report 'appropriate to the circumstances' and, with the patient's consent, give it to a third party. An attempt by GCHQ management to jump the gun and secure access to personal medical records was stopped.

The CCSU and the Cabinet Office reached an agreement whereby no third party, not even the Civil Service medical adviser, would have access to an individual's medical records. He would be allowed only to seek a report from the individual's doctor, and to advise Whitehall security officers on the basis of the information contained in that report. No reference to these negotiations was made in a General Notice circulated by GCHQ management in December 1987. It referred to the original Security Commission's proposal that positive vetting should 'include the subject's written authority for access to *all* his medical records' (emphasis added), thus creating at best a confusing, and at worst a misleading, impression.

The Jekyll and Hyde existence of the union members continued, discriminated against inside GCHQ, fêted outside. When, in 1984, the unions had asked them to play a 'high profile' role it was not seen as an open-ended commitment lasting for years. But the members seemed to draw strength and support from their campaigning in the real world.

Most were not activists or officials prior to the ban, yet out they ventured from GCHQ, speaking at trades councils, branch meetings, public meetings, anywhere that would invite them and listen to them. Unplanned, responding to the many requests, the members built their own network of supporters and contacts up and down the

country. Most often the deepest and most long-lasting contacts were
with the ordinary trade unionists involved in other disputes.

In 1986, after two years of addressing meetings around the
country, supporting the causes of other groups of threatened or
sacked trade union members – Wapping, Silent Night and the miners
– and keeping the GCHQ trade union flag flying at conferences and
rallies, Mike Grindley described what was happening to him during
this time:

You ask if the past few years have radicalized/politicized me. The answer is yes,
though I was a member of Cheltenham Labour Party for some years before
1984. It's not just the struggle that has policitized us further; it's meeting
everyone else also in struggle against this Godforsaken benighted bloody
disgrace of a misbegotten malgovernment. I recall one trip to a miners' support
rally in Reading in autumn '84. After the march and rally, we were taken to the
local UBO for tea and sarnies before heading back home. Fell into conversation
there with a small, pale-faced miner's wife. Originally, she had been against the
strike and had had bitter arguments with her husband about it. But as the weeks
wore on, she became involved in the women's support group and changed her
attitude completely. 'If he goes back now, I'll kill him,' she said. She described
how she'd recently witnessed a picketing miner bludgeoned over the head by
a baton-wielding mounted policeman. He fell backwards on to the pavement
and lay inert and obviously unconscious with blood streaming from the back
of his head against a kerbstone. Two policemen came along before anyone
could get to him and proceeded to kick his ribs in.

We have had it dead cushy compared with the miners, or the printworkers
victimized by Mugger Murdoch, or the Silent Night strikers, sacked by their
employer for going on strike and remaining on strike for over 18 months,
sloughed off by G. Clarke, the bedding magnate. Nevertheless, the GCHQ
TU campaign is fundamental and must be fought with every ounce of our
energy, all the anger at our command, and with the help of every ally we can
muster ... Our belief in trade unionism has been multiplied manyfold by the
tremendous comradeship we have experienced through the last two years
with grassroots TU members across the country. They have been truly
brothers and sisters to us. We in turn have done our best in their direction,
as far as we can. We've learned to speak our minds in public (after our own
fashion), and to say our piece to the telly camera. We've found it true that
there's a lot of good people around in this country – we always suspected it
but now we know it to be very true. On the other hand, my suspicion of the
Establishment has risen tenfold.

We've had a few laughs too, and moments to remember.

All the time GCHQ Trade Unions was becoming more permanent. Jack Hart had 'retired' and taken over as secretary of GCHQ
Trade Unions from Nancy Duffton, who had gone to work in the

NHS. David Gallop replaced Hart as chairman. Jeremy Windust was now a well-established editor of *Warning Signal*, with seventy fort-nightly editions under his belt by the end of 1986. It had even received a special commendation in the TUC's union journal competition. It could not get a real prize as GCHQ Trade Unions was not technically a union in its own right!

No opportunity for campaigning was lost. The union ban was imposed a hundred and fifty years after the conviction of the Tolpuddle Martyrs. By another coincidence, the first town to peti-tion the House of Commons for the release of the Tolpuddle Martyrs had been Cheltenham. The TUC brought out a postcard to highlight the similarity of the two cases. Every year since July 1984 GCHQ union members have joined the Tolpuddle rally and festival in the Dorset village and have become an established feature of it.

One of the most enduring and unsung parts of the campaign was the GCHQ Roadshow. It was established by the CCSU to take the message to union and political conferences. When it was proposed in 1985 Chris Dimmock crept up afterwards and said that he and his wife June might be able to help run it. Chris and June had just got married, both had been married before, and they were naively looking forward to a happy, quiet autumn of their lives together.

By the end of 1986 they had covered eighty-two venues and travelled 30,101 miles – Chris and June kept very precise records. Thousands of pounds were raised, selling mugs, T-shirts, badges, key-rings, pens and even Christmas cards. Their most famous product was local pottery from Bude – animals of all shapes and sizes emblazoned with the GCHQ Trade Unions logo. In 1991, despite undergoing major surgery for cancer, Chris kept going until weeks before his death on 26 July. They had spent half the year for every year of their married life on the road campaigning for GCHQ. By the time of Chris's death they had travelled 90,000 miles, visited 241 venues, stayed away for 733 nights and raised £40,930.

When he knew he was dying Chris bemoaned that he would miss seeing unions restored to GCHQ, although he fought to stay alive long enough to see it. He also apologized to June for the fact that they would never have a 'normal' life together. Just before his death the NUCPS gave Chris and June a unique award – joint honorary life membership. It was unique on two counts, being awarded jointly and in June's case to someone who had never been a member of the NUCPS. When told of the award the weekend before his death – still

From left to right, June and Chris Dimmock with Alan Swale and Mike McClinton at the GCHQ Roadshow stand.

regretting that he would not make the Tolpuddle rally the next day–his main comment was how he thought the standards required to get union awards were declining.

Sacrifices were being made all the time. Those who signed Option B were gradually being transferred out to start new careers; others reached retirement age or left to find other jobs. In January 1986 the CCSU was able to produce details of discrimination against sixteen people. They were refused overseas postings, training and promotion. Any minor way of frustrating them was used, even refusing to write to building societies confirming that they were in regular employment – on the grounds that they soon might not be!

While the government agreed to special pay increases for staff – notably scientists and technicians – to try and stop them leaving GCHQ, staff who refused to leave their unions were forfeiting an increasing amount of money in pay and allowances. In 1985 the Treasury agreed to rises of up to 28 per cent for scientific and technical grades. Union members were doing exactly the same work for up to £2,300 a year less.

One member, Richard Alexander, was also prevented from benefiting from extra pay due to him after he passed two separate promotion boards. As a result, he was being paid £3,940 a year less than he would have been getting if he had given up his membership of the IPCS. As he put it, he was getting 3.5 days' pay for a full five-day week, all because of a union card in his pocket. All of the remaining fifty or so union members were told they would be ineligible for promotion or the benefits of a new salary structure enjoyed by all other GCHQ staff.

GCHQ management indulged in petty moves which without the controversy provoked by the ban would probably have gone unnoticed. Cheltenham Spa was twinned with the Soviet spa town of Sochi on the Black Sea. Cheltenham's mayor in 1986, Conservative councillor Peter Pennell, was a GCHQ official – but not a union member. He planned to accept an invitation to make a goodwill trip to Sochi, but before doing so sought permission from Sir Peter Marychurch. Marychurch wrote to Pennell forbidding him to go on the grounds that the mayor might have been compromised in some way in the course of his trip.

Meanwhile, a feature film starring Michael Caine was being made of John Hale's thriller, *The Whistleblower*, an account of dirty tricks at GCHQ written before the union ban. Not surprisingly, part of the film was shot on location in Cheltenham. The film company placed an advertisement in the *Gloucestershire Echo* asking for extras to appear as part of the crowd in a scene at the town's racecourse. GCHQ management immediately issued a circular forbidding staff to volunteer. Happily, the order was not entirely obeyed– one wonders how many times officials in GCHQ's personnel or security departments watched the film to see whether they could spot a recalcitrant member of staff. Local services, including the Post Office, were also uncooperative in providing background facilities such as vehicles – warned, perhaps, that doing so would be treasonable.

Not content with this process of attrition and discrimination, the government reactivated the threat of dismissal in March 1986. Armstrong had last written to the CCSU in August 1985. Since then nothing. On Thursday, 13 March he announced to the unions that he would be available for a meeting the next day – a euphemism for 'come and see me'.

At 11 a.m. the following morning Armstrong told the CCSU that the disciplinary action was finally about to be carried out – as the meeting was going on the union members concerned were being handed letters by management. The letter contained yet another ten-day warning. When pressed Armstrong told the CCSU that he would not rule out dismissal – it 'was only one, and the extreme one of a very wide range of disciplinary penalties which were available to GCHQ management'.

In forceful mood, the unions demanded a meeting with Sir Geoffrey Howe. It was arranged for Tuesday, 18 March. As usual this latest announcement was greeted by walkouts throughout the Civil Service. So common had the threats become that trade union-ists must have felt like yo-yos, responding to every cry for support in case it was the real one. Although easy to deride, the walkouts and half-day stoppages continued to surprise the government – every time the government got close to decisive action there was a re-sponse. The large majority of civil servants were genuinely aggrieved by the GCHQ union ban – it offended their sense of fair play. There was also concern that the government might try and broaden the ban to include other groups of staff, many of whom worked in sensitive 'national security' areas of work. If GCHQ now, where next? By protesting against the treatment of GCHQ union members, civil servants could also demonstrate a residual, though widespread, opposition to government policies.

The meeting with Howe took place at 5.30 p.m. on the following Tuesday. It turned out to be the most significant public climbdown by the government so far. Howe said that the Director of GCHQ – still Sir Peter Marychurch – had been in contact with Armstrong and had indicated that he 'did not, on present information, regard dismissal as an appropriate penalty in the proposed proceedings for anyone who had rejoined the union in the circumstances of the last months, unless there were factors of which he was unaware'.

The government appeared to have stepped back from the brink, so much so that Denis Healey was able to suggest in the House of Commons that Howe had made himself 'a laughing stock in the country'. Why the government seemed to change its mind over the weekend is not known, unless it was a ploy finally to 'cap the issue'. At the meeting Howe had indicated that the government wanted a period of stability in GCHQ prior to the next election.

To the unions the announcement was a victory, the climbdown was a definite step forward. It seemed to guarantee that there would still be union members in GCHQ at the time of the next general election.

The euphoria of this triumph diverted attention from the fact that

for the first time in modern British history individuals were going to
be disciplined for being trade unionists. In June 1986 GCHQ
imposed pay cuts of up to £2,000 over two years on GCHQ staff who
had rejoined their unions after the Glidewell judgment. The disciplinary proceedings still applied only to these members, but all sixteen
who were disciplined were found guilty in their absence. The fines
were condemned in the press and protested about by the CCSU; but
ultimately they died as an issue in the relief that there were no
dismissals.

22 October 1986 was the one thousandth day since the ban had
been announced. There were about fifty trade unionists left. The
staff association had been dragged off the ground and was now
claiming two thousand members. The Government Communications Staff Federation, as it was called, had announced its intention
to apply for a certificate of independence as an independent trade
union from the Certification Officer – a government-appointed post.
So far the application had not appeared.

Meanwhile GCHQ management continued to rely on the very
individuals whom they claimed suffered from a conflict of loyalties.
At the end of 1986, Richard Alexander was asked to attend a
conference in Washington. Don Clarke was asked to supervise the
installation of new computers. And as late as October 1987, Mike
Grindley travelled to Washington to represent the country at a
multinational conference in the American capital. 'So much for the
"risk" to national security that my continued membership of a free
and independent national trade union is supposed to represent',
Mike wrote on a postcard. Typically, Mike chose a pointedly
appropriate postcard – one of Frederick Douglass, a nineteenth-
century American civil rights activist. The caption read: 'Douglass
sought to liberate all people from the bonds of prejudice, slavery and
war. His writings and life of public service speak as eloquently to us
as to his contemporaries.'

6

The sackings: 1987 to 1989

The object of all legal punishment is not altogether with a view of operating on the offenders themselves, it is also for the sake of offering an example and warning ... the crime is of that description that the security of the country and the maintenance of the laws on the upholding of which the welfare of this country depends, make it necessary for me to pass on you the sentence required by those laws.

Baron Williams, judge at the trial of the Tolpuddle Martyrs, 17 March 1834

The story of the union ban and the dismissals at GCHQ is not only about the sequence of events, the unions, the political arguments and the implications for civil rights. It is also about the individual members of staff who joined the roll call of others in British history who have resisted oppression by arrogant and presumptuous governments.

We end this chapter with the stories of some of the individuals involved, after recounting the sequence of events that led to the exit from GCHQ of the trade union members.

Immediately after the unions lost the case in the English courts, they took the road to Europe – the European Commission of Human Rights. Europe was an important element in the war of nerves with the government. 1986 had seen the removal of the threat of dismissals, at least until an election. There was a degree of optimism about 1987 for two reasons: the European Commission was due to hear the unions' case on 20 January, and there was a distinct possibility of an election.

If the constitutional and legal situation was bad in the UK, surely it must be better in Europe. Was not the British government always being dragged before the European Commission of Human Rights, and had it not been found in breach of the European Convention on Human Rights more than any other country? The right to join a trade union, a basic freedom of association, must be a fundamental human right.

On the face of it, this seemed a more promising avenue. As early as 3 February 1984, the National Council for Civil Liberties – now just called 'Liberty' – advised the unions that Article 11 of the Convention guarantees the right to 'freedom of association with others, including the right to form and join trade unions for the protection of their interests'. The right was subject to limited exceptions – for example, on the grounds of national security; however, any exception was qualified.

This was always known to be a long-term option because individuals or parties must first have exhausted all possible remedies in domestic courts. This meant that the unions could not go to Europe until the issue had been dealt with by the British courts, up to the House of Lords. Despite this, the road to Europe was thought to offer better prospects because of the rights enshrined in the Convention. Ultimately, it would not carry the same legal weight with the British government as the English courts, but its judgment would have to be complied with.

The European Convention on Human Rights is an instrument of the Council of Europe, not of the European Community, as is often presumed. The Convention has two enforcement agencies, the European Commission of Human Rights and the European Court of Human Rights. Both are based in Strasbourg. The Commission considers whether or not cases are admissible – that is, whether they fall within the terms of the Convention. This is the first and often the hardest hurdle to overcome. If the case is admissible then it goes to the Court. Most cases that reach the Court result in decisions favourable to the applicant. The vast majority of cases never get that far, not least because of the time, effort and money involved in the process. In the opinion of Keith Ewing, author of *Britain and the ILO*, published by the Institute of Employment Rights, the Convention has been a disappointment in the field of industrial relations because both the Commission and the Court have read the terms of Article 11 very narrowly.

Following defeat in the English courts, genuine though misguided hope was placed on the chances of success in Europe. Anthony Lester had been employed as counsel for the case. He was one of the few British barristers who had experience of the Human Rights Court – and winning. In the FDA's 1986 GCHQ lecture, on 6 March, he said:

The European principle of proportionality requires a public authority to show not only that it is pursuing a legitimate aim, but also that the means employed to achieve that aim are 'proportionate', or reasonably related to the aim pursued. Thou shalt not use a sledgehammer to crack a nut.

For example, granted that it is a legitimate aim for government to seek to protect national security by maintaining the efficient operation of GCHQ, and granted that civil servants have special duties which necessarily restrict their rights, the principle of proportionality is the yardstick which measures whether the means employed by the government – a blanket ban on trade unions – is reasonably related to that aim. And, since the right to form and join trade unions, and to participate in trade union activities, are fundamental rights, the burden is upon the state to show that its interference with those rights is in accordance with the principle of proportionality, taking into account the needs of national security and of the administration of the state.

That principle of proportionality was not applied by the House of Lords in the GCHQ case, and it can only be invoked by the civil service unions in the pending proceedings before the European Commission of Human Rights, and if necessary the European Court of Human Rights.

When the six litigants travelled to Strasbourg the union members were to have their hopes dashed once again. With little argument or doubt, and after sitting in camera on 20 January 1987, the Commission ruled that the GCHQ staff were excluded from the Convention because they fell within the category of workers engaged in the administration of the state. Like so many other cases, the GCHQ case had been ruled inadmissible.

The applicants were chosen from among the unions banned from GCHQ: Kit Braunholtz (IPCS), Ann Downey (CPSA), Jack Hart (CSU), Dave McCaffrey (SCPS), Dennis Mitchell (FDA) and Jeremy Windust (SCPS). They all travelled to Strasbourg for the admissibility hearings. When the case was declared inadmissible there was no consolation either in the short statement which accompanied the decision or in the more detailed statement which followed later. The *CCSU Bulletin* said at the time: 'Falling back on the catch all "national security" argument, the Commissioners simply folded their papers and went away.' The Commissioners' statement said:

In the applicants' submissions the Government's action was also not 'necessary in a democratic society in the interests of national security' within the meaning of Article 11 para. 2. In particular, no industrial action occurred between 1981 and 1984, when the trade union rights were finally removed. The creation of a staff association provides no substitute since it would not be certified as independent by competent authorities. In any event, the blanket removal of all rights, notably, the right of membership of trade unions and access to industrial tribunals in the light of the binding guarantees which could have been accepted by the trade unions [sic]. Finally, while it is true that according to the last sentence of Article 11 para. 2 lawful restrictions may be imposed 'on the exercise of these rights by members ... of the administration of the State', this provision cannot empower States to exercise unlimited powers to prohibit trade union membership.

The Commission has examined whether the staff serving at GCHQ fall under the terms 'members ... of the administration of the State'. To a certain extent, the meaning and scope of these terms is uncertain and the Commission will not attempt to define them in detail. Nevertheless, the Commission notes that the terms are mentioned, in the same sentence in Article 11 para. 2, together with 'members of the armed forces (and) of the police'. In the present case, the Commission is confronted with a special institution, namely GCHQ, whose purpose resembles to a large extent that of the armed forces and the police insofar as GCHQ staff directly or indirectly, by ensuring the security of the respondent Government's military and official communications, fulfil vital functions in protecting national security.

The Commission is therefore satisfied that the staff serving at GCHQ can be considered as 'members ... of the administration of the State' within the meaning of the second sentence of Article 11 para. 2 of the Convention. It must therefore examine whether the further conditions of the second sentence of Article 11 para. 2 have been met, in particular whether the restrictions at issue were 'lawful' within the meaning of that provision.

The Commission considers that in this light [the House of Lords judgment accepting that the basis of the Government's actions related to the interests of national security] and against the whole background of industrial action and the vital functions of GCHQ the action taken, although drastic, was in no way arbitrary. The measures would therefore also be 'lawful' within a wider meaning of that term in the second sentence of Article 11 para. 2.

For these reasons, the Commission DECLARES THE APPLICATION INADMISSIBLE.

In the aircraft which took them back to London, Richard Norton-Taylor asked the GCHQ applicants and supporters for their reactions:

Don Clarke: 'Je ne regrette rien.'

Tony Bartlett: 'Having exhausted our legal actions, the campaign now becomes a political one, remembering the assurances of all opposition parties. The fight goes on.'

Richard Alexander: 'Whether we like it or not, the question of GCHQ is a political one and nothing else. That means that every civil servant and trade unionist must ask themselves what shade of government can best be relied upon to protect all our reasonable rights.'

Jack Hart: 'The courts may have decided the legal issue, but the moral issue remains. The fight for the right of association goes on.'

Kit Braunholtz: 'This decision underlines the necessity for a convention on human rights to be written into British constitutional

GCHQ Trade Unions applicants *en route* to the European Commission of Human Rights at Strasbourg. Front left is Jack Hart and clockwise are Dennis Mitchell, Don Clarke, Dave McCaffrey, Ann Downey, Richard Alexander, Tony Bartlett and Kit Braunholtz.

law. The fight to achieve this, as well as to reverse the union ban at GCHQ, is now a political one.'

Dennis Mitchell: 'The [Human Rights] Commissioners' attitude is deplorable. The Lords at least gave their reasons. The issue at GCHQ was always far more than the right of staff to belong to a trade union. The existence of a powerful and non-accountable arm of government staffed by a cowed and supine workforce impinges on all our civil liberties and, by extension, those of other Europeans, too, all paying homage to the inscrutable idol "national security". The position of the remnant at GCHQ is intolerable now, but I fear for our democracy if they go.'

In yet another affidavit, Sir Robert Armstrong described GCHQ as an 'extremely important intelligence establishment'. It was vulnerable to industrial action, he said, 'at the behest of national unions who appeared to be impervious to requests to them to have regard to the interests of GCHQ's operations'. He claimed that parts of GCHQ were 'virtually shut down' on 9 March 1981 – the one-day strike called by Civil Service unions in protest against the government's unilateral decision to abandon civil servants' traditional pay review system. Jack Hart challenged this version of events in his affidavit. 'No approaches on the basis [that action threatened GCHQ's operational efficiency] were ever made by management to the local officials of the unions concerned', he said.

Yet again the GCHQ union members picked themselves up from a potentially lethal blow to their morale – there were now no legal avenues left in which to challenge the government. The case could be pursued through the International Labour Organization, but the ILO could not force the government to act. The news from Strasbourg came only three days before the third anniversary march and rally in Cheltenham, on 24 January 1987.

The rally was by this time becoming a fixture in the labour movement calendar. Each year the organization became smoother – give the TUC a march to organize and they are as happy as a child with sand and a bucket and spade. Those attending developed their own traditions; they knew which pub to meet in, and groups could be seen prowling around Cheltenham's array of up-market shops. Despite the occasional protest from a shopowner who thought the march was bad for trade, the marchers were well received. Some former union members from GCHQ watched, a few braver ones joined in. It was not a carnival, but it was always joyful. Despite Europe, 1987 was no exception. John Prescott spoke for the Labour Party, Paddy Ashdown made his first appearance and Tony Bartlett – the new chair of GCHQ Trade Unions – boomed out a typically forthright speech which was enthusiastically received in the packed marquee.

The fun over, work continued campaigning for the return of unions to GCHQ. In November 1986, the unions had organized a weekend workshop for members of GCHQ Trade Unions at the Bear Hotel, Rodborough, near Stroud. They discussed the tactics the unions should adopt and the tasks that would await them. At the CCSU – through the Campaign Committee – publicity material was prepared and the promises of the political parties were dusted off and polished for the 1987 general election.

During the election campaign the Alliance manifesto pledge was repeated by David Steel when he visited the Pittville Pump Room in Cheltenham. The manifesto stated:

Trades unions are an essential element in the protection of the employees' interests, which is why we would return union recognition to GCHQ members.

Our central aim is to make unions democratic and accountable and therefore entitled to positive rights including the right to recognition and the right to strike balanced by the acceptance of their responsibilities to their members and to the wider community.

Unlike Labour, the Alliance had hopes of winning the Cheltenham seat from the Conservative MP, Charles Irving. Irving initially supported the campaign to restore union rights, but fell silent as time went by. Obviously his bread was buttered better as chair of the Commons Catering Committee. While Richard Holme, close colleague of David Steel, tried to win Cheltenham, Labour was trying to win the election. Its campaign and party political broadcasts were presidential in style and included the now legendary film of Neil Kinnock wandering along the cliff-tops. The media liked it, but would the voters?

The union ban remained a political issue. During the election campaign, Norman Tebbit, the Conservative Party Chairman, said: 'there is no fundamental right to belong to a trade union if you are working in a military or security establishment'. Repeating a claim that had been made by Bernard Ingham, Mrs Thatcher's Press Secretary, during the talks with union leaders in February 1984, but since withdrawn by the government, Mr Tebbit added: 'we were forced to act when we found that the trade unions were using industrial action at GCHQ which put at risk the lives of our people, our staff, across the world in an effort to get leverage to raise the pay for other people in the Civil Service'.

A Labour victory was the only chance for the early restoration of trade union rights. Gerald Kaufman – shadow Foreign Secretary – had said at the 1986 Labour Party conference that there was no reason why it should not be achieved by a new Labour administration 'within a very short time'. The Labour Party manifesto stated:

Workers' rights have been eroded, or in some cases removed entirely, during the Thatcher years. We believe that the law should be used to enlarge, not diminish, the freedom of workers to control their environment. We will restore the right to belong to a trade union to every employee – including those at GCHQ.

The Tory manifesto, heavy on 'individual rights', was silent on GCHQ. An article in the GCHQ Staff Association's occasional newsletter had defended Mrs Thatcher and described her opponents as 'political pygmies'. When the Tories were re-elected with an overwhelming majority in June 1987 all the union members' hopes and plans were cruelly dashed. For more than three years, whenever anything had gone badly wrong, the discussion had always returned to the next election and a change of government.

With the prospect of another five years of Thatcher rule, and no chance of a change in policy, it was as if a huge, dark chasm had opened up in front of the Civil Service unions. There was no way back. They could not and would not renege on their commitments to the members, who once again faced the real possibility of dismissal. For the first time there was serious discussion about winding up the campaign – general secretaries were seen wandering about with long faces, muttering phrases like 'it is time to be realistic', 'we should recognize we have lost', 'it was a good fight, but a time has to come ...'.

It was not only among the Civil Service unions that there was a general despondency. Many hopes had been pinned on a Labour government. Many remaining GCHQ members were deeply depressed, though their anger and determination remained: they had not come this far, sacrificed so much, to give up now. Some replanned their lives, others just dug in. After a little while the unions rallied round and carried on, reluctantly picking up their feet to trudge on down the long road.

On 20 June 1987, at the annual general meeting of GCHQ Trade Unions, the CCSU formally renewed its financial and moral commitments to the remaining union members. *Warning Signal* described the meeting in the following terms: 'Nobody could pretend that the failure of the electorate to return a more sympathetic government had not been a disappointment to everyone there, but the mood of the meeting was forward looking.'

There was no doubt, however, that many members were reassessing what they were going to do next – five years was a long time to wait in the hope of a change of government. In the atmosphere of the time, it was not surprising that for some it was too forlorn and distant a hope. In October the *Independent* carried a story on the 'bleak existence' faced by the twenty-eight trade unionists left at GCHQ. The article described the gradual decline in the number of union members since the ban was implemented.

'Natural wastage' had accounted for most of the decline – in the normal course of events retirements and transfers to other government departments had taken place at regular intervals. Also over the years individuals had taken advantage of 'offers to go' in order to change their lives and careers. Perhaps the most extreme case was David McMillan, who quit his job as a discontented radio officer in Cheltenham to become – by all accounts – a very contented game-keeper back in his native Scotland.

The post-election period saw others follow this early example. Richard Alexander, a scientist, went to teach at an outward bound centre in the Lake District. Mike McClinton, a traffic handler (a now extinct communications grade), invested his early retirement money in holiday flats in Spain and went to live there.

In Cheltenham there was the demise of the 'gang of three' – a nickname given by George Toulmin when he chaired the Monday meetings to the first members to argue that there should be no compromise, in particular on the right to strike within GCHQ. The members of the 'gang of three' were Mike Grindley, Ann Downey and Don Clarke. They had become a loose coalition of four – but never a 'gang of four', too many connotations for Chinese linguist Mike Grindley – when the group was joined by Tony Bartlett. However, after the election Tony and Marie, his wife – who had been working in the GCHQ Trade Unions office in Cheltenham – decided to take early retirement and buy a dry-cleaning business on Islay. The island of Islay, off the west coast of Scotland, was Marie's family home and world famous for its peaty malt whiskies. It is debatable whether it was the Bartletts or the whisky which caused the sudden popularity of Islay with GCHQ trade unionists!

Don Clarke was a computer specialist with a sharp and sardonic sense of humour. He had a habit of leaving any meeting which did not start precisely at the advertised time and heading for the bar to wait for it to finish. He left GCHQ to have a year off and has since resumed life working in the commercial computer industry – frustrated by the lack of challenge in the work. Ann Downey, a CPSA activist prior to the ban, left and ended up working for one of the many insurance companies in Cheltenham. A leading light of the campaign, she had just been worn out by it. Of the 'gang of three' only Mike Grindley was left – and with Tony Bartlett's departure Mike was elected chair of GCHQ Trade Unions.

In Scotland union members faced a slightly different problem.

The one remaining outstation in Scotland – Hawklaw near Cupar in Fife – was due to close in 1988. Under a union negotiated agreement, management had given five years' notice of closure. Special transfer, redundancy and early retirement arrangements were available to staff – unless you were a trade union member. The three union members left at Hawklaw – Mark Allan, Alan Chambers and Gerry O'Hagan – were all mobile staff and would normally have been transferred to another part of GCHQ. However, this option was to be denied to union members; they were to be made compulsorily redundant.

While the unions were considering if this would be construed as sacking and hence a trigger for action, Mark Allan decided that he had no option but to take redundancy. He had known this moment would come. He and his wife Jean had planned their own independent survival as a family. The children would carry on their schooling locally, Jean would continue working at the local hospital and Mark would start a new life as owner of the local post office, which they had heard was likely to become available. Aware that the opportunity might arise at any time, Mark had quietly gone off and done the necessary training, and when the post office came on the market the plan was implemented.

It was a cruel choice. Resigning from the union and continuing to work for GCHQ at another station was not an option. But leaving GCHQ meant leaving the campaign. In Scotland the members had, over the years, developed their own campaign. January saw not only a march in Cheltenham but also a rally outside the Hawklaw station. A network of contacts had been established throughout Scotland which was so extensive that nearly as many *Warning Signal*s were distributed from the O'Hagan house as from the Cheltenham office. Invitations to speak at meetings were regular and largely self-generated.

A similar picture of activity – perhaps on a less grand scale than Scotland, but impressive nonetheless – was repeated at the other outstations. Brora had closed early in the campaign; there were no longer any members at Bude or Scarborough; but at Culmhead, Cheadle and in London small groups of members had battled on, very isolated, cut off from the larger group of members and the office in Cheltenham. In the autumn of 1988, when the whittling down process was complete, the unions were left with just six members at the outstations: Gerry O'Hagan and Alan Chambers on gardening leave at the now empty Hawklaw; Roy Taylor and Alan Rowland at Cheadle; Bill Bickham at Culmhead; and Harry Underwood in London at Earls Court.

Pragmatically, the unions had decided that the closure of Hawklaw – on 31 July 1988 – would not be a trigger for industrial action. It was felt that it would be difficult to present the discriminatory treatment of union members as clear-cut victimization. Management were thought to have had a similar dilemma as they took no provocative action over Hawklaw, leaving the members on the payroll while their position was 'being considered'. Since the general election, the fourth anniversary march and rally had come and gone. Inside GCHQ it had been announced that random exit searches of staff would be introduced – some five years after the Security Commission had proposed them in May 1983.

There was a growing feeling that management were going to wait the unions out, just continue the process of reducing numbers by attrition until there were none left. Even seemingly provocative acts – like the SCPS union members at GCHQ taking part in strike action during that union's 1987 pay campaign – were ignored. Good care had been exercised by the eleven members taking action, informing line managers to ensure that there was no disruption to national security. Disciplinary proceedings were threatened, but charges were dropped. In January 1988 compulsory transfers out of GCHQ had been threatened, but again nothing transpired.

The campaign trail had resumed its routine. Trade union conferences were the target in the spring and early summer, concluding with the Tolpuddle rally. In the autumn the concentration was on the TUC, then the Labour Party and finally the latest incarnation of the Liberal Democrats. In August 1988 the one hundredth edition of *Warning Signal* was published.

Ministers who had no direct knowledge of GCHQ continued to make uncorroborated claims. At the time when the government was finally gearing up to sack the remaining union members at GCHQ, William Waldegrave told BBC Radio on 29 September 1988: 'Arriving here as a new minister, it is just not possible to manage a facility like that subject to the sort of disruption it was suffering before.' On 14 October he was interviewed on the *Today* programme. Of the 1979 and 1981 Civil Service pay disputes, in which some GCHQ staff had participated, he said: 'the disputes were nothing to do with GCHQ' – in fact the disputes concerned GCHQ staff as directly as any other civil servants. He said: 'GCHQ is virtually no use unless it runs continuously' – a meaningless statement given that 85–90 per cent of GCHQ staff work a nine-to-five, five-day week. He said: 'GCHQ was constantly out of action' – this is nothing more than absurd hyperbole; more accurately, a lie. Finally, Waldegrave said: 'You cannot run security on a sort of Tuesday and Thursday morning basis' – an insult to staff (including those who later refused to give up their union membership) who worked flat out during crises, and round the clock during the Falklands War.

Ever since 1984 the Falklands War had been hinted at as an occasion when industrial action might have affected national security. The dispute referred to in this context involved the grading of communication and cypher officers in Hong Kong. Overtime was banned, but the work not covered was done by the CCO supervisors – indeed, supervisors doing CCO work had been the cause of the dispute in the first place. In addition, a simple look at a globe would show that Hong Kong is hardly well placed to monitor Argentina and the Falkland Islands. During the war, signals traffic would have been routed through New Zealand rather than Hong Kong.

Interestingly, during and after the Falklands War classified notices were sent to GCHQ staff from 'on high'. The government has never declassified or released their contents, but the sort of comments they contained were 'high level praise', 'never has so much praise been accorded', 'there can be no doubt that this praise has been earned by hard and dedicated work by you as individuals'. A strange choice of words if there had been problems. Brian Tovey, the Director, passed on to staff a personal message of thanks from the Queen. Subsequently, the accusations concerning the Falklands were withdrawn by the government, acknowledging the exemplary record of staff, including trade union members.

Four and a half years after the ban was imposed, on 29 September 1988, the government announced its intention to remove – by dismissal or transfer – all remaining union members from GCHQ. There was no doubting it this time, the moment had come. Ever since 1984 both the TUC and the CCSU had been committed to take action if anyone was dismissed from GCHQ just for being a trade union member.

The commitment was honoured, and 7 November was nominated as GCHQ Day by the TUC and the CCSU. GCHQ Day was planned as a day of protest action with major regional rallies throughout the country. But one thing had changed since the commitment was first given: employment legislation introduced by the Conservative government meant that the unions were hemmed in by legal constraints.

For the day of action on 28 February 1984 the TUC and CCSU had called for support on the Friday of one week and it had been given on Tuesday the following week. There had been no ballot – the call was to everyone who wanted to join in the protest and it involved many unions outside the Civil Service. This time, the law prescribed that all industrial action had to be preceded by a ballot of the members involved. In addition, the laws on secondary action now made it illegal for anyone outside the Civil Service officially to take industrial action – legally GCHQ was a 'Civil Service' issue. One trade unionist could not act to defend the right of another; solidarity was a dirty word – except in Poland.

The first four actual dismissals were announced on 18 October, and they were to take place on 18 November – giving added impetus to GCHQ Day on 7 November. On 3 November Mrs Thatcher was in the Gdansk dockyards in Poland making a speech to members of the Polish union Solidarity that can only be described as hypocritical. She said:

Experience teaches us that you will only achieve higher growth, only release enterprise, only spur people to greater effort, only obtain their full-hearted commitment to reform, when people have the dignity and enjoyment of personal and political liberty; when they have *freedom of expression, freedom of association, the right to form free and independent trade unions* [emphasis added].

With anyone else the words would have stuck in their throats; Thatcher had no such problem.

Despite its need for the British government's support, Solidarity issued a statement condemning the British government's decision to sack trade union members at GCHQ. The statement said: 'We appreciate the British Government's stand on trade union rights in Poland and their support for Solidarity, but the British Government's legitimate concern and welcome sympathy for our struggle could only gain greater authority if they apply the same standards to British workers.'

The first four British workers to be dismissed by a British government for belonging to a trade union were Mike Grindley, 27 years at

GCHQ; Graham Hughes, 31 years in the Civil Service; Brian
Johnson, 32 years at GCHQ; and Alan Rowland, 9 years at GCHQ.
All four had served in the forces, three in the RAF and one – Alan
Rowland – in the Army.

To help the campaign by the Civil Service unions to win a vote in
favour of industrial action, the contract with advertising agents
Delaney, Fletcher and Delaney was dusted off and adverts were
produced for the national press. The content of the adverts was
undeniably effective, although their impact was limited by the
TUC's financial constraints.

The ballot campaigns in the Civil Service unions got off to a bad
start. The unions had decided to exclude their members outside the
Civil Service from the ballot because of fears about legal action. The
contrast with 1984 was stark. Then the whole trade union movement
could be involved without a ballot. Now it was just the Civil Service
and they had to be balloted. The TUC was reduced to calling for
support for the protest march and rallies and hoping that there would
be unofficial action. Unions such as NALGO – representing local
government workers – and the Transport and General Workers'
Union put out calls for their members to support the marches and
rallies. Later in the campaign the NALGO National Executive Committee risked legal action and authorized its members to take strike
action on GCHQ Day. The EETPU, now no longer part of the TUC,
announced that it too would ballot its members over industrial action.

The limited nature of the action reduced its effectiveness in the
eyes of ordinary trade union members in the Civil Service. 'If it is just
us – not the whole trade union movement – and only for one day,
what is the point? It will not change the government's mind.' Just as
big a difficulty for the unions was the passage of time. Any shock
provoked by the sackings had been greatly diminished – there had
been so many false alarms that when they eventually took place it was
almost an anti-climax. Four and a half years had taken the sting out
of the response. It was perhaps this type of assessment – a belief that
they could ride any storm – that led the government finally to act.

As GCHQ Day approached – a name suggested by Delaney,
Fletcher and Delaney years earlier to avoid the disapprobation
attached to the phrase 'day of action' – interest and publicity
concentrated on the individuals. When the government had made its
announcement on 29 September there were eighteen trade unionists
in GCHQ. Three – Bill Greenhalgh, Frances Pearce and Steve

This week Brian Johnson was sacked from his job at GCHQ, the Government's intelligence gathering centre in Cheltenham.

He has to leave because he refused to give up his membership of a trade union.

The order for his dismissal came from the Government.

They say his membership of a trade union is a threat to national security.

But they have offered no evidence to support such a claim.

Instead they say that trade unionists 'might go on strike.'

So it seems that, after 32 years loyal service, Brian Johnson has been sacked for something he might do, rather than something he has done.

The Government could of course have asked the unions for an agreement that would guarantee national security at all times.

But they didn't even talk to the unions before imposing the ban.

And when the unions volunteered such an agreement the Government still refused to talk.

Perhaps it was because they know, as everybody does, that traitors are not found among the ranks of trade unionists.

They generally come from a quite different class of people.

But whatever the Government's motives their actions fly in the face of the democratic values that this country has traditionally upheld.

The kind of values in fact that Brian Johnson and his colleagues at GCHQ had spent most of their lives defending.

Until they were betrayed by their own government.

WHILE HE WAS BUSY DEFENDING OUR COUNTRY THE GOVERNMENT STABBED HIM IN THE BACK.

FOR FREEDOM'S SAKE SUPPORT GCHQ DAY. NOVEMBER 7TH.   *TUC*

A TUC advertisement from the *Daily Express*, 21 October 1988.

Wilkie – were 'offered' compulsory transfers to other government departments, which were accepted with varying degrees of willingness. Another trade unionist was described in the *Guardian* as an 'unlikely rebel with a cause'. He was George Toulmin, a statistician and pure mathematician. George's problem was that he was too old to be sacked. To his great regret he was due to retire, and did so on 31 October.

Artwork from a mug produced by GCHQ Trade Unions to commemorate the fourteen sacked trade unionists. Top row: Mike Grindley, Graham Hughes, Brian Johnson, Alan Rowland, Robin Smith. Middle row: Gerry O'Hagan, Dee Goddard, Bill Bickham, Roy Taylor. Bottom row: Clive Lloyd, John Cook, Harry Underwood, Alan Chambers, Gareth Morris.

Of the fourteen remaining trade unionists, the dismissal of four had already been announced. Disciplinary action was then announced against a further six members – Bill Bickham, Alan Chambers, John Cook, Clive Lloyd, Roy Taylor and Harry Underwood. These six had rejoined their trade unions after the victory in the High Court. They had already been disciplined and fined once for belonging to a trade union; they were now to be tried once again – the hearings were due to start in the week beginning 14 November. Of the others Gerry O'Hagan, who had not worked since the closure of Hawklaw, was given compulsory early retirement – that is, sacked – at the age of twenty-eight. Robin Smith was not sacked immediately, but rather was told to report to the Royal Signals and Radar Establishment Malvern on 30 November. He refused to do so on the grounds that he did not consider that trade union membership constituted reasonable grounds for compulsory transfer – particularly as GCHQ was short of staff in his department!

The closer GCHQ Day got, the shabbier the government's action appeared to many observers. On 30 September the *Gloucestershire Echo* printed an editorial which summed up the attitude of many:

The truth ... is really that the Government is prepared to bully a handful of individuals, who cannot possibly do it any harm, because it is determined to achieve a total victory. To underline one of its own cardinal principles, that it must always be seen to win, it is prepared to demand that they either swallow their pride or lose their livings.

It is mean and shabby manoeuvring that shames the Government and shames Whitehall and, at the end of the day, will leave the GCHQ unionists with their own pride and their own principles still honourably intact.

One month later, on 1 November, the *Guardian* came off the fence in an article by Hugo Young:

It is a matter of record that few if any strikes are ever supported in the national press. This is naturally true of Conservative newspapers ... But it is also true of non-party papers and writers. We may sometimes support the cause but our almost invariable tendency is to wring our hands and press the case for sweet reason when somebody proposes to do something unpleasant about it. I cannot recall a single strike of which I have written with whole-hearted, or even lukewarm, approval. Having consulted a custodian of the *Guardian*'s allegiances over the past two decades, I conclude that its record is pretty much the same.

Over GCHQ, I feel differently. The cause is just and the gesture appropriate because, after more than four years' disputation over the right to work for GCHQ and belong to a union, no other expression of meaningful disgust at what the Government has done is available.

But this attitude was not shared by some Civil Service unions, or even by the much-vaunted EETPU. The results of the ballots were announced in the week beginning 31 October. The two biggest unions in the Civil Service, the CPSA and the NUCPS, and the Northern Ireland union NIPSA had voted to take strike action. Between them these three unions represented a clear majority of Civil Service trade unionists. Most disappointing – not least for its General Secretary Bill McCall – was the IPCS vote. IPCS represented four of the fourteen sacked union members. Its members voted against strike action by 13,826 to 5,633 votes. Less surprisingly, the FDA also voted against action – it would have been unheard of for senior civil servants to have voted for such action. IRSF, the Inland Revenue union which had no members in GCHQ, voted against taking action, but by the narrowest of margins.

The potentially depressing effect of these results, coupled with the failure of the EETPU to deliver its long-promised industrial action, could have been enormous. It was not. GCHQ Day was a major success. It did not bring the country to a halt, but it did demonstrate continuing and widespread support, in the TUC's words, 'for the right of workers at GCHQ to belong to a free and independent trade union'.

Warning Signal reported that over seventy rallies had taken place throughout the country. All were well attended – including by many who would not or could not take industrial action. There was no fatalism among those attending the rallies, just anger at the government and support for the fourteen. The number taking industrial action among civil servants was very high. Over 80 per cent of NUCPS, CPSA and NIPSA members stopped work, while large numbers of IPCS and IRSF members refused to cross picket lines. Outside the Civil Service, dockers at Tilbury, NALGO members in London, Manchester and Birmingham, teachers in South London and miners in South Yorkshire all took action. The fact that the Tilbury dockers took strike action on GCHQ Day was given by the Port of London Authority as one of the reasons for them being sacked at a later date.

GCHQ trade unionists were scattered to the four winds to speak at the rallies, most of which were also addressed by CCSU and TUC representatives. The London rally in Central Hall, Westminster, was packed with 2,800 people, and a further 2,000 were unable to get in. It was addressed by many of the great and the good, including Neil Kinnock and Liberal Democrat MP Robert Maclennan. Mike Grindley also spoke, but refused to be described as one of the great and the good, preferring his wife Isabel's suggestion, 'the short and the stubborn'.

At the rally Mike Grindley let loose the pent-up emotion caused by five years of hostility from his employer and government:

We resent utterly and completely the accusation that the trade unions we are proud to belong to are any threat to national security, and from our inside knowledge we know that they have never been so. The traitors come from the old-boy network and elsewhere.

No government has the right to say to its employees that your democratic rights have been removed;

No government has the right to pick and choose who shall or shall not retain the right to join an independent trade union; and

No government should ride roughshod over ordinary people in this disgraceful fashion.

Many of the forcibly de-unionized workforce at GCHQ are *not* happy with their lot, and are in many cases appalled at how the government have treated the remaining trade unionists – they feel our presence at GCHQ perhaps keeps away some management excesses since we are a voice to the outside world.

We will *not* bend the knee, and with your support we shall eventually win the fight.

The first sackings were due to take place on 18 November, but the fate of the six trade unionists who were to be disciplined had not yet been determined. The six in question were those who had rejoined their unions since the ban had been imposed. Clearly, the government still believed they would attract less sympathy than the others because they had earlier accepted £1,000 for giving up their statutory rights. GCHQ maintained that they were in breach of the conditions of service they had accepted when signing Option A – not to be a union member. In the warped logic of GCHQ there was something dishonest about this change of heart: management could not accept that it was exactly the same principle – the right to belong to a union – that the 'rejoiners' were upholding.

The hearings of Alan Chambers and Roy Taylor were to take place on Tuesday, 15 November and those of John Cook, Clive Lloyd and Harry Underwood on 22 November. Bill Bickham was tried *in absentia*, having refused to attend the hearings on the reasonable grounds that he did not consider trade union membership to be a disciplinary offence. Harry Underwood represented himself; the other four were represented by Hugh Lanning.

There had been some discussion about whether to attend the hearings. Was to do so to accept that membership of a union could be an offence? Also it was inconceivable that the hearings could result in anything but dismissal – if they had already announced dismissal of some members, how could they do anything less to those they were disciplining? The real fear, though, was not about dismissal, but that management would be vindictive towards them, would penalize them in some additional way. Moreover, tactically, the unions wanted to take the cases to the Civil Service Appeal Board at a later stage, and it was therefore better to go through the process. The decision was left to the individuals and five opted to go, perhaps not realizing what they were letting themselves in for.

The hearings would not have been out of place in a novel depicting some totalitarian state of the twenty-first century. This impression was reinforced for Lanning on arrival at the Oakley GCHQ site in Cheltenham. Since the last time – five years previously – that he had been inside Oakley, it had had a new security complex built at the entrance, enlarged to speed up the processing of staff cars in the morning, reinforced to counter terrorist attack and adapted to cope with random exit searches. The security guards were now uniformed – before the Security Commission had recommended they become uniformed, the security staff had been dressed in civilian clothes in order not to draw attention to GCHQ sites. Now they had so successfully drawn attention to the place that it presumably did not matter – a low profile was no longer possible.

Despite the changes, the security system was not foolproof. When Mike Grindley was disciplined in 1987 about an article Paul Routledge had written in the *Observer* – an article which could have been more carefully written if the innocent were to be protected – management had refused to supply a record of the second hearing. To counter this, Lanning had thought to take along the little tape recorder he used for dictation. The hearings – in A Block in Peter Little's office – began with management declining to provide a record of the hearing, and this was followed by an outburst at the suggestion that the hearings might be recorded. 'How did that recorder get on site? They are forbidden.' It seemed rather hypocritical of GCHQ to complain about clandestine recording, but in the event no recordings were made and management agreed to repeat anything at dictation speed if notes were required. The recorder was not confiscated and Lanning's bags were not checked on this or future visits.

After this entertaining opening, the hearings took a more predictable path to their inevitable conclusion. The charge was as follows:

Notwithstanding that you accepted the terms and conditions applicable to all staff at GCHQ as outlined in GN 100/84 and now embodied in EP 101 Ad [the staff regulations], you joined a national trade union in breach of the condition which prohibits membership of such a union. In spite of the disciplinary proceedings which resulted in one increment in your salary being withdrawn for a period of two years and subsequent warnings given by letters dated 30 June 1988 and 29 September 1988, you have continued your membership of such a union both during the currency of the above penalty and subsequently.

Before the charge was read out every member was asked if – 'even at this late stage' – he wanted to change his mind. Harry Underwood declared himself to be unrepentant; Clive Lloyd said, 'Not in the slightest.' Then a further statement was read out – at dictation speed – trying to distinguish these hearings from the earlier ones. It was conceded that the statement was based on legal advice; indeed, they were taking the members through the disciplinary procedure because of legal advice.

The union's case was similar at each hearing. It argued that the outcome of the hearings was predetermined, that they were a charade and a pantomime. They could not decide not to sack these members having already announced the sackings of others. The three-person disciplinary board was not amused – especially when John Cook and Clive Lloyd started referring to 'Nazis' and 'Nuremberg trials'.

It was argued that the members had a fundamental right to belong to a trade union. Management replied that they could: the staff association. The justification for the ban was challenged – disciplinary action was inappropriate and they had already been disciplined for the offence of being trade unionists. More substantively, the six had only signed GN 100/84 under duress – the threat of dismissal. In Clive Lloyd's case, Little accepted that pressure was necessary 'otherwise staff would not have accepted such a fundamental change'. Although it was accepted that it was legal for them to rejoin when they had – because Glidewell had ruled the ban invalid – staff had been advised that it was 'unwise'. The fact that the Director had declared dismissal to be inappropriate in 1986 cut no ice. Nor did the fact that it was five years since the ban, and that the union members who had remained at GCHQ were clearly not regarded as a security risk. In response, management maintained that it had tried to be fair and insisted that the disciplinary board had 'no brief' as to what decision to come to or what penalty to impose.

Between the two sets of disciplinary hearings – on 15 and 22 November – the first dismissals took place. Over four hundred people gathered outside the gates of GCHQ, Oakley, on Friday, 18 November 1988, between 2.30 and 3 p.m. – the time, it was thought, when the first group of sacked union members would be making their last exit from the site. But the department had ensured that those outside the gates would not be able to cheer them as they left. Graham Hughes had been told to leave on Tuesday, Alan Rowland had been shown the door two days before at Cheadle, and Brian Johnson had been forced to leave early on Friday morning. Mike Grindley had not been allowed on site since his positive vetting had been removed in November 1987. Despite this a message went out on the internal tannoy inside Oakley: 'This is a security announcement – the police have informed us that there will be trade unionists outside the gates at 3 p.m. this afternoon.' The gates were shut and GCHQ sealed itself off – management obviously thought trade unionism was a disease that might afflict their staff.

The Brodsworth Colliery Band, from Doncaster, led the four sacked members and supporters around the corner to the Priors Farm playing fields. Among other appropriate numbers they played 'The great little army'. It was a very emotional occasion as Mike

Grindley, Brian Johnson and Graham Hughes all spoke of how they felt about the way they had been treated. Alan Rowland, although present, did not speak as he felt he had had his turn when he cycled out of CSOS Cheadle earlier in the week. Norman Willis, Leslie Christie and others spoke in support. But it was not the general secretaries who caused the emotion; it was the simple dignified statements of the ordinary people who had sacrificed their careers and their way of life for the principle of union membership.

They did not see themselves as heroes, but they had been tested for five years and had not been found wanting. Their behaviour belittled the action that was taken against them. They had resisted and frustrated government policy for a long time. Other disputes had come and gone, but the GCHQ issue remained. Dismissal was meant to be the last resort, the final solution, but the government was to discover that trade unionists in GCHQ would still not go away.

Meanwhile the disciplinary proceedings were wending their way towards the inevitable conclusion of six more dismissals. At the last disciplinary hearing – Clive Lloyd's – on the following Tuesday, 22 November, a statement was read out by Lanning which sought to sum up the feelings and emotions of everyone.

Trade unions were never imposed on GCHQ staff, they were invited in by them, they joined them voluntarily and ran them directly.

Trade unions were needed then to defend the common interests of staff, that need remains today.

Trade unions acted as a guarantee that neither GCHQ management nor GCHQ as an organization could abuse its unique role and position.

The Prime Minister said in Poland on 3 November that she believed in the right to form free and independent trade unions.

Yet in GCHQ trade unions are supposed to be intolerable precisely because they might be independent enough, they might be free enough to do something the government or management does not approve of or agree with.

Freedom of expression and freedom of association are not truly freedoms if it only means freedom to agree and freedom to join approved organizations.

Trade unions remain legal organizations in this country. They are still a part of British democracy.

The government and GCHQ cannot on the one hand claim to defend that democracy yet deny it to GCHQ staff. You cannot defend democracy by removing it.

You cannot destroy the idea of, the wish and the need for free trade unions simply by sacking and disciplining trade unionists.

No government department, not even GCHQ, is an island. GCHQ cannot and should not isolate itself from society totally. To do so would be to make it unreal and unsafe.

Free trade unions will return to GCHQ. The government and management made this probable when they unilaterally took away staff's right to
belong to a trade union. They guaranteed it when they sacked trade unionists
last Friday.

The only way to remove trade unions from GCHQ was to convince staff
that they did not need them. All you have done is prove that they do.

To be a trade union member is not an offence, nor will it ever be in a truly
democratic society.

Today the wrong people are being disciplined. Last week the wrong people
were sacked. They are the wrong people because they have done nothing
wrong.

The guilty ones are those in Washington, Downing Street and in the office
of the Director of GCHQ who conceived, hatched and implemented the plot
to ban trade unions.

Their plot will fail because they saw an enemy where there was none; it will
fail because they distrusted those that they must rely on; and it will fail
because they used force and compulsion when they should have used
discussion and persuasion.

So long as staff in GCHQ have free and independent minds, the potential
for trade unions to return remains. If that possibility ceases then GCHQ has
no future, just a past. Trade unions will come back to GCHQ, not from the
outside but from within it, not as an enemy but as a friend.

A final message for you to decode: *Au revoir.*

The GCHQ campaign was full of times when it was necessary to ask
what was to be done next. As the dismissal process dragged on there
was little discussion or dissent, it all seemed reasonably clear cut. The
results of the ballots on industrial action made it clear that there was
not now – if there ever had been – a basis for further industrial action.
A lobby of Parliament was organized for 30 November – described
by former Labour MP Alf Dubbs as the best organized he had ever
seen. As each member was sacked he or she was met by supporters
and the press. The traditional march and rally were rapidly ap-
proaching and now took on a new significance.

Almost as an afterthought, while the unions were mobilizing for what
they hoped would be their biggest ever march and rally, the government
made another statement. On 8 December the Prime Minister announced that the introduction of the polygraph or lie detector into
GCHQ was to be abandoned. The sacked members – Mike Grindley
in particular – felt that it was a victory for which they could claim some
credit. If it had not been for the union campaign, both inside and outside
GCHQ, they felt the polygraph would have been introduced. The other
victory attributed to the GCHQ campaign concerned its impact on the
government's industrial policy in the public sector.

For years Conservatives had been calling for action to be taken against the power of trade unions in the public sector. The public service strikes during the so-called 'winter of discontent' – frequently blamed for the demise of the Callaghan government in the 1979 general election – were quoted as the reason why unions in essential services needed to be curbed. The most commonly proposed remedy was to limit the right to strike. GCHQ was seen by many as the first step in a concerted attack on public-sector unions. The assumption was so widespread that Sir Geoffrey Howe had been persuaded specifically to deny it in the early days of the campaign, shortly after the ban was announced back in 1984. Whitehall does not deny that options were considered. The fact that the GCHQ ban had caused such a furore, had taken so long to implement, and was generally regarded as a serious mistake both at home and abroad made the government think twice about similar moves they might have taken against other unions in the public sector. Certainly many supporters from all sections of public service were grateful not to have suffered the same treatment as the members at GCHQ.

The fifth anniversary GCHQ march and rally in 1989 was the biggest and the best yet. Well over ten thousand people attended, marching through Cheltenham to Montpellier Gardens, where the speakers included, for the first time, the leaders of both the Labour and (Liberal) Democrat parties – Neil Kinnock and Paddy Ashdown. Kinnock's speech was listened to particularly attentively for the commitments he would give. After a typically wide-ranging speech he concluded by repeating the pledge which had been made many times before:

The next Labour government will restore trade union rights to GCHQ, we will restore to GCHQ unions their rightful place in consultations and negotiations about conditions of work at GCHQ and we will restore the tradition of mutual loyalty and respect at GCHQ which existed before the government ban.

For most people, Kinnock and other trade union and party leaders would be a hard act to follow. But the star attraction of GCHQ rallies had become Mike Grindley. Politely bearing unoriginal remarks about his diminutive stature and his habit of using a carrier bag plastered with GCHQ Trade Union stickers as a briefcase, his turn to speak would prompt a warm and genuine standing ovation – not only for Grindley, but for all the sacked members. Grindley's speeches are always his own creations, but the quips and jokes are sometimes the product of consultation with Jack Hart. This year there were two quips of his own in the speech. Referring to Thatcher's comments in January 1984: 'She says there is an unbridgeable gap between the positions of the government and the trade union movement over GCHQ. We say there is an unbridgeable gap – between Thatcher's ears!' The other was a message for the government: 'They think they have finished with us, but we have certainly not finished with them!'

Of the remaining unionists, Dee Goddard was sacked on 12 January 1989. 14 February 1989 was chosen as the day on which the appeals of the six members who had been disciplined and who now faced the sack were to be heard. The appeals were to be conducted by the Director of GCHQ, Sir Peter Marychurch. In *Warning Signal*, on the day before the appeals, it was reported that one of the six had already been removed from the formal list of staff for his station; another found his pay slip had been written in biro, having been removed from the computer. Management claimed that these actions were without prejudice to the outcome of the appeals. The feeling of predetermination led to 14 February being dubbed in advance the 'St Valentine's Day Massacre'.

John Cook was the only member who chose to be present at his appeal. It took place in C Block in the Director's office. Cook and Lanning were allowed to make their own way up to the office, the banned union member 'escorting' the banned union official. There was no tape recorder this time, though no one checked.

The Director's office was not especially grand and opulent; indeed, it was rather grubby and seedy in appearance. Lanning had first met Marychurch at a reception just before Christmas 1983. It was an annual event alternately hosted by management and the unions, a civilized part of industrial relations practice in most government departments. Then Marychurch had been bemoaning how hard it was to convince the Treasury that he was entitled to a London flat like other permanent secretaries. The problem was that, as Director of GCHQ, he was only a deputy secretary. The fact that he had regular business in London and more need than London-based permanent secretaries was apparently not convincing enough to the Treasury. Judging by his office, he did not appear to have had much clout since then.

Marychurch said very little. By now John Cook was warming to these hearings, reminding the Director of earlier meetings they had had. The one real exchange took place when Marychurch demanded to know whether he was being accused of being a liar. The answer was a not very convincing 'no'.

The issue was whether or not Marychurch had already been told to implement the ban and proceed with the sackings, and whether the outcome of the appeal was therefore predetermined. Marychurch maintained that he was considering the cases on a *de nouveau* basis, that no conclusion had been reached. He said throughout that he had acted independently and that the government had not given him any instructions. It was conceded that he was not lying in stating that he had no *specific* instructions to sack the union members or to reject their appeals.

What was inconceivable then – and remains inconceivable now – is that political authority and agreement had not been given to go ahead with the sackings. The ban had needed prime ministerial approval. It had been Sir Geoffrey Howe – not GCHQ management – who had backed away from dismissals in 1986. It was known that, in the aftermath of the ban, an inter-departmental committee had been established to monitor the handling of the situation. That the Director of GCHQ was left to his own counsel in these matters is simply not credible.

As expected, the Director rejected the appeals against dismissal. Not only were the officials dismissed, but they were also discriminated against compared to the other union members. The other union members had been dismissed on the same terms as if they had been made redundant. The 'rejoiners' were dismissed without compensation. In implementing the decision, GCHQ management displayed a lack of sensitivity which was remarkable even by its own standards. Unlike the previous sackings, where notice had been given, the members were forced to leave the site immediately and told not to return.

Bill Bickham reported for work as usual at Culmhead in Somerset on 22 February only to be intercepted at the gate and taken away to a room where he was debriefed and had his pass removed. He was then led to his locker and told to take away his personal belongings before being led out of the gate. 'It was all over in twenty minutes,' he said.

John Cook was sacked after completing his night shift. Earlier he had asked for time off but had been told that he must work the shift

Gareth Morris leaves GCHQ, Cheltenham, for the last time.

because of a staff shortage. At the end of the shift his pass was taken away from him and he was escorted off site. Neither Bickham nor Cook was given the opportunity to say goodbye to friends. Cook said: 'This is a shabby way to be treated after twenty-two years of loyal service.'

The last trade unionist inside GCHQ was Gareth Morris. He was dismissed on 2 March 1989. *Warning Signal* described the event:

Heavy morning rain had cleared just in time for the sun to greet Gareth as he walked out of GCHQ, ending over 40 years of continuous union membership in the department. As he approached the outer gates, once again closed by security staff as they had been three months earlier when the first sackings took place, he paused briefly and defiantly raised his bag which was festooned with trade union stickers. This was the bag which throughout the five years had been used to carry literature to the union table in Oakley canteen.

As he emerged from the gate he was greeted by his mother, girlfriend and loud applause from his colleagues in GCHQ Trade Unions and from headquarters officials from NUCPS and IPCS. He was immediately surrounded by reporters, TV cameras and photographers and for half an hour security staff looked on in embarrassed amazement as Gareth was photographed, filmed and interviewed.

Morris said: 'There's a lot of sympathy in there for the people who have been sacked, some of it at a very senior level. Morale is at rock bottom.' At the rally afterwards Peter Palmer, then NUCPS President, remarked that the government had intended to deunionize GCHQ in five weeks. It had taken over five years – a gross political misjudgement. Since full-time union officials were present, the social gathering that then took place was technically a breach of conditions of service for all those present who were still employed by GCHQ – some of Morris's colleagues from inside GCHQ had joined him by this time. Employment-related matters were discussed. This was an offence.

Robin Smith – then a 32-year-old scientist, now a full-time union official with IPMS – was removed from GCHQ on 29 November 1988 and 'compulsorily transferred' to the MoD's Royal Signals and Radar Establishment Malvern. Ironically, it was a site where GCHQ had a 'lodger' unit and it generally had close links with GCHQ. Smith was sacked on 7 April 1989 – sacking number 14 – as he had refused to go through with the pretence of a transfer. Technically, Smith was dismissed by the MoD. The nonsense of the action was underlined by the fact that one of the posts which he was 'offered' in the RSRE was with the Speech Research Unit, which was itself deunionized in 1984 when it was part of GCHQ. It had since been transferred to the MoD, and union membership there now seemed to be acceptable.

Those GCHQ staff who refused to give up their union rights formed an unlikely band. Over the years the authors have talked to or interviewed those who were sacked and many other union members who were involved. Norman Willis, General Secretary of the TUC, from the start became involved both politically and emotionally. Although others in the trade union movement – both the leaders and the rank and file – were well aware of the issues at stake, they were bemused by the assortment of individuals who became the focus of a campaign and controversy that has attracted the headlines and caught the imagination of so many for so long.

There was Alexander Hamilton, a member of the FDA, who opted for early retirement. Acknowledged on both sides of the Atlantic as a brilliant cryptanalyst, his decision prompted even Washington and the National Security Agency to question the wisdom of the ban. His talent was such that he gave his name to a code-breaking system.

John Cook joined GCHQ after serving twelve years in the RAF.

When he first came to Cheltenham in 1967 he was not really interested in trade unionism, but his colleagues assured him that it was in his best interests to join. He says now:

I find it ironic to think that in 1984 those self-same colleagues were so quick to give up those same union rights which they were so eager for me to take up ... In 1982 I played my part in the Falklands War. I was a trade union member at the time and no one accused me of being a threat to national security. It astounds me to think that the Prime Minister believes that only Tories can be true patriots. My own father was a trade unionist and gave his life for this country in the Second World War. He was fighting for democracy then, and I am fighting for democracy now.

The values I was taught as a boy have been my guiding light throughout my life. I was taught that this is a free country where we have freedom of thought, freedom of expression and freedom of association. Mrs Thatcher was a hypocrite – supporting Solidarity in Poland, and yet at the same time denying her own countrymen and women those self-same rights ... Without people with strong principles and strong values, a country slowly loses all dignity. If the government really believes in democracy, it should stop pandering to the Americans, lift the ban at GCHQ and let the workers there decide for themselves whom they want to represent them.

Kit Braunholtz of the IPCS wrote an open letter to Marychurch in February 1984 through the columns of the *Guardian*:

I think that the strength of my feeling is due to the fact that I have worked at GCHQ for nearly 30 years, over half my life, and it is the only employment I have ever had. I tend to identify myself with GCHQ and its achievements (or at least I did until three weeks ago), and it makes me angry to see the damage that has already been done by the decision ... The damage consists, of course, in the disastrous drop in staff morale which has resulted from this demonstration of your lack of confidence in our loyalty and dedication, together with shock at the brutal way in which a pistol has been held to our heads ... I believe that the reason for this disastrous decision is poor communications. It is of course difficult in an organisation like GCHQ to tell people as much about what is going on as one would like. But the habits of reticence and half-truths – desirable as they are in some of our professional actions – have I believe spread unnecessarily and dangerously into the area of staff management. We do pass down patronising pats-on-the-back after we have collectively pulled out all the stops in some crisis or other, but there is far too little information given to staff, and too little consultation ... For over 25 years there was never a thought of striking, and only the present government has managed to generate enough militancy among civil servants to make even token strikes possible ... To be perfectly frank, it seems to me that the timing of your announcement, which has puzzled nearly all observers, is due not to incompetence but to a desire on the part of the government to strengthen further its position vis-à-vis the Civil Service before the next pay round, together with a mistaken belief by you and your advisers that this measure would help you overcome the resistance to imposing the polygraph test on GCHQ staff ... In my view, the government has done more harm to GCHQ's mission than the unions ever could have done ... We are supposed to be in the Communications and Intelligence business, but it is a lack of these that has caused the trouble!

The CCSU's media campaign picked up this theme. 'At GCHQ the Government listen to everyone except the people who work there', said one poster in support of the TUC's GCHQ Day on 7 November 1988.

Harry Underwood of the NUCPS was one of those sacked. Roy Pennison, who described himself as the longest surviving member of GCHQ, wrote to Underwood, who had served with him for over thirty years:

You can take credit for many years of loyal service to the Crown, and I regret that this should have been forgotten by some who joined GCHQ long after us ... I have every regard for your professional skill, your personal integrity, and your continued loyalty to GCHQ in spite of severe provocation. I respect the right of individuals to join the trade union of their choice, in Britain as well as in Poland, and without the kind of victimisation which you have had to endure. I cannot accept Mrs Thatcher's statement that membership of a trade union results in a conflict of loyalties ... Security has never been endangered, and this is confirmed by the fact that security clearances of GCHQ union members have not been withdrawn. The decision was purely political, and so is the action being taken against you.

George Toulmin is a pure mathematician. The subject of his Cambridge doctoral thesis, written before he was called up as a private in the Intelligence Corps, was the transfinite dimension in topological spaces. He reads, but insists he cannot speak, nine languages, including Latin, Russian, Welsh and Hebrew. He appeared an unlikely rebel. Just four years from retirement, he readily acknowledged that, a bachelor with no dependants, he massively underspent his income. That might have persuaded him to opt for the quiet life. Here is Toulmin in his own words, writing in the *Warning Signal* of 3 September 1984:

I have never felt it was remotely possible to undertake 'to resign from membership of any trade union to which I belong' and 'not to join a trade union or to engage in its affairs' [the words of Option A]. But why did I feel this strongly? Certainly, as long as I can remember, I have vaguely approved of unions in general, and had the Tolpuddle Martyrs firmly docketed as

Good Men; ... Why should I suddenly feel impelled to become a mini-
martyr?

Most of us in this country lead a pretty comfortable life – compared to most
elsewhere in the world now and almost all in earlier times. It seems to me we
have to thank for that many people in the past who have been prepared to
stand up to challenges of one sort or another – the Three Hundred against
Xerxes' million, the monk of Wittenberg against a corrupt and tyrannical
Church, six men of Dorset against an oligarchy. We may have hoped we
should not have to do the like, but we owe it to them to stand up in our turn
to be counted when a challenge does come. If it is in some ways a very little
challenge – we have not to fear the sword, fire, or transportation – so much
the less excuse for ducking it. One thing is sure – if we duck a little challenge,
someone else will soon face a bigger one. Now, whether the union ban did
constitute a challenge to be met can be argued, and I am not trying to argue
the point here. After all the argument, it comes down to a matter of the
individual conscience ...

So much for 'why?'; whether I regret it is an easier question. Of course, I
don't, and I don't think I shall ever do so. Quite apart from feeling I have
done the right thing, I have gained enormously from it. The campaign has
been a great new interest in life; I've made many new friends from among the
most capable and loyal employees of GCHQ; Norman Willis, Tolpuddle,
and Alistair Graham, are no longer mere names to me; and incidentally I
have been introduced to skittles, taken up tennis again after 27 years'
inactivity, and become a blood donor ...

Later, contemplating the government's claims about a 'conflict of
loyalties', he said he had no difficulty in finding a community that was
admirably free of such conflicts. After prostrating himself on the
lawn, he noted: 'All those fine little ants, busily trotting back and
forth, have no idea in their head but loyalty to the nest and the queen.'

Jeremy Windust, chairman of the SCPS GCHQ branch, took a
leading role in the early campaign against the ban, and was the first
editor of *Warning Signal*. He wrote this personal account in the
Guardian in August 1985:

I was assigned to GCHQ by the Civil Service Commission in April, 1975.
Fresh out of college, this was my first job. Before I had even been shown my
desk, I was given an introductory briefing which included the recommenda-
tion by management that I join the union appropriate to my grade, which I
duly did. In 1979, I volunteered for shift-working and was in work over the
Christmas holiday when the Soviets rolled into Afghanistan. Over the next
5 years on shifts, I had just one Christmas Day off to spend with my wife and
children. I was working a 24-hour shift rota throughout the Falklands
campaign. My performance must have been up to standard since I came off
shifts on promotion in 1983.

So when Sir Geoffrey Howe cited in justification of the Government's banning of unions, that union action had damaged the national interest during the Falklands crisis, I felt not only angry, but personally insulted. And although he was forced to retract that bizarre accusation, the mud sticks. One tabloid had a picture of us as 'THE REBELS', and there can be little doubt in anyone's mind that trade unionists at GCHQ are part of the Prime Minister's 'enemy within'.

I am no hero; neither am I a rebel. The grotesque stereotype of a trade unionist crouching on a picket line with a rock in his hand is not one that I recognise. I am an ordinary junior manager in the Civil Service with a mortgage on a semi-detached Victorian house and a second-hand estate car parked in front. My wife [Elaine] is a full-time student at a local college, and with school uniforms to buy for 3 children, I am one of the millions who find their salary does not go quite as far as it used to. And I have, for the last 18 months, been under extended notice of dismissal. Added to the strains on family life, the breaking of friendships and the loss of trust in senior management at GCHQ, must be the vast waste of human resources. Many specialists have already gone to greener pastures in the private sector – one GCHQ manager has described his computer section as 'unmanageable' because of the rapid turnover of staff. On top of this loss, the Government seems quite prepared to exacerbate the situation by getting rid of the remaining trade unionists, regardless of the effect on the operational capacity of the department. These people have anything up to 40 years' expertise and experience in highly esoteric fields, and are often quite literally irreplaceable. I know the American community working in Cheltenham were advised not to get involved in discussions or comment on the union ban, but some have been quite frank in their astonishment that GCHQ could part so easily with highly respected and dedicated colleagues of many years' standing simply because they would not sign the despised option form. Others are astonished at letters that have been received by union members refusing them training, rejecting them from overseas posts, or threatening disciplinary action.

When the Prime Minister and the Employment Secretary [then Tom King] are asked what is to be done about the remaining trade union members at GCHQ, as they often are, they respond invariably that we will be found jobs elsewhere in the Civil Service or be offered early retirement. They are the words of ministers in a quandary. They must know that all those staff who had indicated on their option form that they would be willing to move departments and who have received acceptable offers have now gone, as have all those who agreed to early retirement terms. Those of us who are left enjoy our work at GCHQ and know that, to the best of our abilities, we are making worthwhile contributions.

Mike Grindley won a classics scholarship to Cambridge after national service in the RAF. During his national service he took a course in Chinese before being posted to Hong Kong, where he spent the time monitoring communications. He did little work at Cambridge, scraping through with a 'special' degree – worse than a third.

'I moved to Cheltenham', he recalls, 'to join a place called GCHQ ... I knew about GCHQ from my time in the RAF and it was the only place I could think of where I could use my Chinese in a modern up-to-date fashion. My starting salary in 1961 was £768 a year as a temporary executive officer.'

For about eight years, Grindley concentrated on linguistic research, helping to build up a Chinese–English technical and scientific dictionary:

I loved the work and learnt an enormous amount. Since that period and until they sacked me, I carried out detailed analytical work and reported on matters connected with China. I produced original technical aids, acted as special problem solver for customers in Britain and abroad, and pioneered new research. I set my own pace and was left completely alone to get on with the job. Now I'm left completely alone by GCHQ *not* to get on with the job! It's a funny old world, as Margaret Hilda Thatcher said.

Grindley turned up to the local strike meeting in February 1973 – the occasion of the first-ever Civil Service strike. It was prompted by the Heath government's pay policy when Civil Service rates were running 20 per cent behind those in comparable jobs elsewhere. He was the only GCHQ SCPS-level official on strike on that day – the rest were GCHQ CPSA members. He describes himself as a 'democratic socialist', adding: 'It is important that all main strands of politics and opinion are free to work at a place like GCHQ. It is part of the necessary checks and balances there.'

On 8 July 1987 eleven SCPS members at GCHQ received a letter from management stating that 'on June 8 and 9, 1987 you absented yourself from your workplace during your working hours without authorisation in order to take industrial action'. This followed a warning letter in May threatening disciplinary measures if they took further part in the joint SCPS/CPSA action over pay and conditions.

Grindley and Don Clarke responded in typical fashion. Threats against them, they said, were based on GN 100/84, an 'immoral document'. They were not subject to GCHQ's 'new conditions of service' because they did not get the benefits of the new pay system and promotions due to them. In August 1987 Terry Gill – the official in GCHQ's Establishment Division who had been given the task of dealing with both the 'rebels' and the media – wrote to Grindley stating that the general Civil Service policy of not taking disciplinary proceedings against staff who took part in official industrial action had clearly been 'disapplied in relation to GCHQ'. He added, however, that management had decided not to pursue disciplinary action 'on this occasion'. Clarke noted in typical style: 'We smashed the fascist bastards again!'

But for Grindley developments were to reach a climax. On 8 November 1987 an article in the *Observer* under the by-line of Paul Routledge referred to a classified circular written by J. D. Rue, GCHQ's security director, admitting that new random searches – finally introduced following the recommendations of the Security Commission in 1983 – 'will have a lower capability against the professional spy'. The only form of exit searches that could catch a spy, he added, were of a kind that would 'constitute an unacceptable imposition on staff'. Routledge made a great deal in his article about the ease with which he had been given a photocopy of the front half of the circular and quoted Grindley, who made the intelligent comment that the best procedure was positive vetting – 'once you are in, trust the people'.

GCHQ management seized the opportunity: Grindley had copied a classified piece of paper and shown it to a journalist. No matter what the content, in this case totally harmless and already in the public domain, Whitehall always takes a stricter view of officials showing outsiders papers than anything that may be passed on orally. For a start, the evidence is clear. On 30 November 1987 Grindley received a letter from the head of personnel security at GCHQ informing him that his positive vetting security clearance had been withdrawn – a move that effectively made him redundant. 'I can no longer rely on your good sense and discretion on security matters', the letter read. The contents of the *Observer* article were cited as the most serious security 'breach'. But Grindley was also told that he was guilty of other 'security lapses': he had revealed 'confidential information' about GCHQ in an interview published in April 1985 – a reference to an article in the NIPSA journal which indicated that there were seven thousand employees at GCHQ, information which was indeed quoted by Thatcher in a parliamentary answer on 20 October 1988; he had failed to report immediately to GCHQ's Security Division 'contact with members of Communist or Trotskyist organizations' – a reference to a discussion with a *Morning Star* reporter, a discussion he freely admitted to in *Warning Signal*, at the Irish Confederation of Trade Unions conference at Cork; and he had given 'further indiscreet information' in an interview published in October 1987 – a reference to an article in the *Independent* which said that Grindley was a Mandarin Chinese expert and was going to address a conference in the USA, information which had already been published.

Grindley wrote back to GCHQ strongly denying that he had compromised security in any way. 'I have never divulged anything which would damage national security and I would not think of doing so', he told Gill. It had always been recognized at GCHQ, he added, that general issues and principles contained in classified documents could be discussed provided they were in a 'sanitized' form. All the issues cited by GCHQ security had already been made public, some even officially, and in any case the regulations specifically allowed civil servants to comment publicly in a union capacity on matters concerned with working conditions. His comments, and those in the Rue circular, had been echoed almost identically in the Security Commission's 1983 report. For example, the report specifically said that random searches were 'unlikely to frustrate the trained and determined spy'.

On 25 March 1988 Grindley was informed that he had to tell GCHQ management if he intended 'to be away from home overnight or longer'. The letter also specified a further charge against him, namely that he 'participated in a radio programme without authority'. This was a reference to a BBC Radio 4 series, *My Country Right or Wrong*, which consisted of a series of general discussions about the work and lack of accountability of security and intelligence services in Britain and the USA. The government had obtained a High Court injunction against the series, contrary to the advice of Admiral Bill Higgins, secretary of the D Notice Committee, on the grounds of national security. A year later the government dropped its claim, suddenly announcing that the series did not harm national security after all. For the sin of taking part in the programme, Grindley was fined £500. After twenty-seven years of valuable and loyal service, Grindley was finally sacked on 18 November 1988.

They put the letter through my door and I went down and picked it off the mat at about quarter to eight. I was expecting it, of course. I rang up Peter Jones [CCSU Secretary] and went to the GCHQ Union office at Clarence Street – Jack was away that day. There was a lull for a bit in the office and then 'bang'. That was probably the busiest day of my life. At one stage, I was being interviewed by Central TV; there were two radio interviewers waiting, a journalist wanting an interview, and I was six behind on the answerphone.

Grindley believes strongly that GCHQ should be monitored by a parliamentary oversight body:

Nothing should exist in a vacuum. GCHQ is an extremely powerful and secret place. If things went wrong it could be extremely dangerous. There is no lifeline to the world outside now the unions have been banned. To a lot of people there that is one of the things they miss. I bumped into a man in the corridor early in 1986. He as good as grasped me by the lapels and said: 'It's all right for you, you've got your self-respect. I felt I had to sign. Can you tell the people out there how it is for people like me ... It's like we are in a jumbo jet that's been hijacked with the doors locked and we don't know where it's going to.'

But in common with the rest of the sacked union members, Grindley is extremely wary of discussing GCHQ's role and operations. He believes that there have been some changes since 1984 and adds:

I think some of its roles are going to become increasingly unnecessary. I'm not going to expound on this. Since it is a large powerful organization, it won't close down those bits of it that are doing things no longer necessary, and it will always look for new roles to keep its own empire going. This is what a bureaucracy does, isn't it?

Grindley has put his name down for twelve different technical translation agencies. On the day we talked, one had rung him with something about marine engineering. It was the first commission he had had for several months.

Robin Smith says he 'fell into GCHQ' in 1978 after studying physics at university, believing he was joining a Civil Service establishment carrying out research and development 'in the field of communications security'. He joined the Communications Electronics Security Group, responsible for developing cryptographic equipment to protect British diplomatic and military communications. The CESG, originally part of the Post Office, was transferred to GCHQ in 1969 and moved to Cheltenham in 1978, where it now employs about three hundred people at the Benhall site.

Smith says he soon discovered that 'there was a little bit more to GCHQ than I thought', although he did not deal in intelligence. 'I have never seen a piece of intelligence in my life,' he says. In 1985, a year after the union ban, he was assigned to a priority research project which was seriously delayed as a result of staff shortages following the ban. He was then offered a post at the Joint Speech Research Unit, which was moved to Malvern after the ban. Manage-

shortage in this area could be remedied if the JSRU posts were
transferred to the MoD. JSRU's work is not considered as secret as the
rest of GCHQ's operations. But Smith declined the offer, sticking to his
principle that all GCHQ officials in Cheltenham should have the right
to be members of a union.

He joined the IPCS in 1979 at a time of deteriorating industrial
relations throughout the Civil Service. He took part in the one-day
strike on 9 March 1981, and collected strike levies in his corridor. It
was his section which he assumes the government was referring to
when it said that 'whole areas' in GCHQ were shut down.

It was being economical with the truth. It did not matter whether that area
consisted of two people or fifty. Certainly in my division more people were
out than were in for one day and we were shut down. I mean it shuts down
Friday evening to Monday morning every week, bank holidays and so on. It
was non-urgent work. In a project of four years, one day in your research
programme is nothing. We did not get pleas not to go on strike or anything
like that. Divisional administration came round on the Friday to everyone
and said, 'Are you going to be in Monday or not?' and placed a tick next to
those who were. In fact, local management went on strike with us.

On 25 January 1984 a brown envelope appeared on Smith's desk.

Our first reaction was bewilderment before anger set in. Being scientists, we
tend to look at things logically first, and when I looked at it I was trying to
work out what the hell it was all about. I just could not see why they were
doing it. We just downed tools, as it were, for the rest of the day. What
actually hit me more than the actual banning of unions was the withdrawal
of employment protection ... We chatted about it and after a while somebody
said, 'Ah, polygraph' and I thought 'Yes, that's right.'

Smith remained a member of his trade union 'for all the reasons,
civil liberties, the whole lot, and the simple fact of being unable to see
or comprehend why they were doing it'. He became more convinced
as he listened to what he calls the 'wishy-washy' arguments of the
hoverers who eventually took the £1,000 and stayed. Smith, meanwhile, passed two promotion boards to the senior scientific officer
(SSO) grade, but he was told two days after the judgment of the
European Court in Strasbourg that he would not be promoted.
Management delayed telling him for fear that it might in some way
count against its case.

Shortly before he was finally sacked – with GCHQ security
wondering whether they would have to manhandle him out – he was

approached and asked if he was interested in a job with a private company which did contract work for GCHQ, needed his skills and had taken on a former colleague, who had taken the £1,000 and quit GCHQ. The company said they would have liked to have taken him on, but told Smith that there would be embarrassment if they did so.

Looking back, Smith says there were a lot of good people, both moral and competent, working in GCHQ. But he has a different view of the management, describing them as 'gutless' and 'spineless'; 'they would do whatever they are told without question'. Smith, now a full-time IPMS official responsible for recruiting new members, says he had no problems working on communications security, but believes that GCHQ should be made more accountable. 'I suspect there are things which go on there which should not.'

Brian Johnson describes himself and his wife as 'Mr and Mrs Anybody'. He joined the RAF as a technician, following in the footsteps of his father. Then he moved to GCHQ, with which he was already familiar from his time in the RAF, spending much of his time fixing faulty electronic equipment. He first became actively involved in his union, AGSRO, in 1980 when he became the first secretary of the Health and Safety Committee at GCHQ. He voted Conservative in 1979, but soon became thoroughly disillusioned with Civil Service management in general, and GCHQ management in particular. He says he was shocked in 1981 by the way the government unilaterally abandoned the Civil Service's Pay Research Unit, which compared pay in the Civil Service with that of others doing similar work in the private sector. Johnson recalls: 'I became disillusioned between 1979 and 1981. In fact, I was so disillusioned I wrote to Lord Soames [then minister for the Civil Service]. I actually handed in my resignation at that time. Unfortunately senior management talked me out of resigning.'

He, too, dismisses the government's claims about the effect of industrial action in 1981. 'When action was taken, management would announce how many people they needed to cover any important work.' There were no letters from management. There was nothing that caused him concern during that period. He says of the ban:

I did think about it and I tried to fathom out why it was done. The only conclusion I could come to was that it was a political decision, taken by the Thatcher government and that it was the first step towards their obvious hatred of trade unions.

I felt confused about it. I discussed it with my wife. We had a long talk about it and I would even admit I cried about it. To a degree I was surprised. It was a strange feeling at least for a week. There were an awful lot of people feeling the same. I would say there was far more work lost at GCHQ within the first fortnight of the trade union ban announcement than there ever was over industrial action. Workshops came to a standstill. It was all very scary. It was an unreal world.

Among Johnson's hobbies is studying the history of the two world wars:

The thing that upset me most was the feeling that what I was being asked to sign away and be paid for was exactly what those men had given their lives for – freedom and democracy – and I still feel that. To me, the people who died in those conflicts died fighting for what I believed in – that more than anything made it impossible for me to sign. My wife said she understood how I felt and we sat down and worked out that if I got the sack immediately we probably had enough money in the bank to last six months. My wife said we could manage with six months' money and therefore there was only one thing I could do. It is all thanks to her.

Johnson says his family was very supportive. His eldest daughter is married to a GCHQ official. He was not in favour of signing, but had family commitments – it caused no animosity between them. 'I had one particular friend who up until the signing date didn't know what he was going to do. Unfortunately in the end he decided to sign. At no time did he ever try to persuade me to sign. In fact the only people who tried to change my mind were the management.'

Clive Lloyd had left his union, the CSU, as a result of a row with the union's local representative. He signed Option A to protect his job, he says, and he believed that he could not fight since he was no longer a union member. 'Afterwards I felt sick,' he recalls. He says he knew he made the wrong decision. He rejoined the CSU on the day the law lords rejected the unions' appeal. He recalls how a senior GCHQ official came up to him and said how much he admired his decision.

Lloyd, a cypher officer on round-the-clock shift work, says of the 1981 action: 'There was no adverse effect. It was discussed with management way beforehand. We discussed what should be covered and what needed to be covered on the understanding that if there was a national emergency, we would be back in.' Like some of his colleagues, his experience has made him much more cynical: 'I used to be a strong believer that Britons never will be slaves. In fact I watched the Last Night of the Proms last Saturday and they sang *Rule Britannia* and I said to my wife: "that load of crap".'

Despite his bad back and kidney complaint, Lloyd joined the others speaking at meetings and rallies up and down the country. He was elected a Liberal councillor in Cheltenham, and became a minister in the Spiritualist Church. Spiritualism, he says, makes individuals responsible for their actions and they have to work things out for themselves. That gave him a certain strength.

I have to say that what I have appreciated most about the unions is their concern for you as an individual. You do have down days and it's nice sometimes when you get a phone call – or a letter – saying 'how are you?'. That shows the human side of trade unionism. It's not just a question of pay and conditions – it is about brotherhood. You are part of something. We're all in this together.'

7

The aftermath: 1989 to 1991

Workers and employers, without distinction whatsoever, shall have the right to establish and, subject only to the rules of the organisation concerned, to join organisations of their own choosing without previous authorisation.

Article 2, Convention No. 87: Convention concerning freedom of association and protection of the right to organize, International Labour Conference; ratified by the United Kingdom government, 27 June 1949

After the sackings came the long wait for the next general election. It had been six months from the start of the dismissal process – 29 September 1988 – until the last trade unionist was sacked on 7 April 1989. Now the unions were left with little to do but wait. The general election did not have to take place until July 1992 – over three years away. The key task was to maintain GCHQ as a political issue so that it was kept on the agenda of an incoming government. There was no easy or obvious way to achieve this objective. But GCHQ had two advantages. It was an issue that united the TUC – all unions could, indeed had to, say that they supported the right to belong to a trade union. And for the Labour Party, GCHQ was its best bet for a positive union issue. The ban was an unpopular government action in the first place, it would be cheap to restore trade unions to GCHQ and, most importantly, it would not clash with Labour's proposals for legislation covering trade unions.

If GCHQ had become merely symbolic to those on the outside of the campaign, those for whom it was very real did not mind. The effect was the same, the campaign just kept on trundling along. The Roadshow kept on going, and political conferences were used to promote the issue through motions and fringe meetings. The office and the members became expert at finding a GCHQ angle to anything and everything. Whenever GCHQ was mentioned in the news, GCHQ Trade Unions in Cheltenham – mainly staffed by Hart

Mike Grindley in the GCHQ Trade Unions office.

and Grindley – was phoned for a comment. After the sackings there were few big news stories, but they were no longer needed. It was a case of being patient, plugging away, making the most of every little campaigning opportunity.

The approaches to the Civil Service Appeal Board were just such an opportunity – another occasion when the government would be forced to defend its action. The first six appeals to the CSAB were heard on 29 March 1989. The board was made up of three people drawn from a panel of trade union and management nominees, plus a chair. The majority of union members were represented by Alan Shute, Assistant General Secretary of the NUCPS, and Jenny Thurston, Assistant General Secretary of the IPMS. Management's case was put in a very low-key, matter-of-fact style by Director-designate John Adye.

In the CSAB's report there was strong criticism of GCHQ management's discrimination against union members, particularly over pay. But, by a 2–1 decision, the appeals were turned down. The board members were clearly influenced by the decision of the House of Lords in 1984 that the ban was legal. The majority argued that the government's refusal to accept ILO rulings – even though it was a signatory to the relevant ILO conventions – did not mean that the dismissals were unfair. The board, as many had expected, had looked at the procedures and the technicalities, but it would not consider whether the ban and the sackings were right or wrong. With its future in some doubt anyway, it was probably more than its life was worth to challenge the government's decision.

The appeals of the 'rejoiners' were heard on 6 July 1989. This time Lanning and Thurston did battle with the much more argumentative Peter Little, John Adye now having succeeded Sir Peter Marychurch as Director of GCHQ. The appeal board once again upheld the dismissals by a 2–1 verdict. But it did express 'concern' that the rejoiners had not been properly compensated when compared with the other union members. This led to a minor victory when, later in the year, GCHQ offered them additional *ex gratia* payments. It still did not amount to full compensation under Civil Service terms, but it was the first time that GCHQ had been forced to admit that it had perhaps done something wrong.

Another body which consistently said the government was wrong over GCHQ – and which was just as consistently ignored – was the International Labour Organization. Based in Geneva, the ILO has been a specialized agency of the United Nations since the Second World War, and as such its primary function has been to build up a code of international labour law and practice. ILO standards are established by the annual International Labour Conference in the form of conventions and recommendations. If a state ratifies a convention, it undertakes to maintain national law in full conformity with its terms.

In early February 1984, the TUC had written to the Director-

General of the ILO requesting he 'convey to the Committee on Freedom of Association of the Governing Body as urgently as possible this complaint by the General Council against the British Government for having breached Convention 87.' The complaint went on to spell out the details of the government's actions and the unions' response and concluded: 'The TUC regards the action with the most grave concern as removing the most basic trade union right of all in Britain where working people formed the first trade unions in the world in the eighteenth and nineteenth centuries.' It was a concern to be shared by representatives from around the world, used to condemning many totalitarian countries but not the UK, the birthplace of trade unionism. Apart from real concern on the GCHQ issue, there was fear about the impact the action would have on the ILO's standing. If the right to join a union could not be retained in Britain, what hope did the ILO have with other countries? It was a question that remained unanswered as complaints about the Thatcher government queued up to be heard.

The unions recognized that the weakness of the ILO procedures is that they rely on moral suasion, that they do not have the force of law. Their strength is that they are obligations voluntarily entered into: certainly the government has fought mightily to fend off international condemnation by the ILO.

As it had done throughout the various GCHQ hearings, the government defended its action on the grounds of national security. In practice the main issue the Committee on Freedom of Association had to decide was whether the complaint was covered by Convention No. 87 or, as the government maintained, by Convention No. 151.

Convention No. 87, Article 2, states that 'workers and employers, without distinction whatsoever, shall have the right to establish and, subject only to the rules of the organisations concerned, to join organisations of their own choosing without previous authorisation'. The only exemptions to this, permitted by Article 9 of the convention, are the armed forces and the police. To come within the scope of these exemptions the workers concerned have to be recognized under national law or regulations as part of the army or the police. The committee concluded that 'this does not appear to be the case in relation to civilian employees at GCHQ' – a view directly contrary to the one taken by the European Commission of Human Rights. The United Kingdom was the first country to ratify the convention, which came into effect in 1948.

Convention No. 151 is a later convention specifically concerned with public employees. It has a wider exemption clause than Convention No. 87. Article 1, Paragraph 2, of Convention No. 151 states that employees engaged in work of a 'highly confidential nature' could be excluded from the right to associate. If the government could get the GCHQ case covered by this convention then it would be on firmer ground.

Unfortunately for the government, Article 1, Paragraph 1, states unequivocally that Convention No. 151 'applies to all persons employed by public authorities, to the extent that more favourable provisions in other international labour Conventions are not applicable to them'. The committee concluded that Convention No. 87 did apply, that GCHQ employees were not excluded from its provisions. As a result it:

- urged the government to reconsider its position on the usefulness of further negotiations;
- reiterated that workers at GCHQ are entitled to join the organization of their own choosing in accordance with Article 2 of the convention.

This decision, taken in 1985, was not accepted by the government, which sought to challenge it, in 1986, through the Committee of Experts on the Application of Conventions and Recommendations. This senior body of legal experts upheld the decision of the Committee on Freedom of Association. The outcome of both committees' considerations of the issue was reported to the annual conference of the governing body in 1987. In accepting the report the conference recognized that a breach of international law had been committed.

There is no real enforcement procedure for the ILO conventions. However, for what are regarded as gross or persistent violations of the conventions there is a special form of condemnation, the 'special paragraph procedure'. In June 1989 a report by its Committee of Experts listed eight abuses of employment rights by the British government. In relation to GCHQ the Report said: 'The Committee notes with regret that 13 employees at GCHQ have now been dismissed because of their refusal to give up membership of the union of their choice.' It went on to urge the government to reconsider its position on negotiations with the unions, and reaffirmed that workers at GCHQ were entitled to join the organization of their choice in accordance with Article 2 of ILO Convention No. 87.

The ILO issued a unanimous statement which concluded with the hope that the next report by the British government would contain 'decisive development in the situation in compliance with the convention'. Later on in the conference, the government narrowly avoided being included in a special paragraph in the report. The vote was 60,398 to 56,845 against naming Britain in this way, with 9,555 abstentions. The British government had put heavy pressure on its allies to vote against the special paragraph procedure. Nevertheless, it came under attack from a wide range of countries including West European and Commonwealth representatives. For procedural reasons the issue was not considered by the ILO in 1990.

One of the British government's responses to the charge that it is denying staff the right to belong to a trade union is that they can join the staff association, the Government Communications Staff Federation. The GCSF was now claiming to represent over 50 per cent of GCHQ staff. But ever since its inception it had suffered from a serious defect – how could it prove that it was independent, that it was a real trade union and not a sweetheart organization?

It was an understandable desire. Many of those involved in the staff association had been genuinely persuaded that it was better to have some organization to represent staff than no organization at all. They felt they were doing a necessary and honest job, and the constant jibes must have grated. Perhaps in response to this frustration, the GCSF set out on the path to try and prove that it was independent. In the process it proved that it was not.

Trade unions in Britain are regulated by a Certification Officer who, though appointed by the government, has independent status. Virtually any organization representing employees can register and be placed on a list of trade unions. There are no hard-and-fast criteria – it is a bit like buying a business name, anyone can do it. But there is a separate procedure whereby trade unions can apply for a certificate of independence from the Certification Officer. This is more rigorous: applicants have to demonstrate that they are independent of management. GCSF went out to try and show it could satisfy this test.

It is unlikely that the initiative was encouraged by GCHQ management or the government, since it contained the seeds of a catch-22 situation. If the GCSF failed to obtain the certificate then it would undermine the government's case. If it succeeded and genuinely demonstrated that it was an independent trade union then surely it would have to be banned! And, if it was not banned, why could staff not join other independent trade unions, such as those that the government had banned back in 1984? At the disciplinary hearings Peter Little had implied that there was a policy decision not to try to obtain a certificate of independence for GCSF. 'The TUC and CCSU would vote against it,' he remarked.

In fact, neither the TUC nor the CCSU has a vote in the proceedings, but the CCSU was entitled to submit its views on the GCSF application. This the CCSU duly did. The submission explained the history of the ban and how management had been instrumental in setting up the staff association. CCSU made three key points:

- The GCSF constitution prevented it from affiliating to any political or trade union organization.
- All GCSF officers were GCHQ employees on secondment.
- The option form which all staff were required to sign – on pain of dismissal – included the following clause: 'I understand, however, that I may join a Departmental Staff Association approved for the time being by the Director GCHQ.' In other words, GCSF was under management control.

On 18 December 1989 the Certification Officer, Matthew Wake, rejected the GCSF's application. He said he need look no further than the GN 100/84 circular and the conditions of service of GCHQ staff. These made it clear that they could not belong to a union or staff association other than one approved by the Director. He rejected the GCSF argument that the Director's approval could not be withdrawn. He also made it clear that there were other aspects of GCSF's make-up which cast doubt upon its independence under the law, but which at this stage did not need to be considered fully – these included the status of the GCSF officers, who were dependent on management for their continued employment.

Decisions of the Certification Officer can be taken to the Employment Appeals Tribunal, which has equivalent status to the High Court, and ultimately to the House of Lords. The GCSF has lodged an appeal, but at the time of writing no date has been set for a hearing. Not content with an appeal, the GCSF also sought to enhance its case by changing its constitution to allow it to affiliate to outside organizations. In October 1990 the head of the Civil Service, Sir Robin Butler, expressed concern about the rule change and about GCSF's training and printing links with the EETPU, which had been expelled from the TUC but was affiliated to the Labour Party.

It fell to Sir Geoffrey Howe, then Leader of the House, to make a statement on the issue to the Commons. It was almost his last act as a member of the government before he discovered that there was a conflict of loyalty between being an independently minded person and a member of the Thatcher cabinet. As he said in the speech which paved the way for the overthrow of Thatcher in November 1990, perhaps he should have realized this earlier. Seven years earlier!

Howe's statement almost certainly put an end to GCSF's claim to independence. He said: 'There are no formal links between the GCSF and any other trade union. It was made clear to the GCSF from the outset, by the management of GCHQ, that affiliation to any outside body was not acceptable and that remains the position.'

The danger and irony of the EETPU trying to steal a march had not escaped the notice of the Civil Service unions. Liaison followed by full affiliation to the EETPU might be a lifeline for the GCSF to try to set itself up as an independent union after an election. This led the Civil Service unions to ask the Labour Party what its attitude would be. It was a potentially awkward question since the EETPU was affiliated to the Labour Party and the Civil Service unions were not. The slightly ambiguous answer came from Roy Hattersley, Deputy Leader of the Labour Party, when he addressed the annual conference of the NUCPS in Blackpool in May 1990.

Hattersley first promised that a Labour government would return full trade union rights to GCHQ staff. He then went on to say: 'For my own part I have no doubt that when unionism is restored to GCHQ the unions which ought to have the first opportunity to recruit members are the unions which were organized there when the ban was first imposed.'

Suspicions about the EETPU were not the only motive for the unions to get organized properly. If the unions were to recruit members and get back to their previous levels – a modest 58 per cent overall – then they would have to overcome a number of obstacles. Many – about 40 per cent – of the staff now at GCHQ were recruited after 1984. GCHQ had a retirement bulge during the 1980s – many of its staff, especially radio grades, had been recruited in the years immediately following the Second World War.

The climate and atmosphere in GCHQ has been antipathetic – perhaps actively hostile – to unions for a long time. Doubts will remain about whether joining a union is a good career move. Management, and possibly the GCSF, will oppose the return of trade unions. The Security Service and the US administration will not be keen. Staff themselves will need a lot of convincing – to them unions will be strangers from a strange land. Even those former members still working in GCHQ might be made uncomfortable by the return of their unions.

When the ban was imposed, there were six non-industrial and a full range of industrial unions in GCHQ. All GCHQ staff are now considered to be non-industrial, so it is unlikely that the industrial unions will return. Among the non-industrial unions, two mergers have taken place since 1984: IPCS and AGSRO are now IPMS, and CSU and SCPS have become NUCPS. NUCPS and CPSA have discussed the idea of a merger, but have never quite made it to the altar. IPMS currently plans to become part of a wider federation with groups outside the Civil Service. Confused? Not half as much as GCHQ staff might be if they were faced with such an array.

The need to be well organized prompted the Civil Service unions to see if they could agree on one union returning to GCHQ to represent all staff. It would have made a lot of organizational sense, but the suggestion raised sentimental and political issues as well as straightforward rivalries. The unions could not agree on this: four unions – NUCPS, IPMS, FDA and CPSA – will be going back. Hopefully the unions will remember that they have fought together to restore union rights at GCHQ, not simply to participate in the glory of the return.

When unions return to GCHQ – in whatever shape and form – it will be an intriguing meeting, a reunion of lukewarm friends after a period of eight or more years. But before any meeting can take place, one further change is necessary – a change of government. This seemed closer towards the end of 1990 when the two people who had, above all, engineered the ban – Margaret Thatcher and Geoffrey Howe – conspired to bring about their mutual downfall.

The GCHQ ban came up for the fifth consecutive year at the ILO annual conference in Geneva in June 1991. The government had lobbied furiously in an attempt to tone down criticism of the GCHQ union ban, but to no avail. Although there was again widespread support for naming the British government in the ILO's special paragraph procedure, however, Ken Thomas, the former CPSA General Secretary and now the TUC's ILO representative, took a tactical decision. It was better, he believed, to attract even broader support for a statement attacking the government. His analysis proved correct.

At the end of a three-hour debate of the ILO's Committee on the Application of Standards in a packed conference hall, four hundred ILO delegates – from governments, employers' organizations and trade unions – voted unanimously in favour of a resolution which contained the strongest criticism yet of the British government's action. The delegates expressed 'deep concern' at the lack of dialogue between the government and the unions, they regretted that they were obliged 'once again to request the Government to have discussions in the shortest possible time with the trade unions with a view to finding a solution to the problem which would be in full conformity with the Convention', and they expressed the hope that the ILO's Committee of Experts would be able next year to report substantial progress in Britain's conformation with the ILO convention on the right of freedom of association.

During the debate speaker after speaker – union representatives from as far afield as Panama, Poland and Uganda, government representatives from the United Arab Emirates, Norway and the Netherlands, employers' representatives from all over the world – criticized the British government. For the government, Peter Brannen, the Department of Employment official responsible for international relations, was reduced to arguing that, if there had been a breach of the convention, it was of a purely technical kind. He stated: '*No one had been murdered, tortured, raped or jailed without trial*' (emphasis added).

What was most significant was that government representatives from the USA and Australia – two of Britain's senior partners in the secret signals intelligence pact involving GCHQ – spoke out in favour of the resolution criticizing the government for not negotiating with the unions with a view to overturning the ban. 'The strength and the moral authority of the Committee', the US government representative said, 'were derived from the fact that it operated on the basis of dialogue and consensus.'

A few days later the new Prime Minister, John Major, replied to a letter from Norman Willis, TUC General Secretary. Willis had written in his letter in May that if the government was really so convinced of its interpretation of international law then it should take the issue to the International Court of Justice in The Hague. He appealed to the Prime Minister to invite Sir Robin Butler, head of the Civil Service, to reopen talks. On 25 June Major, rehearsing the old canards about national security and the 1984 SCPS and CPSA conference votes against 'no-strike' agreements, replied that the unions could raise the issue at their periodic meetings with Butler. 'But', he added, 'I am afraid I find it difficult to see that any useful purpose would be served by such discussions.'

By the end of 1991 few of the original participants in the GCHQ dispute were left. The most enduring were the union members themselves. It was now over two years since the sackings and nearly eight years since the ban, and still the waiting was not over. First they had to wait for John Major to have the nerve to call an election; then they had to wait for the result.

8

The future

It is to their eternal credit that when their integrity and their patriotism were insulted, when their jobs and civil liberties were threatened, they stood out and are still standing out.
Neil Kinnock at the GCHQ Trade Unions fifth anniversary rally,
28 January 1989

They can't do that, surely? These were many people's first thoughts on hearing of the government's decision to ban unions in GCHQ: the unions are recognized; people must have the right to belong to a union if they want to; they cannot sack someone just for being a union member.

What the government's announcement revealed was just how threadbare the rights of trade unions and the individual are. The government acted solely on the basis of executive power, no legislation was required, yet there appeared to be nothing that could be done legally to constrain them. The very first legal advice obtained on 30 January 1984 concluded: 'the only support that can be offered to your members is that if they decline to sign the forms the government may have to think again if a sufficient number of them remain steadfast'. There was no obvious and instant legal remedy.

At the time of the ban the unions represented 58 per cent of all staff. Staff were officially encouraged to join the appropriate trade union, and unions had been representing staff in GCHQ since 1947. The easiest part of the process was to 'de-recognize' the unions: that is, to withdraw their rights collectively to represent and negotiate for their members in GCHQ.

In order to sweep away all the collective bargaining arrangements the government simply had to write to the unions informing them that they were no longer recognized. Although the English courts considered the question of whether or not the unions should have been consulted (see Chapter 5), there are no statutory provisions covering the recognition of trade unions. The government or any other employer is free not to 'recognize' or to de-recognize any union, whatever the number of employees who are members. Section 11 of the 1975 Employment Protection Act had contained some complex and protracted recognition procedures. But even these were of no help in the GCHQ situation as they had been repealed in 1980.

What about the rights of individuals? Are these any better than those of unions? The Employment Protection (Consolidation) Act 1978 says that employees can claim reinstatement and compensation if they have been unfairly dismissed. Any employer must give reasons for the dismissal and show that the action was reasonable. Under the Act, dismissal for being a member of an independent trade union or wanting to take part in its activities is automatically deemed to be unfair. Individuals can therefore be protected if they are dismissed for:

- being a member of an independent trade union, or proposing to join one;
- taking part in its activities 'at any appropriate time'; or
- refusing to join a trade union that is not certified as independent.

If individuals are pressurized to such an extent that they are forced to resign, they can claim constructive dismissal. If they remain at work, they can claim compensation for action short of dismissal – victimization – if they can show it was intended:

- to prevent or deter them from exercising the rights outlined above;
- to penalize them for doing so; or
- to compel them to join a non-independent union.

These rights are indeed fundamental. But they have two serious limitations. Although dismissal for union membership is an 'inadmissible reason', it is very difficult to prove. The burden of proof is on the individual to show that union membership or union activities were the reason for dismissal. The other limitation lies in the remedies.

An industrial tribunal can order reinstatement, re-engagement or compensation if a union member has been unfairly dismissed. If the order for reinstatement or re-engagement is ignored then extra compensation can be awarded. The employer cannot ultimately be forced to take anyone back, merely to pay more for not doing so. In cases of victimization, compensation is in effect the only remedy.

So in British law there is no positive, enforceable right to belong to a union, just provisions aimed at dissuading the employer from preventing union membership. In the circumstances of GCHQ, with thousands of potential cases, this might have deterred a less intransigent employer. But the government had an ace up its sleeve. Section 138 of the Employment Protection Act covers 'Crown employment'. Clause (4) provides that:

For the purposes of this section, Crown employment does not include any employment in respect of which there is in force a certificate issued by or on behalf of a Minister of the Crown certifying that employment of a description specified in the certificate, or the employment of a particular person so specified, is (or, at a time specified in the certificate, was) required to be excepted from this section *for the purpose of safeguarding national security*; and any document purporting to be a certificate so issued shall be received in evidence and shall, unless the contrary is proved, be deemed to be such a certificate [emphasis added].

This meant that the employment protection legislation applied to Crown employees (except for the armed forces, who were a separate case), unless they were excluded on grounds of national security. To so exclude them, the minister has to issue a certificate. It was this provision which Sir Geoffrey Howe used, at a stroke taking all GCHQ employees outside the scope of the Employment Protection Act and its limited protections for trade union members. It was for the loss of these rights that GCHQ staff were paid £1,000, less tax.

The final grounds for individuals to consider were their conditions of service – their contract with the employer. Did this not give employees the contractual right to belong to a union? It did, but the government had thought of this too. GN 100/84 unilaterally changed the conditions of service of all staff and, as we have seen, rendered them liable for dismissal if they failed to comply with its provisions. Was this not a breach of contract, or at least against the common law principle of natural justice? As a defence against this – before the courts suggested it use the defence of national security – the government relied on the ancient device of an Order in Council. This derives its power from the royal prerogative and is essentially legislation on behalf of the Crown. It does not have to go through

Parliament. One of the things that can be covered by Orders in Council is the conditions of service of civil servants.

It remains the case that it is not illegal for employees at GCHQ to be members of a trade union. However, if they join one they are in breach of their revised conditions of service, can be dismissed for the offence and are not allowed to take their case to an industrial tribunal. Nor are they entitled to any compensation for the loss of their job. To achieve this, all the government had to do was write to the unions withdrawing their recognition, sign the necessary certificates taking away their protective rights, and issue an Order in Council changing the staff's conditions of service. There is not one single statutory right to prevent this and, as we saw in Chapter 5, there is no common law remedy either.

The labyrinthine world of the International Labour Organization is remote and has had no direct influence on the government's behaviour over GCHQ, but it is not without influence elsewhere. When the European Community decided to draw up its own Social Charter, more correctly known as the 'Community Charter of Fundamental Social Rights', it had to have regard to the ILO conventions of which the EC countries are signatories.

Article 11(1) of the Charter states that employers and workers shall have 'the right of association in order to constitute professional organisations or trade unions of their choice for the defence of their economic and social interests'. The Action Plan associated with the Charter asserts that 'the right to freedom of association and collective bargaining exists in all member states of the Community'. This is despite the ILO's condemnations of the British government. It goes on to state that the responsibility for the implementation of these principles 'rests with the Member States in accordance with national traditions and practice'.

The Social Charter is part of the 'social dimension' being considered by the EC in parallel with the 'free market' to be introduced in 1992. The British government adamantly resists the Social Charter, arguing that it will undermine all the good work it has done, particularly in relation to curbing trade union powers.

Britain's EC partners, endeavouring to persuade the British government to accept the Social Charter, have made substantial concessions. As we have seen, international law is a battle of exemption or 'safeguard' clauses. General principles are easily agreed – to whom they are applied is bitterly fought. One of the concessions sought and obtained by Whitehall was on the definition of which groups of workers would be excluded. Charter Article 14 now reads: 'Each member state shall determine the conditions and rights for the application of articles on freedom of association, collective bargaining, and the right to strike to the armed forces, police and *civil servants*' (emphasis added).

Allowing for the possible exclusion of civil servants in itself offends the principle confirmed in the GCHQ case at the ILO, namely that freedom of association applies to civil servants. The government clearly had the GCHQ case in mind in seeking this concession. Whatever the strengths and weaknesses of the Social Charter, it does not provide an easy long-term remedy for the staff of GCHQ.

This has been demonstrated further by the difficulties the GCHQ union members have run into with a petition they took to the European Parliament. Before the concessions on the Social Charter there was a good chance that the case would be debated in the European Parliament. Now, however, the government's action is not in obvious contravention of the Charter. Its chances of further progress, not in itself important as it was mainly a campaigning venture not a legal one, depend on arguments over who is and who is not a civil servant. Since practice varies considerably throughout Europe as to whether or not groups such as teachers or postal workers are civil servants, it is possible that some general principles will have to be established. It cannot be all public servants; should it be just those senior staff who work closely with government, or everyone a country calls a civil servant?

To rely on this arcane argument would make clutching at straws seem a sensible policy. For GCHQ trade unionists there is no European cavalry waiting to come to the rescue. The ILO might condemn the government, but the European Convention on Human Rights did not protect them and the EC is extremely unlikely to be a strong ally. The solution – if there is to be one – remains this side of the Channel.

The Liberal Democrats have been consistent supporters of the GCHQ cause. They might still have an important role to play in restoring trade union rights to GCHQ. This could be one condition for supporting a minority Labour government. The Conservative Party has changed its leader, but not its policy over trade unions or

GCHQ. The main hope for the unions and GCHQ trade unionists lies in a Labour government.

Tony Blair, the young and enthusiastic shadow spokesperson on employment, told the 1990 GCHQ Rally in Cheltenham that 'the first act of a Labour government' will be to restore trade unions to GCHQ. Leaving aside the formal position that it would be the responsibility of the Foreign Secretary to implement the decision and that the following year he said 'one of the first acts will be ...', it would certainly make a lot of sense politically.

GCHQ has been a popular trade union issue – people have supported the notion that the freedom to join a trade union is one Britain should have, whether or not they personally want to belong to one or agree always with what trade unions do. The unions themselves have united around GCHQ as a common cause, seeing the ban as an attack on their fundamental right to exist. Support for the restoration of trade union rights at GCHQ has been a consistent thread of TUC policy. The miners, Wapping, Silent Night – many of the long-running union disputes – have come and gone, but seven years later the GCHQ campaign continues.

If an incoming Labour government was looking for a single issue to show good faith to the trade union movement, GCHQ would be it. Restoration of union rights would, at a stroke, fulfil a pledge; it requires no legislation and it has no adverse repercussions for its policy on trade union law. Just as trade union rights were removed administratively, so they can be restored in the same way. Three simple acts would be sufficient:

1. Change the conditions of service of all GCHQ staff restoring their right to belong to a trade union.
2. Cancel the certificates issued under the Employment Protection Act, giving back to GCHQ staff its protections.
3. Recognize the appropriate independent national trade union(s) to represent and negotiate on behalf of GCHQ staff.

None of these acts requires legislation, but each has problems associated with it.

It was reported in *Warning Signal* that, when visiting the Earls Court station as a newly appointed Director of GCHQ, John Adye – when asked to comment on the latest opinion polls and the prospect of a Labour government – said that whatever the government trade

Neil Kinnock, addressing the fifth anniversary rally, pledges that the next Labour government will restore trade union rights at GCHQ. Also on the platform, left to right, are Tony Christopher, former General Secretary of the Inland Revenue Staff Federation, Mike Grindley, Paddy Ashdown, leader of the Liberal Democrats, and Leslie Christie of the NUCPS.

unions will not set foot inside GCHQ again. Should Labour win at the next election, it will be an interesting test of principle and commitment on the part of both Adye and the Labour Party to see what happens. Both pledges cannot be right, and in a democracy you would expect the government to prevail.

Putting aside the democratic and constitutional impropriety of his attitude, Adye was referring to the campaign that will be waged by GCHQ management and Whitehall. With echoes of *Yes, Minister*, new ministers will be initiated into the secret world of the intelligence services, the high-tech world of GCHQ. There will be top-secret briefings, special damage assessment of the industrial action – and in addition the American card will be played. It will be a seductive and persuasive campaign, and one which management is obviously quite confident of winning. It will be a major test of a Labour government's resolve to show that it is prepared to assert its democratic authority and insist that trade unions are restored.

Assuming that this test is withstood – political expediency is a potent weapon – restoring the conditions of service of staff will not repair the damage that has been done to the lives and careers of those affected by the ban. Those sacked will need to be offered reinstatement. Wages, salaries, pensions and direct financial losses will have to be made good. Consideration will need to be given to the impact on individuals and their families, to lost promotions and career opportunities. However judged, seven or eight years is a long time out of a working life. How this compensation is handled, and whether it covers just those sacked or all those who refused to leave their union, will be matters for discussion. But the principle of seeking to remedy the harm done should not be. For those involved, the return of their rights will probably be enough; for the government it should not be.

Cancelling the certificates signed by Sir Geoffrey Howe will give back the limited rights that existed before the ban. It will not, however, prevent similar action being taken again, at some future date, by administrative action. To prevent this, the Employment Protection Act would have to be brought in line with ILO Convention No. 87. In this way any future government wanting to turn the clock back would have to change legislation, not just declare its decision. There would also be some value in trying to improve the EC Social Charter, so that there is an international fall-back with adequate force to restrain a future government.

There is the wider question of whether or not the protections for the freedom of association are strong enough – the example of GCHQ and the practice of the last ten years indicate that they are not. The solution to the problem lies in the debate about trade union rights and general legislation. The lesson of GCHQ is not to leave any holes for a government to creep through. There is a strong argument for a positive right to belong to a union, and the issue will be how it is enforced.

Restoring the appropriate, independent national trade union is not as easy as removing it. As the world has moved on and there have been mergers among the unions and changes to GCHQ's pay structure, the unions will have to decide exactly how recognition is restored. There is much to be said for management and the unions reducing the number of unions recognized in GCHQ. This is a problem for the unions to resolve – the current debate is not about which union represents staff, but about whether any union is allowed to.

A more substantial problem is the staff association. Set up by management, it has now been run by GCHQ staff for over five years and is reported to have about 50 per cent of staff in membership. Whether these are former union members or not is irrelevant, as are the motives of those who have tried to run it. The problem with the staff association is not who its members are or who runs it, but its lack of independence. Its very existence will be a problem to a new government, and for the unions it will be a constraint on their ability to reorganize. A prolonged membership battle is probably not desirable for either staff or management.

The objective set should be an orderly return to trade union bargaining, while still allowing individual staff the choice of joining a union or not. One possibility, which would not be liked by either the unions or the staff association, is to make recognition conditional on negotiating a transfer of engagements – the technical term for a takeover of one union by another. There could be a period of overlap during which the unions and the staff association would be expected to negotiate terms for transferring staff association members to the union(s). Co-operation would be the price both parties would be expected to pay. For the unions a failure to co-operate in negotiating fair arrangements could put at risk recognition. For the staff association a failure to co-operate would mean a complete withdrawal of recognition and a loss of what they had built up.

Whatever method is agreed, an orderly transition or a free-for-all, the biggest problem will not be the unions or the staff association, but the GCHQ management. It was GCHQ management which said that unions should be banned. It was GCHQ management that implemented it – the present Director, John Adye, signed GN 100/84. There will be many, including GCHQ staff, who will not believe and trust the same management fairly and honestly to implement the reintroduction of trade unions. There will remain a fear that membership of a trade union will be a constraint on career progression, that there will be a covert policy of dissuading staff from rejoining. There is also the fact that GCHQ will have been without trade unions for over eight years, that the culture will be a de-unionized culture. Many staff will have been recruited since the ban and therefore will never have worked in a GCHQ where trade unions operated.

To overcome these problems and genuinely to restore something akin to the status quo prior to the ban will require a massive change of heart by GCHQ management. One way to test this would be to require GCHQ management to co-operate with a programme of positive action in favour of trade union membership. This might involve allowing access to GCHQ staff in a controlled way, but at an unprecedented level, including allowing time off for trade union education courses. Management could be given a target of restoring trade union membership back to its 1984 level. In the context of the positive encouragement of trade unions, management should be allowed to negotiate a disputes and arbitration procedure with the unions. This could include safeguards for genuine essential services. But it should be a balanced agreement, freely entered into and democratically endorsed by GCHQ staff. It might pick up some ideas from the draft CCSU agreement, but that agreement should be regarded as history – it was rejected by the government and it was also proposed under the duress of the union ban.

It might be that a management so implicated in the policy and committed to the principle of a ban on trade unions inside GCHQ could not accept and implement such a programme. In this case, it could do the honourable thing and resign.

The final question is whether there should be statutory arrangements covering the granting and withdrawal of trade union recognition. In the 1991 GCHQ Anniversary Lecture, sponsored by the FDA, Brenda Dean (then General Secretary of the print union SOGAT 82) suggested picking up a proposal floated by Professor Keith Ewing of King's College, London. She described the proposal as worthy of closer attention.

Under Ewing's proposal, individuals would have the right to union representation regardless of the level of membership:

- With 10 per cent support a union could require the employer to provide deduction of union subscriptions from pay and other appropriate facilities for union representatives.
- With 20 per cent support a union would acquire rights to be consulted on certain issues.
- With 50 per cent support a union would have representation and bargaining rights on behalf of its members.

Other issues remain to be resolved, such as enforcement of any recognition arrangements and whether such an approach would encourage de-recognition when membership fell below certain levels. The point of referring to this debate is that, in the context of

GCHQ, the objective is not simply to restore the right to belong to a trade union to GCHQ staff. It is also to ensure that such action can never be taken again, at GCHQ or anywhere else.

From the very beginning, it was clear that the government – or, to be more accurate, Mrs Thatcher and some of her advisers – considered the ban on trade union membership as of little moment; no more significant, perhaps, than fiddling around with the structure of Whitehall, or deciding on a new by-pass. They could not grasp the elementary fact that it was a matter of taking away fundamental civil rights by the use of outdated, absolute power and without any reference to Parliament. The government hoisted the flag of 'national security' and the courts – including the European Commission of Human Rights – backed away. The government got away with it, at a price, and for a time: for how long, we still do not know.

The GCHQ union ban, and the way the government handled it, is considered by many as a wretched chapter in the chronicle of the Thatcher administration, the first true indication of the kind of government over which she presided. The many who found the ban abhorrent included ministers, MPs and senior civil servants. They accepted it, some of them sycophantically, some cynically. Many GCHQ staff were presented by the government with an outrageous choice: loyalty to their conscience or to their jobs. That was no real conflict of loyalties; rather it was a conflict between principle and pragmatism. That the flag of opposition continues to fly is a tribute to those few, too few, individuals who never gave up.

Their actions, their speeches, the letters they wrote to *Warning Signal* and the national press, are testimony to the anguish they suffered and the pressure they were forced to confront in standing up for their basic rights, as individuals have done throughout history. The least any government – indeed, the whole country – owes them is the restoration of those rights. Those few who resisted the appalling pressures placed on them to surrender their union membership, and who were finally the victims of vindictive sackings, established a bridgehead preventing the government from taking similar action in the public sector. But the story of the GCHQ union ban, and the lessons we can draw from it, are about much more than that. The ban raises the whole question of the rights of individuals against the state, and of how the courts shy away from challenging an executive which cries 'national security!'.

A new government must resist the pressure it will certainly face from Whitehall, GCHQ management and the USA to maintain the status quo. That government must argue that if the United States wants to maintain its intelligence links with GCHQ – ties which Washington values greatly – then it can do so on British terms.

The restoration of human rights at GCHQ would set the tone of a new administration. It would be more than a fulfilment of a pledge to those GCHQ staff who refused to give up their trade union rights. It would be a symbolic message that a new priority would be given to protecting civil rights. It could also demonstrate a new commitment to calling government to account. No part of the executive, or area of activity by agents of the state, should be immune from parliamentary scrutiny. As Stansfield Turner, the former CIA Director, says in his book, *Secrecy and Democracy*:

It is not good enough for intelligence agencies to be accountable to the Executive. There is a need for a responsible body outside the executive branch to make sure that the Executive is not over-enthusiastic in seeking to obtain information important to the national interest. Over-enthusiasm, as we have seen, may lead to excess.

Democratic oversight would help to restore public confidence in, as well as understanding of, intelligence agencies – and, indeed, GCHQ does have a proper role, especially in verifying internationally approved arms control agreements. By the same token, the need for accountability is even more essential as intelligence agencies, as well as military commanders, put themselves at the mercy of increasingly sophisticated technology.

It is becoming more difficult for CIA officers at their desks in Langley, Virginia, or GCHQ analysts in Cheltenham, to interpret the information which sophisticated technology provides. Too much blind faith, too many resources, have been put into SIGINT technology – hoarded by GCHQ – at the expense of old-fashioned HUMINT: human intelligence supplied by individual judgement. As we have seen during so many crises, including the Gulf War, SIGINT may give you the enemy's capability; it will not give you its intentions. But even these judgements should not be left to individuals who have a monopoly of select information but who live in a secret world and are not held to account. They know they need not share a knowledge which gives them power without responsibility.

Their power and influence ranges from the exotic – the management and manipulation of international crises – to the mundane – the vetting and surveillance of ordinary men and women. The role of those working in intelligence agencies by definition involves the use of covert means to intrude upon privacy and individual freedoms: this is one of the ironies of the story of the GCHQ union ban. GCHQ holds information not only on those whom it may regard as genuine threats to 'national security', but also on individual citizens simply because of their positions or political beliefs.

It is an uncomfortable reality that democracies, as well as dictatorships and authoritarian regimes, are going to have security and intelligence services, if only to safeguard the democratic system and their citizens against physical threats – notably terrorism. But experience has shown that, without a robust system of independent oversight, the gathering of 'intelligence' is wide open to abuse. Intelligence agencies are unable to resist the temptation to indulge in activities that have no place in a democracy. According to our democratic tradition, it is up to Parliament to rein in an overmighty executive, and for the courts, applying the principles of common law, to strike a balance between conflicting interests. During the litigation over the government's attempt to suppress *Spycatcher*, the memoirs of the former MI5 officer Peter Wright, Mr Justice Scott commented in the High Court on the government's argument that the courts had no role in adjudicating disputes about the disclosure of information concerning the security and intelligence services:

No question of a balance between the proper requirements of national security, on the one hand, and of freedom of speech or of the press, on the other hand, arose. I found myself unable to escape the reflection that the absolute protection of the security services that Sir Robert [Armstrong, the government's chief witness in the *Spycatcher* case] was contending for could not be achieved this side of the Iron Curtain.

The observation is all the more pertinent as that curtain drops and the cold war is over.

The government fought, and lost, the *Spycatcher* case in the civil courts. But it tried to repair the damage in its new Official Secrets Act, a statute which introduces into criminal law an absolute, life-long duty of confidentiality on members and former members of the security and intelligence services. There is no 'public interest defence' which allows an individual to claim loyalty to the general good, to the country as a whole, above loyalty to that dangerously vague concept called 'the Crown'. The argument over the GCHQ ban was not directly concerned with this – indeed, as we have seen, the GCHQ union members maintained a discipline which would have been the pride of any Trappist monk. Yet the issues are related: the government says 'trust us' to ensure that intelligence agencies, including GCHQ, do not abuse their power. How can one trust a government to protect our freedoms if it deprives of those freedoms the very people who are supposed to safeguard them on our behalf?

Special laws may be needed for the intelligence agencies. But it is not for the government or the agencies themselves to pick and choose when the law applies to them. A balance has to be struck, but for Parliament, the courts and the large majority of GCHQ staff to acquiesce in a government's diktat is unacceptable in any democracy. The story of the ban raises fundamental constitutional issues, including – given the ruling of the European Commission of Human Rights – the kind of rights that should be introduced in Britain. But no law will be enough until we have learned how to control technology, democratically and effectively.

Appendix 1

The letter and GN 100/84

Government Communications Headquarters
Oakley Cheltenham Glos GL52 5AJ
Telephone Cheltenham 21491 ext
D/8489DQ/1501/29A
25 January 1984

From: P H Marychurch – Director
To all members of staff

The purpose of this letter is to tell you of an important development which will affect us all in GCHQ. Our future work will depend on its success.

Ministers have recently decided that because GCHQ must be able to work in secrecy and to provide a service on which the Government and our allies can confidently rely at all times, it should be freed as far as possible from the dangers of its operations being discussed publicly (for example at industrial tribunals), and from the risks of industrial action. For this purpose, certificates have been signed by the Foreign and Commonwealth Secretary excepting GCHQ staff from provisions of the Employment Protection Acts. This is further explained in GN 100/84, a copy of which is enclosed.

The general effect is to limit (as in other British security and intelligence services) the right of the staff to have recourse to an industrial tribunal, and their rights in connection with union membership and activities. Other conditions of service relating to pay, allowances, etc. will remain unchanged as explained in the GN. But in recognition of the fact that staff are being deprived of certain rights previously enjoyed, Ministers have agreed that a financial payment of £1,000 (to full-time staff) will be appropriate for those who remain at GCHQ. Part-time staff will receive a pro-rata payment. This also is explained in the GN which I urge you to read carefully.

E Division is ready to provide any further information and advice which you may need but, as the GN explains, you have the opportunity to seek a transfer elsewhere if you do not wish to remain in GCHQ. Many of you will I know wish to consult your families before making up your mind, and I urge you to do so, drawing on this letter and the accompanying GN which are both unclassified. You must of course not reveal any classified information.

In making their decision Ministers recognised the critical importance of the work of GCHQ. The value of that work depends on the dedication, loyalty and professionalism of individual members of staff: I hope that all of you who are affected by the changes will wish to stay with GCHQ, so that we can continue to provide the high level of service which is of such vital importance to the country.

When you have made your decision, please fill in and return to the Establishment and Personnel Officer the attached option form. This should be done as soon as possible, and not later than 1 March 1984.

P H MARYCHURCH
Director

GN 100/84
25 January 1984

GCHQ : CHANGES IN CONDITIONS OF SERVICE
INTRODUCTION AND SUMMARY

1. This notice explains certain changes relating to employment in GCHQ which the Foreign and Commonwealth Secretary is announcing in the House of Commons. Briefly these are that the Government has decided:

   a.   that it has become essential to except staff from the provisions of certain employment legislation on the grounds of national security;

   b.   that recognition of existing trade unions in respect of employment at GCHQ is to be withdrawn;

   c.   that accordingly GCHQ staff will not be permitted to be members of any existing trade union;

   d.   that staff who remain at GCHQ will receive a financial payment in recognition of the loss of rights previously enjoyed;

   e.   and that staff who do not wish to remain at GCHQ are to be given the opportunity to seek a transfer elsewhere in the Civil Service.

The Director is writing to each member of staff inviting acceptance of the revised terms and conditions of service.

PURPOSE AND NATURE OF THE CHANGES

2. GCHQ's work must be conducted secretly and must provide a service on which Her Majesty's Government and our allies can rely with confidence at all times. With these requirements in mind, Ministers have reviewed the status of GCHQ within the Civil Service and the conditions of service of its staff. It has been concluded that an organisation whose publicly acknowledged responsibilities include intelligence work should in certain respects be treated differently from other parts of the Civil Service.

3. Ministers believe that those engaged in this kind of work should not come within the ambit of legislation which could lead, for example, to details of GCHQ's operations being discussed before an industrial tribunal. The Secretary of State for Foreign and Commonwealth Affairs has therefore signed certificates under section 138(4) of the Employment Protection (Consolidation) Act 1978 and section 12(4) of the Employment Protection Act 1975 excepting GCHQ staff on national security grounds from the application of those Acts. This means that none of the provisions of the Acts will now apply to GCHQ staff. In particular, they can no longer make a complaint to an industrial tribunal in connection with dismissal or restrictions on trade union membership and activities. The provisions relating to disclosure of information to trade unions are also no longer applicable to GCHQ. But individual rights and provisions on many other matters covered by the Acts will still be separately available to staff (as explained in paragraph 6 below) under the Civil Service Pay and Conditions Code.

4. Ministers have also decided that organisations involved in vital intelligence work should be freed as far as possible from the risk of industrial disruption. They have decided that recognition should be withdrawn from all existing unions in respect of employment at GCHQ and that accordingly it will be a condition of service that GCHQ staff will not be permitted to be members of trade unions other than a Departmental Staff Association approved by Director GCHQ. In future, disciplinary action may be taken against anyone involved in industrial action.

5. Although GCHQ staff will not be permitted to belong to any existing trade union they may wish to form a Departmental Staff Association to represent their views and look after their interests. The precise form of the Association would be for staff to consider and make proposals for approval by the Director. Consultation and negotiations between Staff Association representatives and GCHQ management could be conducted within a system modelled on the present Departmental Whitley pattern, covering the same range of subjects as under existing arrangements. Representatives of a Staff Association could be authorised to represent and advise individuals on request in personal cases. Staff with experience in Whitley matters will be invited to take the lead in discussing new arrangements and entering into consultation with management.

OTHER CONDITIONS OF SERVICE

6. It is not practicable to mention each condition of service individually, but those terms and conditions which do not relate to trade unions or trade union membership or activities or industrial action will continue to apply. For example, provisions relating to pay, allowances of all kinds, leave, overtime, overseas service, FWH arrangements, time off for public duties or maternity, and the Principal Civil Service Pension Scheme (PCSPS) will still apply. GCHQ staff will continue to be members of the Home Civil Service, but will be recognised as a separate group for whom the Treasury and MPO will be prepared to consider changes in structure or conditions which are justified by GCHQ's operational requirements; in this context the plan to introduce a Departmental Class for Scientists and Engineers is mentioned at paragraph 10 below. Existing qualifications and appointments will continue to be recognised. Transfers between other Departments and GCHQ will still be possible.

7. GCHQ staff will continue to be subject to the security regulations and procedures prescribed by the Government and by Director GCHQ from time to time. These will include any recommendations of the Security Commission accepted by the Government.

IMPLEMENTATION OF THE CHANGES

8. GCHQ Staff
New entrants joining GCHQ will be appointed on the basis of the new terms and conditions. It is hoped that all existing staff will want to remain with GCHQ. They will be required to confirm their wish to do so, but will be given the alternative of seeking a transfer elsewhere in the Civil Service. An option form for signature, to record their decision, is being sent with the Director's letter to all staff who expect to be in post on 2 April 1984.

9. MOD Scientists currently employed at GCHQ
MOD Scientists employed at GCHQ who wish to continue to work here are invited to agree to be transferred from MOD to GCHQ and so to become full members of this Department, while retaining such reserved rights for consideration for employment within MOD as were granted on their appointment to GCHQ. Details of the personnel management arrangements for scientists transferred to GCHQ will be promulgated separately.

10. Departmental Class for Scientists, Engineers and Technicians
Staff will wish to know that approval in principle has been given for the establishment in GCHQ of a Departmental Class which will initially comprise staff now in the Science Group, the P & T Group and TTO/RT grades. New pay scales will be introduced for this class in due course, which together with assimilation terms will be promulgated separately. The effect on existing staff will be that no-one will lose pay and many will benefit.

11. Special Payment to all Staff who continue to work at GCHQ

In recognition of the withdrawal from GCHQ staff of the statutory rights referred to above, a special ex-gratia payment of £1,000 (subject to tax) will be made to all full-time UK-based industrial and non-industrial staff (in grades and equivalents up to and including Assistant Secretary) who remain with the Department and sign the option form to that effect. MOD Scientists who opt to be transferred to GCHQ will also receive this payment.

12. The payment will be made by the end of March 1984 or as soon as possible thereafter to all staff whose option forms, indicating that they wish to remain with GCHQ, have been received by 1 March except that:

   a.   staff who leave GCHQ, for any reason, before 2 April 1984 will not receive it;

   b.   staff who are on probation will be required to serve out their probationary period to GCHQ's satisfaction before receiving the payment;

   c.   part-time staff will be eligible for a reduced payment, the amount due being calculated on a pro-rata basis according to their working hours.

13. Staff who elect to leave GCHQ

For GCHQ staff who elect to leave, the Department will try to arrange a level transfer within the Home Civil Service and the rules relating to reimbursement of expenses on transfer will apply, but those over the retiring age who elect to leave will be retired after the customary period of notice and will receive their PCSPS benefits. GCHQ will make every effort to arrange transfers to other departments and will continue to employ the individuals concerned while this is being done, but if it proves to be impossible, and if at that stage those concerned still wish to leave GCHQ, they will be eligible for premature retirement on redundancy terms.

14. Similar arrangements will apply to MOD Scientists, except that in the first instance an attempt will be made to arrange transfers for them to other MOD Establishments.

15. Any officer who chooses not to remain with GCHQ will until leaving:

   a.   be subject to the Ministerial certificates, and consequently the provisions of the legislation referred to above will no longer apply to him/her;

   b.   no longer be considered for a tour of duty overseas with the Department and his/her name will be removed from the appropriate volunteer lists;

    c.   continue to be eligible to be seen by Promotion Boards but will not be promoted while he/she remains in GCHQ.

16. An officer who requests a transfer out of GCHQ may remain a member of a trade union, but such unions will not be recognised in respect of employment by GCHQ after 1 March 1984 and their officials will not normally be allowed to enter GCHQ premises. Nor will trade union subscriptions be deducted from salary after this date.

17. **Staff who refuse to express an option or to accept an alternative posting**
Any staff refusing to complete the option form or who, after electing to leave GCHQ, refuse to accept an alternative posting will have their employment terminated from a date to be determined by the Director. Such staff who have reached the retiring age will be eligible for immediate payment of their accrued Civil Service superannuation benefits. For staff below that age, accrued benefits will be preserved and brought into payment at the retiring age.

GENERAL

18. Although this Notice gives as comprehensive a range of information as possible, an information centre has been established in A/0807 (Extensions 3129 or 2332) and staff are invited to ring with any queries after they have received their option forms for signature. For those unable to telephone (e.g. staff abroad), written queries, which should be addressed to:

> The Establishment and Personnel Officer
> Information Office
> A/0807
> Oakley

and forwarded via normal channels, will be answered as soon as possible.

J A ADYE
Principal Establishment Officer

OPTION FORM
(to be completed by all GCHQ staff)
Complete either A or B

A. I, ...* have read and understood General Notice 100/84 and wish to continue to be employed at GCHQ. I agree to resign from membership of any trade union to which I belong. I also undertake not to join a trade union or to engage in its affairs or to discuss with its officials my terms of employment or conditions of service or any other matter relating to my employment at GCHQ. I understand, however, that I may join a Departmental staff assocation approved for the time being by Director GCHQ.

Signed   Date

Division/Station   Grade

B. I, ...* have read and understood General Notice 100/84. I do not wish to continue to be employed at GCHQ. I wish to be considered for a transfer elsewhere in the Civil Service.

Signed   Date

Division/Station   Grade

* Insert full name in capital letters.

Appendix 2

The agreement

The following is the CCSU draft agreement on trade union organization in essential intelligence areas in GCHQ. It was rejected by the government.

INTRODUCTION

1. The general objects of the Civil Service National Whitley Council are to secure the greatest measure of co-operation between the State, in its capacity as employer, and the general body of civil servants in matters affecting the Civil Service, with a view to increased efficiency in the public service combined with the well-being of those employed; to provide the machinery for dealing with grievances, and generally to bring together the experience and different points of view of the representatives of the Civil Service.

2. Both Sides attach importance to the improvement of industrial relations throughout the Civil Service and to the avoidance of disputes and disruption. To achieve this, discussions are currently taking place on new arrangements for determining pay; and for arbitration, mediation and conciliation to resolve disagreements wherever they may arise.

3. Within the spirit of these general objectives, the National Whitley Council has concluded this agreement with the purpose of:

(i) safeguarding the continuity of the essential security and intelligence services provided by GCHQ by guaranteeing their immunity from risk of industrial disruption, whether in pursuit of national or of local disputes;

(ii) safeguarding the secrecy of the essential security and intelligence services provided by GCHQ;

(iii) providing for the resolution of disagreements and grievances in GCHQ;

(iv) providing for those civil servants employed in or under GCHQ who so wish to remain or to become members of trade unions, and for their representation.

MAINTENANCE OF ESSENTIAL INTELLIGENCE AND SECURITY SERVICES IN GCHQ

4. It is agreed that it is for the Government to determine what are essential security and intelligence services in GCHQ. Before the Government reaches its determination in respect of GCHQ for the purpose of this agreement, GCHQ management will consult and fully take account of the views of the staff of GCHQ through the local trade union representatives.

5. It is agreed that there shall be included in the conditions of service of staff employed in or under GCHQ a provision that they will take no action which would or might interfere with the uninterrupted operation of essential security and intelligence services.

6. To provide for the immunity from risk of industrial disruption whether in pursuit of national or local disputes as provided in paragraph 3(i) the Trade Union Side will not instruct or ask members employed in or under GCHQ to take any action which would or might put at risk the continuous maintenance, twenty-four hours a day, seven days a week, of essential security and intelligence services at GCHQ.

7. GCHQ management and GCHQ Trade Union Side will consult together to provide agreed machinery for the resolution of disagreements and grievances (as provided in paragraph 3(iii)) affecting either individuals or groups of staff employed in or under GCHQ. Such agreement will require the endorsement of the National Whitley Council.

ACCESS TO INDUSTRIAL TRIBUNALS

8. The Government has issued certificates excepting employment in or under GCHQ of members of that Department or of the Ministry of Defence from the provisions of the Employment Protection Act 1975 and the Employment Protection (Consolidation) Act 1978. The purpose of the certificates is to protect security by preventing access of these staffs to Industrial Tribunals under these Acts. It is therefore agreed that, subject to the provisions of this agreement, the staff concerned shall have the rights and conditions of all other civil servants save that, instead of access to Industrial Tribunals, they will have access to the Civil Service Appeal Board (CSAB) which, for these purposes, will have the powers and authorities of Industrial Tribunals. On such matters there will be an avenue of appeal to the three Advisers on Security whose decision will be final. The National Whitley Council will consider further the powers and authorities of the CSAB and the three Advisers on Security in respect of appeals from GCHQ staff.

CONDUCT OF NEGOTIATIONS

9. It is agreed that:

(i) Departmental union representatives at GCHQ will not give, and full-time or other union officials or representatives will not seek to acquire, classified information about operations, activities or services at GCHQ.

(ii) Negotiations on departmental matters in GCHQ which, in the judgement of GCHQ management, will involve access to such information will be carried out by GCHQ employees acting as union representatives and appointed or elected by union members in GCHQ. Full-time or other officials or representatives of unions at national level will take no part in such negotiations but may provide information on national arrangements which may be relevant. On all matters affecting GCHQ staff alone, the accountability of representatives will be solely to members employed in GCHQ.

(iii) The rights of members of trade unions in GCHQ to have a say in determining national matters which may affect them are preserved, in so far as they are not incompatible with the provisions of this agreement.

CONCLUSION

10. The provisions of this agreement are designed to remove any possibility of a conflict of loyalty for civil servants employed in or under GCHQ by providing for the maintenance of the continuity and secrecy of GCHQ's security and intelligence operations and activities through their immunity from any threat of industrial disruption.

11. Subject to the provisions of this agreement, and to their remaining in operation and effect so as to ensure the continuity and secrecy of GCHQ's operations and activities, the Official Side adheres to the advice given to civil servants about membership of trade unions and under which members of GCHQ staff who so wish will be free to remain or become members of trade unions or representatives of trade unions at GCHQ. The Official Side will continue to recognise trade unions in GCHQ on the basis of the nationally agreed criteria.

Timetable

1981
March: Government unilaterally abolishes Civil Service pay agreement.
March–July: Rolling strikes in the Civil Service.

1981–2
Union ban is proposed, but is rejected by successive ministers.

1983
13 May: Thatcher officially 'avows' intelligence work of GCHQ to the Commons in the wake of the Security Commission report on the spy Geoffrey Prime.
22 December: Secret oral instruction by Mrs Thatcher to Sir Robert Armstrong, Cabinet Secretary and head of the Civil Service, to ban unions at GCHQ.

1984
25 January: GCHQ union ban announced without any consultation with staff. All GCHQ staff threatened with dismissal if they do not leave their unions by 1 March.
1 February: First meeting with Thatcher.
23 February: Parliamentary lobby and second meeting with Thatcher.
28 February: TUC/CCSU day of action.
1 March: Ban imposed; 150 GCHQ staff refuse to give up their rights. CCSU establishes GCHQ Trade Unions and permanent office in Cheltenham.
May: ILO condemns ban as contravening ILO Convention No. 87 governing freedom of association.
16 July: High Court rules ban 'invalid and of no effect'; 150 GCHQ staff rejoin their unions.
6 August: Appeal Court overturns High Court ruling.
22 November: Law lords rule against unions and support government on grounds of 'national security'.

1985
25 January: CCSU/TUC organize 1st anniversary march and rally in

Cheltenham.

1 April: GCHQ management threatens trade union rejoiners.

May: ILO reaffirms its condemnation of ban.

9 May: CCSU submits GCHQ case to European Commission of Human Rights.

9 August: Armstrong tells CCSU that GCHQ will discipline trade union rejoiners.

September: TUC pledges industrial action if any GCHQ trade unionist is dismissed.

1986

25 January: Roy Hattersley and David Steel pledge to restore unions in GCHQ at 2nd anniversary rally.

18 March: Trade union rejoiners given 10 days to renounce their unions; all refuse.

24 March: Foreign Secretary, Sir Geoffrey Howe, backs down and tells unions that 'dismissal is not an appropriate penalty'.

April: Disciplinary penalties announced; 13 fined about £2,000 each.

23 October: 1,000 days of campaigning.

1987

20 January: European Commission of Human Rights declares unions' case 'inadmissible'; CCSU and TUC pledge to continue the fight.

June: Some GCHQ trade unionists again threatened with disciplinary action for taking strike action. Charges later withdrawn.

22 June: Following the general election, CCSU and GCHQ trade union members pledge 'the fight goes on'.

1988

January: Compulsory transfers out of GCHQ threatened.

30 August: GCHQ Trade Unions publishes 100th issue of *Warning Signal*.

29 September: Government announces intention to remove by dismissal or transfer all remaining union members at GCHQ.

18 October: First four dismissals announced.

7 November: Widespread action on GCHQ Day.

18 November: First four dismissals.

8 December: Thatcher announces that polygraph scheme is to be abandoned.

1989

28 January: Neil Kinnock again pledges restoration of trade unions to GCHQ at the largest ever anniversary rally.

2 March: Gareth Morris, the last remaining union member working in GCHQ, is escorted out.

June: Government is criticized by ILO and narrowly avoids 'special paragraph'.

16 July: 2,000 days of campaigning.

December: Staff association is refused certificate of independence.

1991

June: British government is unanimously condemned by ILO.

Bibliography

Aubrey, C., *Who's Watching You?*, London: Penguin, 1981.

Bamford, J., *The Puzzle Palace*, London: Sidgwick and Jackson, 1983.

Ewing, K., *Britain and the ILO*, London: The Institute of Employment Rights, 1990.

Hall, R.V., *The Secret State: Australia's spy industry*, Sydney: Cassell, 1978.

Hodges, A., *Alan Turing: The enigma of intelligence*, London: Burnett Books, 1983.

Jones, R.V., *Reflections on Intelligence*, London: Heinemann, 1989.

Lykken, D. T., *A Tremor in the Blood: Uses and abuses of the lie detector*, New York: McGraw-Hill, 1981.

Norton-Taylor, R., *In Defence of the Realm?*, London: Civil Liberties Trust, 1990.

Richelson, J. and Ball, D., *The Ties that Bind*, London: Allen and Unwin, 1985.

Welchman, G., *The Hut Six Story*, London: Allen Lane, 1982.

West, N., *GCHQ: The secret wireless war, 1900–1986*, London: Weidenfeld and Nicolson, 1986.

Winterbotham, F.W., *The Ultra Secret*, London: Weidenfield and Nicolson, 1974.

Acknowledgements

The authors and publishers are grateful to the following for permission to reproduce photographs and artwork: BBC Press Office, p. 25; Mike Charity, cover and p. 77; Delaney, Fletcher, Slaymaker, Delaney and Bozell, p. 162; *The Guardian*, p. 174; John Harris, pp. 61, 205; Brian Nugent, p. 163; Trades Union Congress, p. 162.

We are also grateful to the Rt. Hon. Denis Healey, MP, CBE, for permission to reproduce extracts from his speech to the House of Commons, 27 February 1984.

Index

227